The RABBI'S WIDOW

Turning Pain into Purpose

JOELLE ECKSTEIN

For more information please contact joelle@k-eckstein.org or +972.50.3477357

First printing 2022

ISBN 978-965-599-805-4

For all the widows who are
at the beginning of their journey,
with love

Prologue

By the time I met Joelle, I had been Rabbi Yechiel Eckstein's Chief of Staff at his organization's Chicago headquarters for four months. I had a solid sense of Yechiel's passion for his calling, his meticulous attention to detail, the blithe star-power charisma that he brought into every room, and his famous mercurial moods. He was a demanding and exacting boss; he had audacious grandiose goals, seemingly impossible expectations, and the demands of my job taught me that I had only ever before been limited by narrower minds. And incongruently to his towering presence in the office, whenever he talked about Joelle, it was with the giddy head-over-heels delight of a man who has discovered his soul mate.

In my first week working with Yechiel, he told me he wanted to expand his nonprofit organization into Korea – a country with few Jews, no organizational footprint and no contacts. He wanted a star-studded inaugural party with 10,000 guests, to coincide with the 50th anniversary of diplomatic relations between Israel and Korea. He already had a tentative date in September for it. A couple of former executives had been trying to make inroads into Korea for several years. He gave me three months and a "no fail option."

It was that September in Seoul that I met Joelle for the first time. I was stage-managing the largest event I had ever been a part of in my life, in a country where I didn't speak the language, celebrating the 50th Anniversary of Diplomatic Relations Between Israel and Korea – two countries I didn't have any connection to except that four months earlier I started working for a rabbi. The entire event nearly came to a crashing halt days before the boss arrived when I made the terrible social faux pas of questioning the bill the organization got for a socialite's flower expenditures for the event, and I had spend a frantic evening writing Israeli Prime Minister Bibi Netanyahu's welcoming speech points because we found out last minute that he would tape a welcome for our event but only if I wrote it. Over one thousand books and CDs of Rabbi Eckstein's teachings and songs (that we had put together and translated in three months) were arriving for the attendee gift bags, and for the past couple months I had been managing Yechiel's expectations that we weren't going to come close to the 10,000 guests he wanted, we were projecting 1000 and that was still astonishing in a country where no one knew us.

I didn't know what to expect meeting her. I had heard stories within the organization from those who had witnessed Yechiel's crushing heartbreak from his divorce years earlier, and the younger woman that charmed him; stories from his family who didn't want her a part of his life. To listen to some of the stories, one might expect a brassy domineering harridan that bossed him around and expected staff to kowtow to her. I was surprised to meet a gracious, almost painfully shy, humble woman who dotted on Yechiel as much as he dotted on her. I was shocked to realize that Yechiel's bombastic, exacting, and mercurial nature softened and relaxed around this beautiful quiet woman. Yin yang.

The event was a smashing success; the organization secured a board of directors, an office in Seoul, and achieved coveted nonprofit status there in record time.

And it was clear to me as Chief of Staff, that for the health of the founder, and for an extra layer of protection for the staff, the organization needed Joelle to be with Yechiel as much as possible. Under her care and protection, Yechiel was calmer, less inclined to mood swings, and with his brutal travel schedule, he recovered from jet lag faster when Joelle was with him. Moving forward, whenever Yechiel was coming to Chicago headquarters, meeting us in Florida for a board meeting, traveling to NYC or LA for events, I would insist Joelle travel with him. He rarely pushed back and seemed happy someone on his staff in Chicago finally got it.

In the months that followed, it was a delight to get to know Joelle on a personal level. I don't know how our first walk came about; I may have offered to see if she wanted to go for coffee and a short walk along Lake Michigan. I knew she didn't have a huge circle of friends in Chicago outside the synagogue, and it was good for me to get away from the rigors and insanity of the office. Beyond the high stress of working for the organization, my personal life was a mess; I started seeing the executive director of the organization whose wife had given him permission because she was having an affair with her female personal trainer. While I didn't share that craziness with Joelle until after I left the organization, she was a source of calm in the middle of the high stress high-wire act that had become my life. Some people have an innate calming influence, and Joelle did that for everyone she came in contact with.

Soon I was having dinners with Yechiel and Joelle whenever they were in town. Joelle and I walked the lakeshore, shopped for boots, tried on wigs and hairpieces along the Mag Mile, or took coffee in the neighborhood. She would regale me with stories of their travels, astonishing and hilarious anecdotes that showed me a side of my boss that I rarely saw at the office. During our dinners, she would share Yechiel's antics or quirks, and I've never seen Yechiel happier, nor laugh so much.

On one spring walk, Joelle and I were heading to the lake path along the tip of Lincoln Park, and she had just cracked me up with Yechiel's anecdotes during their plane ride here, and I blurted, "Joelle, you need to write a book!" I realized when I said it that I was serious. Yechiel's autobiography "The Bridge Builder," was due out in the fall and I'd been reading the drafts, but there was nothing of the wit, humor, quirks and delight of Joelle's stories in what I had read. Joelle dismissed the idea, but I pressed. "Seriously, you could call it, The Rabbi's Wife." She laughed then, and we brainstormed a bit of the stories and anecdotes she could put in the book. Everyone would know the Rabbi's accomplishments and struggles from his autobiography, but who better to tell the softer, funnier side of the man than his wife?

In the years that followed, I continued to meet Joelle for walks, window-shopping, and had dinners with the two of them whenever they were in Chicago. Joelle became more than just the wife of my boss; she became a true and dear friend. And we continued to talk and joke about The Rabbi's Wife. She demurred, saying she wasn't a writer, but I like to think the idea germinated.

And suddenly the world skewed. I got a LinkedIn message from a former colleague. I didn't believe it. Then a text from someone in the organization. Then texts poured in, and the international news confirmed it: Rabbi Yechiel Eckstein had died. I was stunned. I called Joelle. No answer. I was pacing, calling her again and again. I booked a ticket to Israel. When she finally answered, her voice was hollow. Small. She sounded exhausted. In shock. She invited me to come to Israel, but asked me to wait. I was torn. She reminded me that I would never make it in time for the funeral. I could be there for Shiva; I could see her shake her head. If you want, but I think you should wait. I didn't comprehend fully at the time, but understood later. Tens of hundreds of people in and out during Shiva. A tsunami of humanity every minute of every hour for seven days. Already in shock, her life ripped apart, she was wrung out by mid morning, a shell at night. Later, those people would disappear never to be seen again, when she needed support the most. "I think you should wait." And I rebooked my ticket for the spring.

A year after my visit, Joelle and I were reminiscing about her life with Yechiel and she asked me if I thought she could really write a book when she'd never even kept a journal. Of course I said yes. I told her I would be with her every step of the way. "Start small journal entries. Ten minutes every day. Don't judge yourself. No one ever has to read what you write if you don't want them to. Don't judge yourself and don't show them to anyone until you are ready."

She started writing. And The Rabbi's Wife became The Rabbi's Widow.

– TM Derrickson

February 6, 2019

It was a day like any other day, perhaps with a little more flurried anticipation. It was mid-winter and cold when I headed to work. We were attending a wedding in Tel Aviv that evening, and packing for a longer weekend to celebrate our own anniversary. We were moving into a new home later that month. I had been working with architects and was beyond excited that our move-in date had finally arrived. Given the early hour, Yechiel was still in bed, which was understandable – it was going to be a long day.

Like any other day it was a day of lists, of preparation. A day of all the little things one does during the course of any normal day to get ready for the future. Between work calls and on breaks, colleagues asked about the new home, the decorations, or what I was going to wear for the wedding that evening. I made a mental note, a decision of an appropriate black dress I would wear for the wedding that evening, nothing too fancy, something modest, as was my preferred style. I decided to leave work early so we could get ahead of the traffic. Yechiel was to say one of the seven blessings under the *Chuppah* so we had to be there on time, and Yechiel was never on time unless prompted.

On the walk home, I texted a friend about contractors and countertops. I rarely talked to Yechiel during the day and that day was no exception. Our favorite time of the day was in the quiet of the evenings, when we would sit together and catch up on our respective days, usually with a bottle of wine. It would always start with a quick banter of "You go first,"

"No, YOU go first"... it is the closeness of everyday togetherness, the little habits of grins and laughter shared, that pack the hardest punches.

The door was locked when I got home that day, which was strange, because when Yechiel was home the door remained unlocked. And the blinds were up, which was also strange because we never kept the blinds up. I tried my key in the door and it wouldn't fit. Which meant his key was in the lock on the other side. I rang the bell. And waited. I called his phone. I rang the bell again. I was starting to get angry. I had so much to get done before we left and we were going to be late. Did he forget? Was he taking a mid-afternoon nap again? I looked through the window as I dialed him again. He wasn't in the recliner, did he go out? Rang the bell. Again. Ugh. Looked in the window again.

I must have screamed then. Yechiel lay unmoving on the kitchen floor. Banging on the window, screaming before my brain could even process what I was seeing. *Yechiel on the floor.* My cries alerted the neighbor, who rushed to my side and helped me force the window open. I crawled through, and scrambled to open the door for my neighbor who was on the phone with 911. I was on the floor with Yechiel, my neighbor giving him CPR. The world tilted and time blurred. How long did my neighbor perform CPR before the paramedics took over? Yechiel was still unconscious on the kitchen floor. My brain wasn't processing it. Was he breathing? I tried to give them space but a part of me was lying on the floor with him. The important part. He was my life, my love, my past, and my future. Everything was dissolving. *Yechiel was unconscious on the kitchen floor.* I couldn't process it.

My eyes were taking in too much detail to cry. I couldn't scream anymore. I couldn't talk. Autonomous function took over. Someone must have asked for his medical records and I remember logging online to give the paramedics a list of his medications and medical history. Neighbors, passersby, random people, got curious and came up to the door. Some knocked, some just tried walking in. I found myself pushing strangers out of my house while trying to monitor the progress of the paramedics. They worked on him for what seemed like an eternity. So long. Too long. It was shattering. I wanted them to stop. Make it all stop. I tried calling his lawyer to make them stop but the exact details elude me. What felt like hours later, the doctor called it. Time of death.

My world ended.

One is never prepared for the death of a beloved, time rends abruptly and cruelly into "before" and "after." I held Yechiel's hand. I put my head on his chest. This couldn't be happening. His chest didn't rise beneath my head. I couldn't hear his heartbeat. I was swamped with fear. My body grew numb. My brain, numb. My guts churned. A terrible realization: *I can't do this. I can't live without him.* I stilled. *I can't do this alone.* A prayer. A beseeching. The overwhelming terror of knowing I would be alone from this moment on. And I was suspended in the numb void in between before and after, my soul screaming for time to stop. Just *stop.*

"I love you. Remember to pack a weekend bag." Those were the last words I told Yechiel before kissing him goodbye.

Dear God, please no. It can't be the last.

One of my neighbors sat on the staircase. I didn't know her name, and I tried to remember why she was there. She sat in the middle of my house like she belonged here but I didn't know who she was. It would be a year and a half later when I would see her unexpectedly, and I would finally piece it together: she was my neighbor, yes, but she also answered calls as a paramedic. She had been a calm presence. She had stayed with me in the kitchen as I was on the floor next to Yechiel. I don't know for how long. I lost all sense of time. Was it still daytime? Was it night? I couldn't move. I didn't care. Eventually, I must have looked up, "What do I do now?"

"I think you should call someone," she said.

Who do I call? I didn't want to call anyone. The one person I expected to help me through any trauma was… gone. I couldn't. I felt that the moment I called someone, this… this would all be real. And it couldn't be real. My thoughts cycled through all the neighbors and people that had come into the house today. Who tried to talk to me, sit with me – I hadn't let them. I was unable to talk. My brain cycled through friends, coworkers, and family. It was overwhelming. I would have to tell people. I would have to relive this over and over with each telling. I felt like I was suffocating.

I finally called my children. "I need you to come. Now. I need you here with me." I don't remember saying any more than that. I knew they would. I didn't know if I could bear it but knew instinctively I needed them.

No, no, no… now what?

I called my brother-in-law. When he answered the phone, I could not find the words. My brain refused to say the words. I kept asking, "Are you sitting down?" and he kept responding, "Yes, what happened?" I was shaking my head. I passed the phone to the paramedic. She had the words and was the one to tell him they had done everything possible but could not save him. I heard him scream through the phone. I closed my eyes and lay back down on the cold floor next to Yechiel's body for the last time. I held his beautiful big hands. I just wanted him to wake up. I needed him to wake up. *This can't be happening.* We had so much planned. It just was not possible.

"I love you. Remember to pack a weekend bag." "See you later." I don't know how long I lay there. Just holding his hand.

I did not sleep that night. I could not stop crying. Every time I got close to sleep, I would jerk awake as if falling off a cliff. Heart pounding, gut wrenching, and my eyes would cry again. My brain was a torment of reliving the day. My children were staying with me, and it was some comfort, but still felt like it was a rollercoaster I was on alone. It is customary to bury a body immediately, especially in Jerusalem where funerals are usually held just hours after death, or the next day at most. It seemed impossible. The weight of the deadline was like a boulder on my chest.

Shiva would begin right after burial and I needed help to prepare the house. The only one I could think of to help me with the house was our longtime housekeeper, Pedro. I had lost track of time by the time I called him, and I know it was way too late in the evening. My throat ached and I could not get the words out. I could not say that my husband... that Yechiel... had died.

"My husband had a heart attack." I managed.

"Oh, is he going to be okay, what do you need?"

"I need you to come right away to help us get the house ready for *Shiva*."

He was there in a half hour. We had to get the house ready for *Shiva*, put all the boxes away in the basement and extra furniture to make room for all the visitors that would be coming. He would also arrange for help throughout the week of *Shiva*. Our house was a neglected mess because we had been in the middle of moving to our new apartment. I suddenly became aware of the walls that needed repainting, the small repairs we had decided against, and the broken appliances we never bothered to replace because the new ones were for our new home. It flashed in my mind that I was no longer leaving this house, this place Yechiel and I had called home for so many years. It was like a physical blow. We were so looking forward to the new place. A future now gone. I shook, I could not think about that now.

I had to speak at the funeral. I had no idea how I was going to; I just knew I had to. Earlier I had sat with my sister-in-law and her husband while he dealt with the mounting paperwork for the funeral, the ambulance. In a fog at the table, he helped me put my thoughts on paper. I did not know how to even begin to write a eulogy for my husband. It was surreal. I gave him a few reflections, and he wrote several paragraphs and emailed them to me. What seemed clear when I was talking, now read clinical and distant on the page.

I cannot do this in English. I could not relate to those words, I don't know why. Time was running out and I was exhausted. I desperately wanted to crawl under the covers and stop the world so I could process everything in my own time. Or at least until my brain caught up. Could I speak in Spanish? My mother tongue?

I guessed it was ridiculous to give a eulogy in a language no one would understand. In a foggy panic, it occurred to me to call a close friend and ask her to translate it into Hebrew so I could get some sleep. Hadas printed it out for me. In Hebrew, it was beautiful, poetic, and sounded more natural to my ears.

Even with the words now coherent I was still going to have to speak them. I avoided public speaking. My legs trembled and my voice would shake. I was always the shy, quiet wife behind the strong charismatic public figure that was Yechiel. Even those times he would bring me to the stage to translate his speeches; I would get terrible stage fright. I had no idea how I was going to do this. In a sense, the immediacy of it all is a blessing - there is no real time to think or process anything.

Too early in the morning, I sat on the bedroom floor with my children around me. I was so thankful they had dropped everything in the middle of their final exams and came to be with me. As we sat there, I read and reread, crying, shaking over the words I would say at the funeral. I could not believe I was going to bury my husband on our anniversary. *We should be walking on the Tel Aviv promenade, enjoying an outdoor breakfast, and going to a concert that evening.* Should I cancel the hotel and tickets? Did I already? Did it matter? My mind was not functioning. I could not see the pages. My brain felt like it was tearing itself apart. I read the words again. Instinctually I knew working through my emotions now, crying through every reading, would inoculate me for speaking it at the funeral.

The ride to the cemetery is hazy. Our arrival, a fog. I did not understand what I was doing there. Colleagues, friends, were hugging me and crying, when just yesterday they were wishing me a happy anniversary. I was not supposed to be here. I could not breathe. All those people, news cameras, photographers. *I am not supposed to be here.*

Maybe that is when it happened. A certain calm took over, *this is not me*. This was not my life. I was not supposed to be here. And all of sudden, my stage fright vanished. I realized my legs were not shaking, even when I focused on thinking about speaking in front of the hundreds of people that were there. It was too surreal. What did all these people matter when my life ended on the kitchen floor? *This is not me.*

My turn to speak. I do not remember walking to the front. Suddenly, I could not speak. Silent. Numb. I was later told that the silence before my eulogy was too long and maybe uncomfortable, some believed I would not be able to speak. After all, everyone who knew me knew that I never spoke in public. Somehow the words came. I spoke but I do not remember speaking. Months later I was shocked to find out it had been all recorded and was available online; I would watch a brief clip of my eulogy, and it was like watching someone else. I did not recognize myself.

I became a different person that day. Time had rent and that day I stepped out of the void between "before" and "after." It was the beginning of the new "me."

The end of "we." I had to learn how to speak for myself. To carry on. To shape a new course. To list and plan for a new future.

I am not physically affectionate to acquaintances or even friends, but all of a sudden everyone was hugging me. I would never allow that before. When I think about it now I'm appalled, *I let everyone hug me*. I was numb, I let them. Later, during *Shiva*, someone would try to hug me again and I would pull away. My reticence would come back, but I let myself be hugged during the funeral.

I was no longer the *Wife* – in one single crushing moment that title was taken from me and I became the *Widow.*

I did not want to leave his grave.

The fresh turned dirt. The incongruence of flowers. I wanted to be left there with him. I wanted to scream… my rage, my fear, and my frustration with the unfairness of it all. I wanted to weep… from the enormity of life. I was exhausted by the battering of all the little inconsequential needs pushing me further away from the moments I had with him.

Jewish law requires immediate burial and I was reeling from the discordant displacement of time.

I changed into my non-leather mourning shoes. As was the custom, my shirt was torn right before the funeral, but I do not remember it. I needed to return home but I did not want to. Returning home meant leaving him there, but how could I? What if he got cold? I was not thinking rationally. Returning home meant a physical step into this new me – alone. Returning home meant facing hundreds, perhaps thousands, of people who would be in and out of our home for the next seven days for *Shiva*. Our home. Home, without Yechiel. Pain flared in my chest and it was hard to breathe. I wanted to sink into the dirt with him.

I was driven back home to sit on a low chair for a week of mourning. I was told what to do. A steady stream of people. The low indistinct murmurs, the clank of dishes, the jarring quiet shuffling of hundreds of bodies invading my space, our home. I could not keep track of my emotions; at times grateful for the distraction, and other times I could have screamed to get a private moment. I became irrationally pissed off at all the food – so much food. Why were people still bringing in food?? The kitchen overflowed and still more came. The thought of eating made me physically sick. Who could possibly eat at a time such as this? Who was all this food for? What were they all thinking? Someone would have to clean up the mess. Take care of the logistics of it all. My stomach burned and my chest was so tight I would gasp for air. My children kept putting hot cups of tea into my hands. It became an anchor, a focus, and a way of grounding. It was the middle of winter and the front door was open. People passed in and out so often the door stayed open and the cold sank into my bones. It was giving me fits, I was freezing. I'm sure I was in shock, but that open door confounded me. I felt like I would never be warm again. My children brought me blankets, cups of tea.

They were always at eyesight. Making sure I had something warm to hold. Something to soothe my aching throat.

I could not imagine it was possible to feel such intense physical pain from loss. The squeezing pain in my chest and lungs that would stab into my guts was a pain I had never felt before and I thought – sometimes even wished – it would kill me. Died of a broken heart – I understood that now.

My son and daughter hovered within reach, very aware of any "point of repair," sensing when the enormity of it all threatened to overwhelm me. *Shiva* felt like being tossed overboard in a storm. The door of our home, open to a swirling tide of humanity surging and ebbing around the house, around me, talking, praying, eating soup, drinking tea, using our bathroom. Every long day filled with people I knew, some I did not, some who had never met Yechiel, very few had ever been to the house – but all with a story they wanted to share, all wanting to give a few moments of comfort. It was a comfort only in that it was a distraction from the inevitable void of loss. I broke down repeatedly. Weeping especially during morning prayers. It was exhausting. Sitting through another story, more tears, more words of condolence that can be anything but.

By the end of the second day, I was running out of patience. I was utterly wiped out, sleeping barely a few hours a night. The constant open door during a week of winter gave me a chill. My heart ached, my body ached. I begged my children to turn off the lights at 9pm and lock the door so people would not come into the house late. After the third night of not sleeping, not eating, I felt like I was floating. Hallucinating. I was given medication to sleep. Sleep was my only sanctuary from the pain, and I was grateful for it. Waking up crying, however, was a new experience for me.

I would not have survived *Shiva* without my children, my coworker and dear friend Hadas, and Judith, my close long-time friend who had flown in from Spain. At the end of each day, after hundreds of people had been through the house, Hadas had the foresight to secure Pedro's housecleaning service. As he worked to put the house back together in anticipation of another hectic day, my little family would sit me on the porch and we would have our own moment of quiet reminisce. Some night near the end, someone handed me a joint. I took it. As the night progressed, I found myself laughing. It was a moment of wonder, a moment of thinking, "What will Pedro think?" We smoked, reminisced, and laughed so much more. It was a rare moment of peace, and I was nearly swamped thinking how much Yechiel would enjoy this moment.

And then, suddenly, the week of *Shiva* was over. The constant flow of hundreds of people every waking moment of the day dwindled to a trickle and disappeared. I thought back on the week. Being surrounded every day. Taking late nights on the balcony with a couple dear friends and my children while the house was put back in some semblance of order for the next onslaught of well-wishers. Some nights they even managed to make me laugh a little bit, over what, I don't remember. Every waking moment, surreal. Every moment felt like Yechiel would come through the front door, asking what we were doing. What would he think of all of this? He would likely try to make me laugh with some mischievously gleeful and probably inappropriate comment. The thought made me smile and my eyes stung.

"I love you. Remember to pack a weekend bag." "See you later." And the crushing pain in my chest came back and left me gasping.

Me too.... at least mine and Gary's last words had "I Love You"... in the sentence preceeding - see You Sunday - have a nice swim. Be safe??? We at least said "I Love You"

The greatest pleasure of life is love.

– Euripides

Unbeknownst to him, I saw Yechiel months before I actually met him. It was 2003, at a banquet in Jerusalem. I was there only because my boss could not attend and I went in his stead. Since it was his organization, Yechiel dominated the podium. He completely captivated me with his speech and his charisma. Even though I was casually dating someone else, I could not stop thinking about him, much like a teenager in love with a favorite singer or celebrity.

As with any crush, I imagined what it might be like to catch his eye. In my mind, our meeting would be electric, fortuitous, and romantic. He would be worldly, sophisticated, and devoted. I knew it was ridiculous to speculate, but who doesn't fantasize and romanticize over a crush?

I was working for a well-known Israeli nonprofit when I met the matchmaker that would finally introduce me to Yechiel. I say "matchmaker" because it was her determination that brought us together, but Dvora actually ran the Israel office of Yechiel's organization. She was bringing in a Spanish-speaking friend from the US that they were courting to be their ambassador for outreach. Because of our working partnership with the organization, and because Spanish is my native language, my boss asked me if I would help Dvora and guide this ambassador around Israel. I was to show her projects around the country, arrange her schedule, lunches, dinners, every activity, and work with Dvora to make sure this woman's visit to Israel was one-of-a-kind.

During this visit, I had taken our visitor out to dinner and let Dvora know where we were. She joined us and as we were eating, Dvora got a call from Yechiel who was overseas at the time. When she got off the phone, she turned to me and said, "Say... did you just say you were divorced?"

"Yes, but I'm seeing –"

"Why don't I arrange for you to meet Yechiel?"

I gaped at her.

I think I spluttered.

I hoped I wasn't blushing.

I wanted to ask her if she was out of her mind, what made her think I had *anything* in common with a rabbi?? My heart fluttered. I laughed it off as gracefully as I could and reiterated that I was seeing someone.

"I'll take care of it, you'll meet." I'm pretty sure I blushed then, and I looked down at my plate, hoping my eyes wouldn't give me a way.

I put it out of my mind. Weeks passed. And then one day Dvora informed me that Yechiel was back in town and he was going to be meeting with my boss. Dvora arranged it with him for me to join the meeting. Yechiel was known to be mercurial and Dvora assured him that having me present would "soften the atmosphere."

When we got to the meeting, Yechiel had not arrived yet. He was notoriously late; Or so I thought. I would discover later this was not because he was inconsiderate, but because his staff would call him in once everyone had arrived. His schedule was back-to-back, 24/6 and every minute was used up. At this meeting, everyone was already sitting, yet Dvora grabbed me before I could claim a seat. She asked me to stand by the door with her. When Yechiel finally arrived, he looked so much bigger and taller than I remembered. Dvora sat me next to him. I was in cold sweats. I barely remember what was said. Yechiel was bombastic, and unsmiling. He had everyone cowed at the meeting. But his hands struck a chord in me. His distinct handwriting. He wrote with such strength I thought he would pierce the paper. Every time he glanced at me, I felt pinned to my chair. It was a look that spoke without words, and I didn't know it at the time, but that look would develop over the years to a point where we knew each other's thoughts. Before I knew it, the meeting was over and he was up and out the door.

Dvora later asked Yechiel if he "had noticed the pretty woman in the meeting."

"Yeah, I did... who was that?"

Dvora told him who I worked for and then directly asked him if he wanted to date me.

"What? Why would she go out with me? Really? I... Okay, arrange it." Dvora said no, and gave him my number to call.

He did not call.

Not that day. Not the next. In fact, it took weeks of Dvora prompting him to finally pick up the phone.

I expected it would be quick and we would both realize this wasn't for us. However, we spoke for an hour on our first call. He was so very different from what I had seen in the meeting. During that call, I immediately felt his compassion, his loneliness. He had no barriers, and poured out his heart – his pain, his hurt. I was overcome with how open and vulnerable he was with me.

We had many long and wonderful phone conversations before we were able to have a first date. I had young children and needed to prepare, to plan a babysitter before being able to go out. Yechiel's schedule was constantly in flux, and tended to be more spontaneous. He stayed in Tel Aviv often because of easier logistics, but Dvora really worked to bring us together. She alerted me every time he was staying in Jerusalem. She kept me apprised of the events he would be attending, his speaking engagements, and she always made sure I had an invite. Once, he was to give a talk to a group near my office and she insisted that I "just had to attend" since it was just a short walk for me. I took a break from work and went for a short while, staying in the back of the room, leaving even before the end of his speech. He asked Dvora if she knew why I left, and she teased him with an, "Oh, you noticed her, did you?"

When we finally settled on a date, he called me. "So, can you pick me up?" I was taken back. Pick him up? Not an auspicious beginning. I wanted romance; I wanted him to take the lead. But, okay, fine, I agreed to pick him up. It was hard to shake how awkward it felt. He was supposed to be worldly, an international traveler, yet he couldn't grab a taxi? I was used to chivalry, European dating standards. I felt a sliver of doubt. Confusion. He couldn't pick me up or meet me at the restaurant? It was a first date, wasn't he supposed to figure this out?

When Yechiel got into my car, he asked where we should go. I was dumbfounded. He didn't make a reservation, or even think about it? There was nowhere he wanted to take me? I was confused. My thoughts scrambled to catch up. I decided to give him the benefit of the doubt. He didn't know the city. I chose a nice place near me, a beautiful restaurant overlooking the walls of Jerusalem.

He walked in like he owned the place. I was to learn this was his way; he was larger than life, gregarious, and exuded confidence. From his initial, "Hi, *shalom*!" to the room, the staff – to his interrogation type questioning of our waiter, "Where are you from, how long have you been in Israel…" All he wanted, all he ordered, was hot soup. "Not just hot, boiling hot. I want the soup boiling hot." He would reiterate boiling – he would never eat the soup if it were not boiling. He wanted soup to make him sweat when he ate it.

I had this impression of a rabbi that was overturned when I met Yechiel for that date. As an introvert, his extreme extraversion would make me squirm but it was also incredibly endearing. I felt like he did not know how to eat, his table manners were sloppy; he would slurp his soup so loudly it was shocking. That night I found out that Yechiel was 17 years older than me, and I nearly fell off my chair. Had I known his age, I'm not sure I would have agreed to meeting him, I already knew what that was like.

To top things off, he did not leave a tip. I was mortified, and couldn't say anything. I think he sensed my discomfort; he realized what he had done and on the ride back, said he would stop by the next day to give them a generous tip and apologize. Despite my discomfort, I knew part of my hesitation was from my own expectations.

I drove him home, dropped him off and then I went home. There was no kiss, no hug, nothing but propriety on that first date.

Yechiel and I had talked on the phone for hours before our first date, and in the months that followed, we continued our sporadic but long nightly, sometimes early morning conversations. During the days or weeks when we didn't talk, my mind kept reliving our chats, how comfortable they were, how much we had in common. There were similarities in the years that shaped up as adults. I arrived in Israel in 1983 at the age of 15. I'm not sure what I was running away from, all I knew is I needed to get away. We shared our memories from boarding school. Life away from home from a young age. I would tell him how I would sneak into the kitchen at night looking for food, he would tell me about living with a family where he was embarrassed to ask for more. In his youth, he had spent a year in Israel and he would describe how once a week they crossed the fields into town to buy a *shawarma* and it would be the best meal of the week. He remembered always being hungry since he left home. We spoke a lot about how those years shaped us, being lonely and away from the love of our parents.

The pain of our divorce connected us very strongly during those initial conversations. We had cried together talking about the loneliness of a Friday night. I loved how friendly he was with everyone, how easily he would start a conversation with anyone. He was open with me in a way I had never experienced before. We spent hours together on the phone and yet I was not sure I would see him again.

Yechiel left Israel a couple of days after our first date. Our relationship that first year or two became sporadic – some might even say uneventful. Often it was just a phone call every other week. It certainly wasn't like the intense, passionate beginnings one reads about in romance novels or sees in the movies. But we connected. And when we connected, we would talk for hours. I loved talking with him, and quickly he became a dear friend. In truth, it felt more like a deepening friendship than a whirlwind romance. He would invite me to come spend the holidays with him in Chicago or to spontaneously meet him in Los Angeles; we had been dating for over a year at that point. It had been several weeks since our last conversation and out of the blue, he called me from LA. He opened without preamble, "I just really, really miss you… I don't know when I'm getting back to Israel, why don't you get on a plane and meet me here?" I didn't hesitate; I was on a plane the next day. We had enjoyed mini vacations in Chicago, LA, Prague, and Barcelona. Yechiel traveled wherever he needed to be for his growing organization, and sometimes I wouldn't see him for weeks. We never spoke about getting serious, or taking things to the next level.

After two years of not knowing what the future held with him, I was becoming unsettled. There was uneasiness in me, wondering if he (*me, we*) were ready to take to the next level or not. Honestly, I wanted stability. I wanted a life partner.

We sat down for a serious conversation. I told Yechiel I could not continue the relationship as it was. We were more than friends, but still not a couple. I wanted to be a couple, but as a rabbi, he could not introduce me as such unless we were married, so I let go.

We did not speak again for two months.

I was okay as long as I knew he was far away. I was used to not having him around. I missed him but it was not painful. However, after a couple months, Dvora alerted me that he was in the country again. I lost my balance. My heart in my stomach at the thought of him in the same city and not see him. I had to find a way to see him.

To take my mind off Yechiel, I had started rekindling the romance I had with a man I had been seeing when Dvora first suggested I meet

Yechiel. He and I were securing our plans to go to Sinai for a vacation. Moreover, I started to think this was a step toward my future. One day, unexpectedly, Yechiel called. In one of our previous conversations, he mentioned a set of books on Jewish thought that meant a lot to him: Strive for Truth by Rabbi Eliyahu Dessler. He was calling to say he had the books and wanted to know how to get them to me. As was his habit, he had taken out a recorder and added a voice note to his to-do list. I was taken back, touched that he had remembered and thought to still get them. Any not that made it into his voice-it would get done. Not always immediately, but he would get to it eventually. I thanked him. In the brief conversation that followed, I told him of the man I was seeing and our impending vacation. I heard it in his voice immediately. He got jealous. "What? Sinai? Sounds exotic, can we do that sometime?" I was confused and told him so. He asked if we could meet.

For our meeting, I deliberately chose the most romantic place in Jerusalem. This time I told him to take a cab and I would meet him there. I figured if it were going to be the last time I saw him, I would make it the date I thought I was going to have the first time we met. To my surprise, when I arrived, Yechiel was already there. Yechiel was never on time. And not only was he on time, *he had gotten there before me*. This would be the only time in our dating and married life when this would happen. I knew at that moment that it was a huge gesture from him.

During dinner he confessed he was distraught because he realized he was losing me. "And I don't want to lose you. Please bear with me. I can't promise you anything right now. But I'm telling you two things, I don't want to lose you, and bear with me. Give me some time."

I said okay.

"I'll bear with you, but don't push it."

"Are you giving me an ultimatum?"

"I'm just being honest. I don't want to wait forever."

So we agreed. I didn't go to Sinai, and I started dating Yechiel again.

Now, days later, after what was to be our 12th year wedding anniversary, after I found him on our kitchen floor, on the last night of *Shiva*, I again climbed the stairs to our bedroom. His side of the bed is flat, empty… tidy. His overnight weekend bag is open. His clothes lay out on the bed. His shoes are just where he left them. He had been packing for our anniversary trip. I crumbled. I didn't know it was possible to have so many tears.

I keep finding myself stifled by the company of others and then crippled by loneliness when I leave them. I am terrified and I don't even know of what, because I have lost everything already.

– Veronica Roth, *Allegiant*

Just like that, *Shiva* is over, the house is empty; my children are going back to their lives in Tel Aviv for a couple of nights, to return on Thursday through *Shabbat*. During this time, my brother arrives from the States. His visit had been pre-planned, a gift from Yechiel and I to celebrate a milestone birthday. Instead of a celebration, my brother, the organizer par excellence, started rearranging and cleaning up what had remained untouched since the day Yechiel died. Even after the nightly cleanings during *Shiva*, the house was a total mess. My kitchen looked trashed. My brother is tidying up. Papers, containers, leftover food, chairs everywhere. The entrance tables, side tables, covered with papers, condolences, booklets, the leaves of hundreds of people who had been through our house in the past week.

This is all too soon. As he tidies up, I try to reason with him.

I beg, I plead, and yes, I scream at him.

"You cannot remove any of my life with Yechiel!"

I am not able to do anything but stay in bed. My brother is firm. He removes the overnight bag that was on the bed, the shoes, and the clothes Yechiel had laid out to pack.

"I will take them out again later." I thought to myself.

He insists that I need this cleansing, that I would thank him someday.

Over the next couple of days, we go through the closets together, packing up everything that looks old and dusty, and clothes Yechiel has not worn in years.

Pedro will come to pick them up and donate.

My brother goes into Yechiel's bathroom. I cannot bear to watch as he removes all of Yechiel's personal items – his toothbrush, cologne, medications...

As my brother slowly put the house back in order, he was careful to leave the happiest, less overt, reminders of my husband's presence in our house. The books Yechiel was reading, with the bookmark in them, still occupied the area by his chair. His reading glasses still rested on the side table in the living room.

Jewish custom dictates the mourning period is one year, yet for a spouse the custom is different. Just one month. *One month...* it was inconceivable. The reasoning behind this being that a grieving spouse should start to find some kind of normalcy as soon as possible, out of fear of becoming accustomed to being in mourning. I would carry this pain for the rest of my life.

One month. I was barely functioning. Given that I just had thirty days of "official" mourning, I pushed off everything. I hardly left the house. I tried going to the office for a few hours just to try to distract myself but I would only last about an hour before I broke down crying. Coming back home knowing that nothing awaited me there was indescribable. I did the bare minimum and pushed away anything that was not urgent. The mail, bills, lawyers, any and all paperwork would have to wait.

I felt his presence with me at every moment. I felt his loss every second. Evenings, our together-time, were the hardest. Climbing into bed and looking at the empty side was excruciating. The silence was deafening and so hard to live with. A friend shared with me that she left the lights and television on all night just to fill in that space. I adopted the idea of leaving on the lights but was still unable to turn on the TV, or even touch the remote. It still had his fingerprints on it, still sticky from changing channels while he ate. He would snack at his recliner while watching the news. Crumbs, spills were a daily event around the recliner and I desperately missed cleaning it up.

Today, the living room feels like nobody lives here.

Those first few weeks without Yechiel were torture. This nightmare was just starting. Every first of everything. The first *Shabbat*.

Shabbat was magical with Yechiel. It was his day to get lost in time and he took me with him. He was always racing the clock, cramming everything he could before sundown, only turning off his phone after he made sure he called his family. Once the sun went down, he was able to shut his mind off of work, even if his email inbox was full and had important matters left unattended. On Saturdays, it wouldn't matter what time he woke up, he could sleep for over 12 hours. He worked so hard during the week, his rest was crucial. I would often go to the synagogue on my own, and he would sometimes still be sleeping when I returned. There was never a schedule on *Shabbat* day; this was his special "island in time" as he called it. I never knew what time we would eat; it was sometimes awkward when we had guests and we all had to wait until he was finished praying. I can feel him there, always in his special place on the balcony. He always stood in the same place, unless it was raining and he would stand outside the small covered porch by the front door, but always outdoors.

When my eyes caught those special places where he would pray, I expected to see him standing there.

I wasn't going to hear him make *Kiddush*, the blessing of the wine, on that first Friday night. This is more than I could bear. I loved putting my head against his chest to feel the vibrations of his singing. I would thank God each week for that moment. Those moments kindled a strange feeling, as if something was telling me that those moments would not last. I made an effort to take a snapshot of each special moment for remembrance later. That first Friday night at my brother in law's home, I sat with my children on each side of the table and held their hands so hard I thought I would break them. The rest of the family was also around the table. Looking around that table, I saw they all had their spouses, and my loneliness nearly gutted me. My love would never again be by my side. I would never again rest my head against his chest and feel him singing. Looking around the table, I realized I was the only one that would sleep alone in bed that night, and every other night that followed.

They say time heals all wounds, but that presumes the source of the grief is finite.

– Cassandra Clare, *Clockwork Prince*

For the first ten years of our life together, Yechiel dreamed of opening a unified social 911 network of support that covered all of Israel. He wanted the grassroots one-on-one help. Some ideas worked for a while, others failed, but he persevered.

He was finally able to launch his vision in February 2016. He directed his staff to organize the opening of this safe haven where any person in urgent need could call and receive immediate assistance. We were both excited; I asked him if I could volunteer there.

I started the next day. We had a week to prepare before 25 operators would begin the month-long basic training for the call center. I helped prepare the nametags, training folders, and the schedule. I thought I would continue to volunteer a few hours or one day a week. I was very wrong. On the first day of the actual training program, I realized the job was not so simple. I would have to go through the entire two-week basic training and learn how to answer calls and operate the computer systems necessary to register the calls. A few hours were just not going to be enough.

Our tags identified us by first names only, so mine just said *Joelle*. The newly recruited operators did not recognize me as the President's wife, and I did not volunteer the information. I just wanted to be treated like one of the crew. We did trust exercises, role-playing emergency calls, and reviewed scripts. During one exercise, the woman I was paired with was blindfolded and I had to lead her around the room and down the hallways. She was petrified, flinching and timid. Rather than holding her hand like others who were paired up, I tucked her under my arm, and we proceeded slowly. I felt her fear, she barely knew me and yet she had to trust me in her darkness, not being able to see anything. I would remember that later when I was answering phones. To hear the pain, fear, anxiety over the phone. To work with someone through their struggle, gain their trust rapidly and help them as best as we can. We enacted calls, role-playing with each other – when someone is screaming on the phone, when a stranger is sobbing, how do you respond? The weeks of training bonded us, made us feel like a family working toward something bigger.

It was liberating to train alongside everyone else like a regular volunteer. Until the day Yechiel came into the center to welcome the new team of operators. As soon as he appeared, the room went silent. Yechiel had a reputation, and everyone was intimidated and in awe of meeting the big boss.

They expected a serious man, but Yechiel jovially opened the meeting with, "I heard the most beautiful woman is among you." Mouths dropped, hushed intakes of shock rippled around me. All the women in the room blushed. And then he made his way towards me and gave me a big hug. When I pulled away, I could see the confusion in the room. Yechiel then smiled hugely. "I believe you've met my wife."

My coworkers were taken by surprise. But we had already shared a connection during intense training weeks we spent together. I had their friendship. I may have been the President's wife, but I wasn't being paid to work at the call center.

After a full month of training, the hotline was ready to go live. I was a bundle of nerves the night before. We all were. We would be talking to real people, dealing with raw emotions and real issues, and I barely slept. What kind of response would we get? Would it be overwhelming? What if we couldn't help anyone?

I jumped out of bed the next morning and was the first one at the office. We went live.

Ours was the number you called if you were going to be evicted, or if you couldn't pay your electric bill, or if you needed assistance with getting the special foods required for a holiday. It should come as no surprise that initially we got a lot of suicide calls. Desperate people say whatever they can to get help. However, we were not set up as a suicide line. In Israel, if you hear anyone say they are going to harm themselves, by law you have to take it seriously and report it to the police. Our hotline had a partnership with a suicide prevention organization, and when we got such calls, we would bring them on the line and they would take over that conversation – we weren't trained to take mental health calls. I pictured little red flags that we would pull up to let the manager know as soon as a caller was threatening with suicide, but luckily, we found a solution.

Initially we paired up in teams of two until we got comfortable with the live system. No amount of training really prepared us for the daunting task of taking a call – it was fast-paced, it was stressful due the immediate pain from the caller,

and you had to be incredibly accurate. Typing in the information from the caller, listening and being empathetic to the caller's plea, while also checking the database for a solution, all while trying to mitigate risk and defuse a volatile situation. Each day was a drench of adrenalin, and I was exhausted by day's end. Especially in that first month. But I felt galvanized after each call, gratified that I was able to assist someone and the close of every day was rewarding in a work well done. It was something I had never experienced at a job before. It was inspiring. I felt useful. I was actually helping those in great need.

I sat side-by-side in a cubicle with them, took calls like every else, and they treated me as equal. While others in Yechiel's organization didn't know me well, and struggled about how to relate to me, at the hotline, I was just one of the group. I spent my whole days there – I was the first one in the office in the morning, and last one to leave at night. Our friendship just grew from there and over the next three years, they became my family. I became a full time staff, just without a salary or benefits.

The initial manager for the call center left shortly after opening and the management started recruiting for another. The process took a few months. Suddenly one day, we were introduced to Hadas.

Hadas had over twenty years' experience in call center senior management. She had been responsible for over 300 staff in different teams spread all over Israel. At first, she was reluctant to accept a lower job with a team of only 25 operators, but her dream was to switch to the nonprofit sector. She finally accepted the offer, and then found out that she would also manage a volunteer on staff who happened to be the rabbi's wife. She shared with me one day that the fact she was going to oversee the boss's wife made her apprehensive. Her worry proved unfounded. At the moment we met, I felt an immediate connection with her. I found myself hugging her, and knew we would get along great. Hadas herself realized what a resource the President's wife could be, and she was excited to work more closely with me. We scheduled a formal meeting the day after and talked about Yechiel's purpose and vision. She wanted the team to become more effective, and quickly put in a system. She took me in as her right hand, shared with me the outcome of all her meetings, and asked me to be her co-director within a few weeks of her arrival.

For the next three years we became inseparable, and as such, Hadas also became an inseparable part of our house. She joined us often on Friday nights, I trusted her to take care of our home when we traveled. It's hard to describe how integral Hadas was in our lives; she took care of everything behind the scenes. Hadas would cook and fill up the fridge before we landed. She wasn't intimidated by Yechiel and would regularly pop over to our house and into his office, just to say hi.

Yechiel was proud of the systems we put into place and talked about the outstanding work of the call center at every opportunity.

I spent 10-12 hours at the call center every day (when we were in Israel), or on the phone a few times a day with Hadas when we were traveling. The call center was receiving 200-300 calls every day of people asking for help and it was hectic. Each operator at the call center was passionate and dedicated. Answering call after call of people crying or screaming took a toll on all of us. We set up weekly sessions with a licensed therapist so staff could decompress.

The hotline was starting to take a life of its own, a separate organization within the organization. As a call center, it had a business-based management, instead of a nonprofit. We measured length of calls, answered calls versus non-answered calls, number of referrals of callers to other partner organizations, or immediate emergency solutions provided along with cost. In time, Yechiel realized he needed to separate the activities of the hotline from the rest of the organization, and establish a new, separate nonprofit.

He just did not know how. He needed help. In the fall of 2018, Yechiel hired a well-known consulting company to help with the process. First, they conducted a review of all the departments, and although they barely spent time with us at the hotline, they concluded that the social 911 was not in line with the rest of the organization. Of course it wasn't, that was exactly the point – to separate the two.

Yechiel's frustration was clear and obvious. The staff that were in the hallway on the day the company presented him with the final report recalls Yechiel's yelling coming from his office. The walls were almost shaking. They had never heard Yechiel scream like that. The company didn't get it, and they could not understand each other. Yechiel dreamed big and the hotline got back to the grassroots vision he had of directly helping Israel. The hotline was a direct line to those in need, unlike other programs in his organization that just handed out money to partnering companies. A social 911 helpline was his big audacious vision and he was not willing to let it go just because an outside report said it did not fit.

In the days following Yechiel's death, all I could think of was, "Thank God for Hadas and thank God I have my job." I had been working full time at the hotline since February 2016 and it had changed my life in so many ways. I was so grateful to have a warm place and a family of such caring co-workers and to care for the most vulnerable that would call in every day. I went back for an hour at a time after *Shiva*, sometimes two hours – whatever I could handle. I didn't last much without crying in that first month. The first time I opened my computer and saw an email from Yechiel, I fell apart. I would never again receive an email from him. I needed to get back home immediately. My safe place. I rushed out, blindly making my way back.

"I am going to be ok." It was like a mantra I kept repeating to myself.

When people asked how I was doing, I started answering, "I'm going to be okay." For myself, I needed to stay with a positive answer, a positive message, even if I really disliked that question. Instinctually, I knew that having a routine, having a purpose was what I needed. And I was grateful for a job that gave me that; even if it would take me time to work back up to being there full time.

The organization Yechiel had founded decided otherwise.

Just a few short weeks after Yechiel died, Hadas got notice to start the process for closure of the hotline. I could not understand what was happening. Yechiel wanted to establish a separate organization and this decision was confusing to me. The management said they wanted to focus on a core mission, and that the hotline was not part of it. I offered to volunteer in another department.

"We appreciate the time and commitment you put in, but we are moving in different directions and wish you much success in whatever you choose to pursue."

And just like that, I was unceremoniously released. In all intents and purposes, fired from Yechiel's organization. Less than a month after he died.

To say it was devastating is an understatement. *Betrayed*. Heartsick. For weeks I could not function. I was barely holding on before, and this felt like being kicked while down. Unnecessary and brutal. It paralyzed me.

I had a desperate urge to connect with other widows. Women who would know what I was going through, who understand my pain, and see how they are doing. I needed their advice. I called an acquaintance and every widow I could find.

Grief can destroy you – or focus you.

– Dean Koontz, *Odd Hours*

My neighborhood communities in Jerusalem rallied around me. They made sure I was never alone for *Shabbat.* I do not know how I did it. I went to people's homes, some I barely knew. I would hold my tears as much as possible, but I was not always successful. I felt like a zombie just accepting invitations without thinking, and eating with people just to be distracted for a couple of hours. All I felt was that I could not be alone. I needed a reason to get out of bed, get dressed and out of the house.

Those first *Shabbat* invitations got me out of the house. I started going out during the week as well, I kept as busy as I could meeting people and came back home exhausted in order to go straight to bed. I had no occupation at home. I tried reading, but I could not get through the page. I would read a paragraph and realize I did not remember it. It was surreal, this lack of focus, this fog. I struggled against it. I read and reread the same page, still not understanding the words. I didn't know what was happening to my brain. I later learned the term "widow's brain." But during those first months, I thought I was losing my mind. I could not read a simple letter or email without rereading ten times to try to understand.

The memory fog was more acute than I could express in words. My brain's lack of retention bled into every aspect of my every day. I came to rely on Hadas to keep me level. She would patiently repeat herself for me. Remind me often of appointments, conversations, tasks and minute details of my day. I started carrying a notebook with me to write everything down, just so I could remember the smallest things.

Choices. Decisions. "You can be the director of the movie – the movie that you choose to be your life." Hadas loves repeating this, a spectral moving through the numbness of my brain. We are not just watchers of our own movie – we get to direct it. We get to choose, to change whatever happens to us, whatever happens does not need to determine what our life looks like. I need to decide what I want my life to look like.

I could not choose other people's actions, but I could learn to control my *reaction.*

It was just one month after Yechiel's passing. ONE month. Raw grief. I could not feel anything besides the pain of losing my beloved husband. The pain took over any other feelings. But something inside me knew, somehow I felt that I needed a purpose, a goal, something to focus on. However, I could not think of anything that gave me 'butterflies' like the hotline did. I did not want to look for another job. I could not bear the fact that something that Yechiel cared so strongly for would not continue. I tried talking some sense into the director general. "I can take over the hotline, let's register it under a separate entity – as Yechiel was already thinking of doing – and continue." Yechiel had already approved the budget for 2019 so I could not understand the reasoning behind the decision to close such a lifeline for Israel. I had no say; I was just a volunteer – no longer seen as Yechiel's wife.

A lawyer friend suggested that I fight for my rights, that I was not just a volunteer. I gave 12-hour days in the position of co-director without pay, yet I had no capacity for a fight. My husband was dead. My world imploded. And now I watched his dream shatter. I did not want to be in a place where I am not wanted. I walked away.

I needed to do something in Yechiel's memory. Touching the lives of Jerusalem residents, people who otherwise had nowhere else to turn. Doing what Yechiel truly loved.

My mind went to a moment when he saw an old woman with her groceries at the bus stop in the rain. *Why was she out struggling in the rain in the first place? Where was her family? Did she even have any family?* Yechiel stopped the car suddenly, causing the car behind to almost crash into us before angrily honking his horn. Yechiel was not paying attention; he only had eyes for the little old woman in the rain. He got out of the car, stopped a cab, paid for it and helped the woman in.

That was the essence of Yechiel. That was the level of service he wanted for all Israelis. I knew what I had to do.

Two are better than one [...] for if either of them falls down, one can help the other up.

– Ecclesiastes 4:9-10

A few months before Yechiel died, I was commuting once a week to Tel Aviv to take a public speaking course. He talked me into it, the hotline was expanding, which meant I had to run more meetings, to present and speak more, and I always felt so awkward. I had to get over the burgeoning anxiety I felt about presenting to even just a few people. I was so passionate about the hotline but I did not know how to talk about it. Hadas had been teaching me a bit, training me on the broader points of public speaking and would offer tips on all my presentations, "At this point tell a story," or "for impact, now is the time to make this point." And she really tried to teach me how to make an impact during a presentation, but I was still very, very uncomfortable.

I had been at a work retreat when one of the speakers, an actor, told us that we can actually decide who we want to be in front of people. Decide what your character will be in front of people, and be that character. She encouraged us to take an acting course and mentioned that she was one of the teachers at a school that carried a public speaking course. A light went through me that day, and I felt like I needed to break out of my shell. After her talk, I went up and spoke to her. Later, with Yechiel's encouragement, I signed up for her course. A 10-week course required me to drive an hour each way to Tel Aviv, spend four hours in class, before driving back home to Jerusalem at 10pm. I was nervous about the drive, especially at night, and the intense time commitment, but Yechiel knew my stage fright and insisted it would do me good.

That first day it was a small group. It was scheduled to have a different topic every week, learning a specific skill with a certified teacher: voice, body language, structure, incorporating humor, etc. That first night, she asked each one of us to stand and introduce ourselves. Stand and talk? OMG. I cannot do that. I was shaking. They allowed me to sit. Just that first time.

I persevered and made it through the course.

One night, I arrived at school and was looking for parking around the neighborhood. Tel Aviv's city center is extremely difficult to find parking. I was winding my way on the narrow streets looking for an empty space, when I slowly made a right turn into yet another street. A huge truck was parked obscuring the road, but there was room around it. The truck had been unloading

so the rear ramp was lifted. Without cargo on it, nor did it have a warning flag, it would be visible in the darkness. As I made my turn, the thin metal of the lift sliced through my windshield. With the sound of breaking glass, I slammed the car to stop, the heavy metal struts abruptly stopped in front of my face.

Time slowed. Light bounced eerily, I was covered in glass. I don't know how long I sat there staring at the steel that came so close to decapitating me. Strangely, all I could think of was I was going to be late for class. I got out of the car on wobbly legs. I must have kicked into autopilot. Took pictures of the truck and car, licenses, called insurance, sent license and pictures of the accident. Left the key under the mat for the tow truck to pick up in the morning. Went to my speaking course. I would figure out how to get back home later. I don't remember much of that night but the sound of breaking glass, facing the metal lift, my heartbeat. It wasn't until the next day that I was hit with the realization of what happened. I started shaking uncontrollably. I was in shock.

I got a call to pick up the car about a week later. I was confused – they were able to fix it? I did not want to see that car again, but I went to the garage. I got behind the wheel, and started shaking. Images of the close call I had, flashes of the accident, traumatized me. I got right back out. I left the car there, called Yechiel and I never got in that car again. It would be several months before I could get into any vehicle again or even drive again. I started taking the bus or the train wherever I went. Yechiel was worried I might never sit behind another steering wheel because nothing he did could compel me to drive. I could not get in the car even if he drove, so eventually we sold it.

One day, driving back after a meeting, Hadas feigned illness. She pulled over and said she was "too sick to drive." Rather than call for help, we switched places and I drove us home. She surreptitiously took a picture of me driving and sent it to Yechiel. He sent back a happy face emoji. He was happy and proud of himself, not only was their plot successful and tricked me back into driving, he had also just learned what an emoji was and enjoyed using them.

I think of that often, and the many times since when Hadas just knew what to do. Now, in order to navigate my grief I had to trick myself into living again. Another moment of life offering me a parable to prepare me for what was to come.

No one ever told me that grief felt so much like fear.

– C.S. Lewis, *A Grief Observed*

Three weeks. Somehow I'm still alive. The pain is almost unbearable. The *Shloshim*, the end of mourning of the first month, is coming up. One week before the end of the first month I'm not functioning. I cannot make it through an hour without crying.

The family will be gathering. We decided to keep it strictly family instead of the customary large event. I'm scared. I haven't seen some of them in a few weeks. I'm afraid of reliving the *Shiva* when we were all together. How will I handle this? Where do I pull the strength? Whom do I hold on to? I am alone.

I woke up in Hadas' house. What was I doing here? How did I even get to her house? I couldn't remember. Last thing I remembered was having dinner with Yechiel's brother and his wife at their apartment in Jerusalem. My head was spinning. What happened?

Hadas tells me I just showed up drunk at her door last night, crying inconsolably. Luckily, I still had enough sense to call her when leaving their apartment, and she realized I could not drive. She ordered a cab for me to her house and had remained on the line with me until I arrived. I honestly don't know what I would have done without her that night. Only Yechiel knew that I should not drink more than one glass of wine, and always watched my glass. Yechiel always drove if we went out. This was my first time out drinking wine without him. He wasn't here anymore to drive us home. What could I do? I was alone in the cold night by myself. I was utterly lost. Embarrassed to go back up to my brother-in-law's apartment. I could not show them the intensity of my pain; they were dealing with their own. I did not want to be a burden and I did not want them to pity me. I don't know how I had the wherewithal to call Hadas. She saved me that night.

And it hurts like hell.

It was like the first day all over again. I cannot bear the pain.

I lost so much more than my husband. I lost the person I need by my side right now. I lost the person who can hug me and tell me that everything is going to be ok. His look – those eyes that spoke without words. That entire past, our future plans. Our special connection died with him, and realizing that I lost my other half is more than painful, like an amputation. Who will I share those special moments with? Who will remember a detail of our time together if I forget? There is nobody to share the memories with. How do I get through this without the loving hug of my husband? Without his shoulder to cry on?

You honor a man by the way you treat his widow.

– John Armor

Yechiel had shared with me the trick he used when public speaking and it had become one of our silent signals: *the switch.* "Turn it on," he would signal to me as he mimicked a switch with his hand. He would literally mimic flipping a switch and turn on his secondary persona: the performer, the public figure everyone wanted to see. He would turn to me and say "It's show time!" and he would dial it up. Then he would enter a room or walk on stage and the atmosphere would change. He would be charged, lit, his presence larger than life. No one could miss his loud booming voice, his charisma, and the fact that he was a big, tall, rather imposing man. He would give the room his all and invest in connecting to everyone. People who knew our travel schedule often commented that we must have seen so many beautiful places, but every trip was packed with events, people, and having to "be on" all the time took it out of him. He was totally exhausted after every event, always needing to rest.

Yechiel didn't really have close friends to unwind with, to share experiences. He often reflected that most people in his life stuck around because of what he could give them. Hundreds of people would claim closeness, but only two called religiously every week to wish him *Shabbat shalom.* It was, in some measure, an aloneness of his own making. He sacrificed everything for his mission, for his calling. Time normally spent with family or friends, he gave to his work. I am blessed to have been by his side and to share his work, because it really was the only way to be near him. His mission and he were one.

After his death, I realized quickly how true it was that he really did not have friends; his belief that everyone just wanted to be near him for their personal interest was true. I was surprised how quickly even his best friend was gone. While it seemed like everyone came out of the woodwork for *Shiva*, only a very few continued contact afterwards. Others expected me to be past grieving, to move on only a few short months after his death.

I felt like everyone dropped me. More than ever, I was "turning it on" so that I did not push people away. Use the switch. Turn it on, pretend to be okay because no one wants to be around sadness. It did not help. I felt the sting of being shunted aside. As if with Yechiel gone, I was expendable. I wondered why I even bothered. Widows talk about this, the lack of friends, friends that one has as a couple, just disappear. Heartbreakingly, Yechiel spoke about it all the time, "People are just around me because they want something from me." No one cared to call him just to say hi, to schmooze. A vast majority of the time, when his phone rang, it was work.

Now, with Yechiel gone, very few called.

I felt the hypocrisy of the hundreds of people who claimed friendship with Yechiel. "*You honor a man by the way you treat his widow. A widow honors her husband by the way she lives her life after he dies.*" It moves me to fresh tears.

Courage doesn't always roar. Sometimes courage is the little voice at the end of the day that says I'll try again tomorrow.

– Mary Anne Radmacher

S*hloshim* – Thirty days. The one-month anniversary of Yechiel's death is approaching too quickly.

Scared. It's been just a few short weeks and each day seems harder than the last. Scared doesn't even come close to describing how I'm feeling. Fear. *Panic.* I am terrified. I am in total denial. *How can I survive this?* The person I need by my side, to hold me and hug me and tell me everything will be ok, is gone. How on earth am I supposed to go through this alone? How can the month be over? It seems like I just found him.

Everything around the house still feels the same. The image of Yechiel walking in through the front door is still so fresh in my mind I still catch myself expecting it. The house even still smells like him. His worn clothes are still in the laundry basket. How can I live my life without him, when my entire day was built around his schedule? A future on my own is still too unfathomable to even contemplate.

Physical pain strikes my chest, as though I tore my heart and lungs. *Shloshim*, it means thirty in Hebrew. 30 days. The term refers to the month after death, period after *Shiva* to the 30-day mark. And it refers to the end of the first stage of the mourning period. The custom in Israel is to put up the headstone, gather at the cemetery to recite Psalms and say *Kaddish*. A meal is also customary. What should one write on the stone? Most of that first month revolved around that question, the family trying to come up with a meaningful text to describe Yechiel's life. This was something I tried to focus on for the past few weeks. Drafts were sent back and forth. We finally decided on the wording.

The family dinner for the *Shloshim* lies under a fog in my mind. I remember we had one big table for all of us. The rest is vague. Being surrounded by the family was comforting, yet the thought of returning by myself to the empty house was devastating. I just wish someone had offered and insisted to stay with me. Maybe they did, but I ended up by myself.

The irony of grief is that the person you need to talk about how you feel is the person who is no longer there.

– Author Unknown

In the weeks that followed I found some comfort – although agonizing and heart wrenching at first - in reading the comments and going through the photos on his Facebook page, many of which I had taken and posted myself. Yechiel didn't even know how to log into his page. I had tried many times to teach him how to, even downloaded the app on his phone, but to no avail. He did not grasp social media, and I gave up trying to explain the difference between like and share, or the difference between a friend and a follower. The social media team in his organization managed his page together with me. They posted content referring to his work, and I took care of the more private posts, especially when we traveled. Yechiel would dictate to me many of his posts, so even if he didn't actually post it himself, every word was his. I would read the comments and private messages to him and would ask how he wanted to respond, then wrote it for him.

I would often film him on video and send it to the office for editing. I got used to filming him everywhere, even when just hanging out at home. Whenever he had an idea, or randomly started singing while having dinner or on a quiet evening at home, I would take out my phone and take a video. He wouldn't even realize I was filming him at times.

Every day after he passed away, I would sit and go through his page, reliving many of the moments we had spent together and remembering our evenings together or many trips around the world. I would spend hours and sometimes through the night just watching his videos and wanting to hear his voice.

Facebook can memorialize a page for a deceased person if you designate it while alive. Widows talk about how important their husband's pages are for them. On significant milestones, holidays and important anniversaries, friends can still write on it. It becomes a digital gravesite of sorts. It was heart wrenching but comforting at the same time. Knowing I had all those memories to look at whenever I needed gave me some peace. I knew they were kept safely there and would always have them. How naïve I was and took that for granted.

Yechiel's page was a public figure page, and without warning his organization decided it belonged to them, and that I – his wife and now his widow- should not have access to it. They removed me as administrator of the page. The social media team I had been working with understood my feelings, but they also had no say. Senior management decided otherwise. Overnight they blocked my access and took down the page. Without warning, that source of comfort was gone.

Luckily, since I was the one who took most of the pictures and videos, I still had some saved on my phone, together with all our private moments at home, but I could not believe the cruelty of it. I did not have the strength or energy to even fight it in court. From that point on I did not trust anyone when it came to Yechiel's property. Now I had to learn to trust only myself, to protect myself and get used to the idea that I was on my own. It is a very slow process; I am learning to take it one minute at a time, not even a day at a time. The hardest part is not knowing where your life is heading, all your plans and the future you had imagined are erased and I have no idea what tomorrow looks like.

Only true love can fuel the hard work that awaits you.

– Tom Freston

Every time I left the house I felt a terrible pain in my heart, a feeling that I was leaving him all over again. When I was home I felt that I was with him somehow. Everywhere I looked I saw him at home. Leaving the house felt like leaving Yechiel behind. A friend made some blown up photos of him and us together and I hung them around everywhere. Even in my bedroom. A full size photo of him in front of the bed looking at me, and even if I cried and kissed it every time, with time it became quite comforting.

Jewish custom has a person in mourning lighting a candle for the period of mourning. There are special mourning candles for this, built with specific thick wicks, and they can withstand stronger than average airflow. Simply put, they do not go out. Everyone in Israel buys them, because we know they don't blow out. The candles are created for specific time lengths and I was buying the seven days candles that stay lit for up to a week, and as per custom, I would light a new one when the candle diminishes. I thought maybe the rabbis stipulated only one month of grieving for a spouse so as not to impose restrictions on an already extremely difficult time for widows. It made no sense to me; I wanted the social padding of a longer grieving period.

I was not able to stop lighting the candle after a month and I kept it lit for the first year. I kept it in the kitchen where he died. The flame greeted me as I came and went. It became my constant, something tangible that I could "do" for him. I was very busy around the candle, I was always making sure I had enough, I checked it all the time, always aware when it was low, sometimes before I went to sleep, if it was too low, I would light another so the candle that was his presence in the house became an eternal flame. I would talk to the candle, I felt closer to him with the candle. It was as if he was watching over me through the candle. Some days, when the windows were closed and the air was still, I would talk to his candle and the flame would move. Was it my imagination? I didn't know, and frankly, I did not care. I would see the flame move and it drew me in. As if an invitation to talk to Yechiel. The flame let me know that Yechiel was with me.

Leaving the house and leaving the candle felt like I was abandoning him, leaving him alone. It was both a comfort and a tie. And then some days it felt like I was losing my mind speaking to a candle. I would have long conversations just looking at the candle, imagining how with each movement of that flame was an answer from him, looking for just a sign that he was still with me. I would try to get back home as fast as I could, spending as little time as I could out of the house. Because he was there, waiting for me. The way back home was often very painful. That dreadful anticipation of an empty house, no movement, no energy, and a deep dark silence that was terrifying.

Life isn't a matter of milestones, but of moments.

– Rose Kennedy

I cannot wrap my brain around how quickly time is moving away from Yechiel. The first holiday was coming up shortly after *Shloshim* and I am beside myself. I am in denial. How can I possibly celebrate *Purim* without him? *Purim*, a joyous holiday commemorating the great victory of the Jews over Haman. *Purim*, when we read the Book of Esther, wear costumes, but most importantly give *tzedakkah* and offer baskets of food and sweets and have a festive meal. In Israel, you will see children dressed up in their costumes, and there is such a festive atmosphere everywhere.

I just want the world to stop for a minute and let me catch up.

As with everything else, Yechiel had his own way of celebrating. He was really strict on some matters and more lenient in others, he had his own red lines in every holiday, and on *Purim* it was the reading of Esther. We were in a different place every year for *Purim* so we really did not have specific customs of our own or habits of celebrating with anyone in particular. The *mitzvot* for *Purim* were not always easy in places where we didn't know anyone. Even finding a place for a festive kosher meal on *Purim* could be challenging. In Buenos Aires one year, we were having our meal at a local kosher restaurant and bumped into a dear couple we had met at a conference the year before. Yechiel was so happy to see them, because he had been wondering how to complete the mitzvah of giving food, and he felt that God had sent them to us!

On *Purim*, the one thing Yechiel was hard-ruled about was the reading of the *Megillah* – the scroll of Esther. As is customary, every Jew has to hear every word of the *Megillah* read directly from the Scroll. It was to be heard twice, once at night, the beginning of *Purim*, and again the next day. Yechiel was strict: he had to hear each word directly from the rabbi leading the reading. He would often stand right next to the reader to make sure he heard it first directly from him, and not accidentally from someone else who might follow along and speak aloud the words first.

With my first *Purim* alone approaching, memories about the incredibly special *Purim* Yechiel and I shared in Amsterdam came to me. It was a cold rainy day. The Jewish people were not really dressed up, just wore masks or other small accessories. Yechiel was running late and I wondered if he had wandered into one of the local coffee shops. The day was otherworldly, a leisurely exploration of the city, and then we met up at the Portuguese Synagogue of Amsterdam. The 17th century building is a breathless work of craftsmanship, high arching windows and intricate woodwork. On *Purim*, they light over 1000 candles on the giant, centuries-old chandeliers. Walking in there at night took my breath away. It seemed we were caught up in the hushed, moving spirituality of the evening. Instead of the usual noise making at every mention of Haman, the community lightly tapped their feet on the floor. It was an awe-inspiring and spiritual evening.

And suddenly, I was overwhelmed with memories of Chicago.

We had landed at O'Hare and arrived in our apartment the evening of *Purim*. We were exhausted from the long trip from Israel. It was snowing heavily, but one cannot postpone reading *Megillah*. All must go to synagogue and hear it from someone who knows how to read it, and it has to be read from a kosher scroll. Thankfully that night when Yechiel found his kosher scroll in our Chicago apartment, he was able to read it himself so we wouldn't have to go out in the snow. It was the only time in all our years together that he read it just for me. It was just the two of us, candles, the windows overlooking the city, and the deep silence of the snow. I took a video of him reading Esther, as I did every chance I could, as though a small part inside me knew that these happy times would end.

Remembering this, I scramble to find that video on my phone. I broke down, but being able to listen to him was indescribable. I still did not know how I would get through the first holiday without him, but this video, his voice, was such an aching comfort for me. For the past two years we had been in Jerusalem for *Purim*, and had been invited to a dear friend for the festive meal. He called to invite me by myself this year, and I thought I could do it. I tried. I went to buy some sweets to bring with me, and walked over to their house. As I arrived and got in the elevator, I felt the pain again and started to choke up. Tears threatened. I really wanted to be there, remember how Yechiel was dancing in that apartment just a year ago, enjoy the *Purim* meal with some friends and not be by myself. I tried as hard as I could but was unable to control it. When I got there, I lost it. I could not stop the tears; they just spilled down my face. I could not even talk. I didn't even get to sit down and had to leave. It was too soon, I was not ready. I cried all the way back home.

I can understand why they did not invite me again the following year.

There are specific situations so powerful that they can overwhelm our inherent predispositions.

– Malcolm Gladwell, *The Tipping Point: How Little Things Can Make a Big Difference*

I soon discovered my power of attorney was only valid while Yechiel was alive. Right after *Shiva*, I realized my credit cards were frozen and I was cut off from any way to buy groceries or pay any of the mounting bills. Since I volunteered my time at his organization, we relied on his income that suddenly disappeared. They remotely erased his phone, contacts, emails, and texts, all gone. Then requested I return the leased car. The months after Yechiel's death felt like Shark Week. One day I was the president's wife, the next day nobody. I was only able to get groceries, necessities, and pay bills through the generosity of family and friends. Months later, they were 'kind' enough to share some of his emails.

It's still all one big fog. Yechiel's phone was cleared of all contacts, texts, and emails because they determined his phone "belonged to the organization." I was not consulted. I was not warned. The pain was unbearable. I almost gave up.

Everyone has a way of coping with difficult situations. The only way I knew to deal with them was to just ignore them.

Like so many years before, I found myself relying on the same coping mechanisms I had as a young adult. When I could not handle a situation, I would just remove myself from it. Run away. After I met Yechiel, he took over whatever I could not handle. Whenever I needed advice, Yechiel had been there for me. He helped me deal with anything. Everything was ok because he was by my side. How could I possibly handle lawyers, banks and bills without him? I just could not. Therefore I did not.

I focused on survival.

Call it a primal instinct, I knew I had to take care of myself and do whatever was good for *me* because no one else would. My life partner was gone. I had to slowly let go of anything or anyone that was not good for me. I slowly learned to fight my own fights; the ones that would help me survive. By creating a goal and looking to find meaning, I started building a *new* me.

I made mistakes along the way. In my fog of grief, I misjudged situations and had trouble communicating. I definitely made the wrong choices. But I tried – I dared. I did the best I could at the time. I became obsessed with plans and ideas that fizzled out. I kept at it, learning along the way. I over-prepared for everything because I could not trust my roller coaster of emotions. I hashed out and reviewed what I wanted to achieve during each meeting, even scripting out exactly what I wanted to say during casual phone conversation. I could not concentrate easily, and even when I was able, I could not concentrate for long. I was forgetting people's names, who they were – even people I saw daily, their names would suddenly no longer be accessible to me. There were times I was afraid I would forget my way home, like I would run an errand and not remember how to get back. I was terrified I was losing my mind. I had to write down everything, my notepad and pen were with me everywhere. In my house, the car, out running errands, and at work. Panic when my memory would go blank during a meeting; fortunately, Hadas was tuned to my state and she would notice my terrified look in time to take over. And we managed.

Somehow, I tapped into a determined place in myself. I was not going to let the fog take over, or let my fear paralyze me. I could not. If survival is fight or flight, I may have run away from a lot but I was still fighting for *me*. Guerrilla tactics with my own brain. I was going to move forward even if I made missteps.

To be kind is more important than to be right. Many times, what people need is not a brilliant mind that speaks, but a special heart that listens.

– The Lubavitcher Rebbe

One day my phone rang and I heard the voice of a young woman asking if she could come over. I was surprised. We were only acquaintances, but she worked for an organization that Yechiel and I knew well, so I agreed. I usually tried to agree to activities or meetings that felt 'safe' or didn't put me at any risk. Often I would ask Hadas to join, especially those early days when I wasn't able to carry on a conversation logically.

The young woman showed up with a huge box full of cakes and cookies and sat down. I thought she just wanted to visit, chat. Then she took a breath and said, "There's a reason I wanted to meet you."

I knew.

I burst into tears and hugged her without even waiting for more. My only small relief in those days was talking to people who knew my pain. Not the pain of grief, but specifically the pain of widowhood.

This young girl lost her husband just a few months after giving birth, and shared how her world looked dark and life was beyond hope. A few years later, she found happiness again. She just wanted to share her message of hope with me. Hope and some slim light at the end of the dark tunnel is what we need in those first weeks and months.

It was hard to feel anything other than pain in those days. However,

I was grateful for her visit. Kindness and caring from someone who did not even know me. Reaching out to bring hope to another widow. A truly good soul just wanting to comfort me.

Those short moments eventually made a real difference in my life.

I have a flashback to right after Yechiel and I were married; one of his close friends died. This friend and his wife lived in our neighborhood, he was one of the two male witnesses for our wedding, and he and Yechiel saw each other regularly. We would see him out for walks in the neighborhood, hand-in-hand with his wife. Whenever he passed our house, he would ring the bell and check in on Yechiel.

One evening he showed up to our house, again delightfully unannounced, and when I opened the door, I realized how very sick he was. Yechiel had known he was sick, but I hadn't realized how far along it was. He was so thin, so frail. That was the last time I saw him, and the image of him at the door stays with me.

Even though I felt badly at his death, and Yechiel was so close to him, we drifted away from his wife.

Today I feel so acutely how wrong that was. I didn't push Yechiel to stay in touch, and I didn't reach out. I wish I had understood more, and although I was not close with her, I regret not staying in touch. At the time, I felt like I was, I felt like I *did* reach out, but I now know I never really understood. I wince when I realize how much pain she must have been in at the time. How very alone she must have felt.

I know I did not do nearly enough.

Everyone keeps telling me that time heals all wounds, but no one can tell me what I'm supposed to do right now. Right now I can't sleep. It's right now that I can't eat. Right now I still hear his voice and sense his presence even though I know he's not here.

– Nina Guilbeau, *Too Many Sisters*

Yechiel used to come home and drop everything he carried on the dining room table. That table was always full of papers, books, keys, and wallet. It was a jumbled pile of his work bag, jackets, and shirts that he took off as soon as he got home, and this chaos was always there to greet us when we walked into the house. Only on Fridays would he clear it off so I could set the table for *Shabbat*. We didn't really use the dining room table during the week, so it didn't really matter to me. Except it looked cluttered, and made the rest of the house look untidy. I tried to clear the room in the entrance closet, or add an extra piece of furniture with drawers and shelves for him to put his everyday stuff away, but it never worked. He just liked to put everything on the table where he could see it. The messy entrance became part of the house.

That table was bare for months after he passed away.

I couldn't stand it.

It hit me every time I walked in the house.

The emptiness and clear reminder that he was not there.

I do not understand why there are some things that serve as triggers and make me break down, while other items around the house don't. The memories associated with every corner of the house are mine alone now, and cannot be explained to anyone else. The table has to be moved. I need everything to stay the same in the house, and yet I find myself slowly changing the things that I cannot deal with. So the table moves to the kitchen where it is not the first thing that hits me when I walk in the house. But his glasses and the book he was reading are still untouched.

Some things change, others do not. I cannot explain it. There is no logic.

But grief makes a monster out of us sometimes . . . and sometimes you say and do things to the people you love that you can't forgive yourself for.

– Melina Marchetta, *On the Jellicoe Road*

The news of Yechiel's death didn't seem real. It was incomprehensible. He wasn't just my boss, he and Joelle were dear friends of mine. Every morning I would wake up, expecting life to be normal, every morning realizing it would never be again. It was such a blow. And I had no idea in the beginning how much our lives were going to change.

The thing I wanted most was to call Joelle and tell her, "See, I told you, it's just a bad dream." But this was not to be.

Joelle had her before and after. It was difficult to witness such an immediate transformation. The first weeks were a struggle. The loss at witnessing her pain. The realization that I had no context to provide comfort for such a loss. In a moment, her life split apart. She lost more than her husband. She lost herself. Her identity as a wife, partner.

Her life's mission entwined with his.

Joelle was the one I leaned on at work. A trusted colleague who managed a large call center with me. I watched this strong, compassionate woman crumble. I saw a part of her die that day with Yechiel. I didn't know how to help her back. How could I sit in front of her and tell her, "it will be okay" and "you are strong." How do you make such meaningless platitudes when someone is shattered? What do you say to a person whose whole world has been destroyed?

After Yechiel's death, I made a pact with Joelle. We would just make it through the day. One day at a time. We wouldn't look ahead because it was too painful and nearly impossible to comprehend. One day at a time. One action at a time. For her, that could be just eating lunch. Getting dressed. Going for a walk. On good days it may be calling the bank, grocery shopping, or cleaning. I tried to be with her. I tried to be with her as much as possible but in the end, many of these things she had to work through alone.

She made it through a week and I planned as many things as possible to keep her busy, keep her mind off the emptiness of the house. We made it like any operations plan we develop for work. It became our mission: fill the days.

It seemed clear to me that Friday nights were the worst for her. Shabbat was normally full of love and warmth. I sensed she started to dread the coming weekend. Those nights when minutes would stretch into hours in an empty house. This beautiful evening was in danger of becoming a dreaded time of loneliness and alienation. It was not easy knowing there were Shabbats she spent alone, when I was surrounded by the cheerful noise of four children in a house full of family. I was always anxious to find out how she was doing after every Shabbat. Saturday after Saturday, it was a long time before Joelle became stronger. She was like a baby, learning her limbs again, standing upright, learning to walk on her own, only to fall and try again.

Her recovery was beset by falls, and every tumble brought us back to the pain of the first day. Only they weren't just minor *tumbles – they were devastating crashes. It's wrenching to witness the pain that keens from the soul. Every milestone, every holiday, every anniversary required emotional preparation. The date always brought a crash, and a week before she could stand up and walk again.*

I've come to think of Yechiel's death as Joelle's too. The Joelle of now is not the Joelle of then. The first year was a rollercoaster. One day she'd be almost normal and the next she'd be a weeping wreck. Her memory and comprehension disappeared. Conversations and meetings with her would progress normally and I would think she understood and was with me, but then she would respond like we never talked. I found myself repeating myself several times a day, for days in a row. She was learning to walk again, and it was a struggle.

At her lowest points, she retreated from the world, when the acknowledgement of reality was too much, she would break down crying, unable to function. She had no space for all the little things that needed taking care of and I realized I needed to help her. Her world stopped, but the rest goes on: electricity, gas, water, phone, property taxes, home shopping – the daily minutiae of life. I reviewed the binders of their accounts at home, everything was registered in Yechiel's name, and his bank account and credit cards were frozen. Past due notices had piled up, debts and alerts began to arrive before disconnection.

I made a list, took Joelle's ID, started calling utility companies, the city, banks all in Joelle's name to start sorting out the charges so she would not be cut off. It was difficult to impersonate her while she was lying on the couch motionless, numb to the world. But I did, I tackled the bureaucracy of companies for her, signed forms, certificates from anywhere possible just to exchange means of payment.

I needed the death certificate and I dreaded asking her. When I touched on it gently, she did not understand what I wanted from her. "A death certificate? Who died?" She was genuinely confused. When I reminded her Yechiel had died, she shook her head. "Yechiel will come back." She was adamant. "He just went for a walk and I know he will come back." Those days were the hardest. The ones when she could not accept that her sturdy and passionate Yechiel was gone.

Several weeks later, Joelle asked me if I would handle her bills for her. She couldn't deal with them; she asked me to do whatever it took to access the money and get it done. I didn't have the heart to remind her that I already had. I had done it all in her presence and she had no memory of it. I just smiled and let her know it was taken care of.

Her healing manifested itself in bouts of frenzied activity. So started the madness in home design. Every day I would go to her home and something had changed. The couch would be somewhere else, the chairs were replaced, and the dining table disappeared. It was a house caught in a storm. As if there was no calm and the changing atmosphere was survival.

Some days I would broach it gently. "It's beautiful, why change?" and she would answer, "This way it's more beautiful." It was as if all of the uncertainty and vagueness in Joelle's mind was trying to find roots, something to ground her.

For a few weeks the house was changing every day until the storm inside her passed, and the house stabilized. She was slowly becoming more stable, stronger. – Hadas Tsarfati

I didn't know why I was going to cry, but I knew that if anybody spoke to me or looked at me too closely the tears would fly out of my eyes and the sobs would fly out of my throat and I'd cry for a week. I could feel the tears brimming and sloshing in me like water in a glass that is unsteady and too full.

– Sylvia Plath

I had to get a death certificate.

I could not. I tried several times. *This cannot be happening. This is not real.* It felt like such a final step, and every step I took toward it meant he was dying all over again. The thought suffocated me. And the more I thought about it, the more I rebelled against it. *Why me? Why can't someone else get it for me?* I found myself at the Ministry of the Interior several times but could not bring myself to enter.

After countless attempts at courage, I discovered the Ministry had a self-service computer near the entrance. A frisson of relief. I did not have to vocalize what I needed. Saying it… *out loud to a stranger…* that I needed a death certificate… *for my husband…* just was not possible through the painful ache in my throat. I went through the motions as fast as I dared. The printer spit out a blue document resembling a birth certificate. I could not look at it. It just was not possible that it had his name on it. To read his name on a death certificate felt insurmountable. I tucked it away in my purse.

In the first year and especially in the first few months, there are everyday moments that will knock the wind out of you. Seemingly inconsequential things that are indescribably painful. Each time I faced one, like picking up a stupid piece of blue paper with Yechiel's name on it, once started I could not do them fast enough. As if I could pretend it was not happening. With every commonplace task completed, I felt a frisson of relief: *I did it, it's over, and I won't ever have to do that again.*

But it was not over.

Yechiel was also an American citizen, and a few weeks later I was told that I needed to go to the American consulate in Jerusalem to report his death and get an American death certificate.

I wanted to scream. *No no no no no, I cannot go through this again.* I railed against it. I pushed it off for weeks. And then I would try again. And again. When one doesn't need to make and keep an appointment for a task, sometimes it's easier to keep putting it off.

I was finally able to get myself there one morning. I got there but could not speak. I still could not say the words. Throat constricted, eyes blurry, I handed over his passport. And burst out crying. I will be forever grateful that the woman behind the counter was gentle and kind. She took note, made a copy of his passport, and then told me she would personally bring the certificate to my home because she lived nearby. Unthinkable. It is hard enough to get an appointment at the American Consulate, who would think you do not even need one to report a death? And even ensuring that I would not have to go back to the consulate? Unreal.

That was my first experience with a complete stranger being kind in those days. Such kindness was rare. I am sure that it is not so much because people don't want to be kind, but just that they don't know how to behave, they don't know what to say. The woman at the consulate even apologized that she had to cancel and invalidate the passport by punching holes into it, but was careful not to punch a hole on the photo.

I sobbed in the car as I made my way back home. Somehow keeping myself together until I reached the house where I screamed out my pain. And I knew I was done. Done for the day. My function was gone. Events like this took everything out of me, left me with no energy to do anything or even care for myself. All I wanted was to hear his voice and look at him, so I would play his videos for hours, repeatedly. I must have watched them thousands of times by now. Hearing his voice was starting to calm me down, even the messages from when we first met, before texting and apps that facilitated communication, Yechiel would leave me long voice messages that I would listen to on repeat.

But sometimes, unexpectedly, grief pounded over me in waves that left me gasping.

– Donna Tartt, *The Goldfinch*

It is the little things that haunt us.

The special wire basket that I got for Yechiel was haunting me.

Yechiel was obsessed with newspapers, and he would try to read three every morning. Sometimes when his schedule was too hectic, if he left the house too early in the morning, or when he was traveling, those papers would pile up in the special wire basket I had bought for him. The basket always had some reading material in it and you would never see the bottom of it. Magazines, printed articles and old newspapers.

Opening the door every day before I went to work and leaving the paper for him next to his recliner is something I still miss. Yet in those first few months when the newspaper was still delivered, it pained me to see it outside on the floor. It also killed me to see an empty basket. So I could not bring myself to cancel the subscription, and cried every day at the sight of them. I did not pick them up either; they would just accumulate on the floor.

We cause ourselves pain by not getting rid of triggers because we want to hold on to anything that was his. He loved getting the newspaper every morning and I did not want that to change. I tried to hold on to anything that reminded me of our life together.

And I could not get rid of the newspapers.

Once, before we left for the airport and I was scrambling to pack some last minute items, I spied Yechiel taking out the garbage. He always felt so good contributing to house chores, (he had two) and I never had to ask. He loved that I always noticed that he had taken out the garbage and would thank him for it. I made a note to thank him, but in the flurry of leaving, forgot. We got to the airport and as we were grabbing our luggage from the cab, I saw that he had brought our garbage too. I was mortified, bemused, *what was he thinking*? Frustrated, *now we had to deal with it and we'd be even later.* And yet I laughed, because *what else can I do, it's one of the beautiful quirks of the man.* He smiled at me, and as if to reassure me, said, "Those are my newspapers." I nearly fell over.

He actually went through security, passport control and into the plane holding a large black garbage bag full of his newspapers. He never cared what people thought, didn't mind that people looked at him. He would often relish in it, making light of trivial social constructs. That morning at every checkpoint, he would ask each security personnel, the check in counter, the flight attendant at the airplane door, "My wife is embarrassed that I'm carrying a garbage bag, what do you think?"

By the time we took our seats, I was too overrun with exasperation and laughter to be embarrassed. He was incorrigible. I loved that about him.

Every flight with Yechiel was special. First, it was a whole ritual of it, starting with the newspapers, of course, carefully put into the back flap of the seat. And he always – always – made the same remark – "Ugh. There is not enough room here". His carry on was inevitably incredibly heavy, stuffed with work material he rarely got to read. He would rummage through the carry on looking for his sleeping pill but given that it was so stuffed, this was always an issue. His large hands would probably fumble and drop the pills as he did nearly every time he would find them in that bag, so early in our marriage whenever we traveled, I would remind him to wear a shirt with a pocket. A pocket to keep the sleep aid safe and he wouldn't have to search for it.

He would then take his shoes off and put them on the top bin next to his carry on, put his Bose earphones around his neck, sit down and used every minute on his phone replying to emails or making last minute calls until he got the angry look from the flight attendant who has already told him twice to shut off his phone. He would then turn to me and say, "Hi! I'm here, let's get away."

Those were the moments I cherished. He would hold my hand and say *tfilat haderech,* the prayer for the traveler, and give me a kiss. Only then would he finally relax, in those moments when he got to shut his phone. He would exhale a loud, "*Aaahhh,*" as though he were alone, unaware that the plane was full. He also never realized you could actually get Wi-Fi on most airplanes and work, or even that you could answer emails that would be sent upon landing. I never revealed that information to him either. Once he had a chance to finally relax, I was not going to tell him he could also work during a flight.

Landing was less of a ritual, more a minor ordeal. He would scramble to look for his second phone and wallet, the ones he used outside of Israel, which meant digging back into the disordered and stuffed carry on. Invariably, he forgot something at home, too many times to remember or count.

Yechiel and I traveled very often for his work, flying every three weeks on average, so that our suitcases were always in the bedroom ready to go. They remain there to this day. Taking the suitcases and his carry on down to the basement would mean accepting the reality that it's over. Deciding not to move them was another way I was letting things just *be.* It was not a conscious decision of making a decision of not doing something – what worked for me was just *not deciding.* A widowed friend gave me advice early on to not make any major decisions in the first year. I extended that to not make *any* decisions in the first year. The suitcases stayed. With his shoes and his bathrobe. It's my sanctuary anyway, my private space. Anyone who would see it would be shocked. I am aware that it is not very healthy for me to be sleeping with a huge portrait of my husband looking at me or to be surrounded by his belongings.

Do not let anyone judge you. You are entitled to grieve as you wish.

Where you used to be, there is a hole in the world, which I find myself constantly walking around in the daytime, and falling in at night.

– Edna St. Vincent Millay

I am missing Yechiel so much today.

It is so much more than just missing his presence. Days like this where I just cannot adjust to this new life. A part of my body is gone and I don't know how to live without it.

Will the empty bed ever feel normal again?

Will the house ever feel like a home again?

How do you change your dreams, leave behind all those old dreams we had of a future together and dream of anything with only me?

It feels like learning how to walk all over again. Learning what I like all over again. Learning to decide without asking for any advice from the closest person to you, the person who knows you best. Some days I don't know myself, doubt everything, not having him around to reassure me that everything will be ok.

The one person I would call, the one person I would ask for advice, the only person I need to talk to right now… is gone.

Even when surrounded by people, I feel alone. There is no hand to hold. And Yechiel had such warm, big hands. I go into my bedroom to his full size photo and put my hand over his.

I keep going back to all the photos and videos, watching them over and over. Some days I can watch one particular video, the same video, a hundred times in a row. It's become a part of my life. There are so many of them. Why did I take all those videos in the first place? Looking back and thinking back, it does not seem normal. Could it be that something inside me felt that the happiness and the dream I was living with Yechiel would not last forever? Being with him was so intense I had to pinch myself to believe it was true; I wanted to hold on and remember every moment, taking mental photos every possible second.

Today it is the opposite. Today, the intensity of him being gone is something I cannot grasp; it is too surreal to believe he is never coming back.

On the mornings when it is especially hard to wake up alone, I watch a video of him saying good morning. We usually only had mornings together when we were traveling. In Israel I was the first one up. Most mornings, I would get up quietly and have a cup of tea downstairs by myself, and kiss him good morning to wake him up on my way out.

Nights are the hardest. The silence in the house is smothering. Nights at home with Yechiel were our favorite times, talking and laughing; he always made me laugh, even when he told me the same jokes over and over. I have the funniest videos of Yechiel at night, one when he was pretending to be an orchestra director. He held up his fork in the middle of dinner, using it to conduct his pretend orchestra. Singing was very much a part of the home, especially on *Shabbat* when I could notvideo him. So I made up for it at any chance I had. Now, whenever I need to 'see' him, whenever I need to hear his voice, in the morning, during the day, or when approaching a holiday, I take out my phone and I watch the videos I have... and I see my Yechiel.

Life is not a problem to be solved,
but a reality to be experienced.

– Soren Kierkegaard

I got through the *Shloshim*. It was too brief a moment that I was cocooned by family. I somehow made it through *Purim*. And then I was alone again. *Pesach*, Passover, was coming up. I had just a few weeks for cleaning and *kashering*, the cleaning out of all leavened products.

Such a purging was the last thing on my mind. I still have the urge to keep changing the furniture around. No configuration feels right. No amount of mixing it up felt like home. As with the table, today my obsession is the recliner. Yechiel's recliner was empty; I could not stand walking in the house where the first thing I saw was his empty chair. Yet giving it away was not an option. Every day I moved it to a different corner. Changed everything around it. Shifted around other rooms. Our kitchen table was in the entrance, then by the back door, at one side of the living room, then the other side. There was no way I was moving to our new apartment by myself, but I could not live in our neglected house. We had planned every detail for the new apartment. We had not gotten keys yet, but we were going to get new appliances, new furniture. In anticipation of new furniture we had gotten rid of much of our old stuff. Now I found myself without a sofa or a dining room table and chairs. The treadmill that was going to be in Yechiel's office in the new apartment was still taking up space in our kitchen.

I should change out the old curtains, get rid of the old clunky coffee table. The walls were in desperate need of paint. So many things that would have happened in the natural course of moving to a new place, I couldn't find the strength to do now. I just kept shifting those around in an attempt to make the house look better, more inviting, more comfortable. Nothing helped. The house was starting to feel like uncomfortable clothes. Until one day I woke up with a near desperate urge to get rid of the treadmill. It was a constant reminder of the day that broke me. It had to go. *Now.* As with everything that needed to be done, I turned to Hadas. I called her nearly in a panic, "Please get rid of it, today!" And I left the house.

Friends who understand and hold your hand during the roller-coaster of craziness are worth more than gold. Without questioning, she took care of it and had it picked up that same afternoon. With the kitchen space now freed up, I could finally put the kitchen table back where it belonged. It was an odd small relief. Somehow putting order around the house helped put some order in my head. Small things, one step at a time. The leak and humidity in the kitchen became urgent, the smell of mildew and creep of black up the walls were starting to really bother me. I guess this is a good sign, *I'm starting to feel things*, notice other things around me and I had urges to do something about them. The numb indifference was lessening its grip on my brain. I was nesting. I just needed to create a comfortable space for myself. To make it mine.

I do what I can by myself. I was too skittish to bring a stranger in to fix or paint anything; it was unthinkable. That level of healing might take months. It was not the fear of strangers; it was the pain and anxiety of having a man in my house when Yechiel never would be again. Months ahead of Yechiel's birthday, I start to think more and more about refreshing our house. Seeing my space slowly transform seems to match the slow transformation in me.

I became more deliberate in maintaining the rituals I shared with Yechiel so I would not forget anything. Some might have interpreted it as being "stuck in my grief". For me, it is the fear of forgetting. I know I have to build a new life.

I am not there yet.

Every week before *Shabbat* I keep the same routine we had together at home. I prepare the same food, I listen to the same songs Yechiel did. He would play them on his phone, the same *Shabbat* songs every week. He would then take out the hot plate – and I smiled, because he never learned how to set the timer – and he plugged in the hot water heater. His only *Shabbat* chores. I struggle to take it out each week from the top closet where he kept it, where only he could reach it. But I don't change it, and still keep it in the same closet, even if it means getting up on a chair to take it down. It was a way to not forget all the same details. I would light the *Shabbat* candles and then kiss him and wish him "*Shabbat Shalom.*" Now, I kiss his big blown up photo in the living room.

We developed a custom of toasting right after candle lighting with scotch in the early days, then switched to vodka after our trips to Russia and Ukraine. Our Friday nights together were special, but in these first months after his death, I am unable to handle the memories, and after lighting candles, I run to the synagogue. I accept all invitations from friends and spend every Friday night surrounded with people to distract me. The bottle of vodka stays untouched in the liquor cabinet for months…

And now, Passover. It was the first big holiday after Yechiel died. I was freaking out. It's a holiday where families get together; sit together around a big table. You must thoroughly clean the house and remove all the bread, crumbs – everything leaven. A holiday with lots of work involved, when the women talk about how far along they are with the cleaning, then get together to coordinate the preparations of the meal to include lots of specific dishes, side dishes – it's all the talk after Purim: the preparation of *Pesach*.

Pessach, when we sit together and read the entire story about our Exodus from Egypt; we recall the time when we were slaves and we celebrate our freedom today. A time of reflection of ourselves, our own thoughts, a metaphor to figure out our own personal "exodus".

I can't do this, I can't bear this.

I could not bear the thought of sitting at a table alone with a big family. As much as I would want to be happy in their togetherness, my loneliness was unbearable. I would not be able to stand it, seeing couples together when I was without. However, I did want to continue my tradition, I *needed* to keep my tradition. Staying home by myself is not an option.

As a cry answered from heaven, the local *Chabad* announced they would be holding a community *Seder.* I immediately called Hadas. After her divorce, she also looked for safe places to spend the holidays away from her children. She was quick to agree to come with me.

It was the fastest *Seder* I had ever been to.

There is a joke that you invite guests over for a Seder meal, but then you don't eat for the next two hours. You invite someone over for a meal but you read to them instead. They see all this food that's been prepared, but you only give them bitter herbs with vinegar. Then they see matzo, and think, *I'm going to eat*, but you only offer a taste of matzo... etc. etc.

Yechiel had everyone laughing at this.

The *Seder* was uneventful. I pushed my feelings away and went through the motions. I got through the first *Pesach* without him, and without crying.

That is all I want in life: for this pain to seem purposeful.

– Elizabeth Wurtzel, *Prozac Nation*

It was not just a call center.

Not to me, certainly not to Yechiel.

Yechiel's vision was an entire operation, a nationwide network to help people with urgent basic needs, including volunteer groups on call with chapters in each city. Yes, there were social workers and the government was responsible for people's welfare, but it just wasn't enough.

Like in too many wealthy countries, the role of social workers in Israel is considered a lesser profession and as such, it's a low paid, underappreciated job. Yechiel was different in that he deeply appreciated social workers. He saw how much they personally gave to families in need, how little they were recognized for their dedication. The average social worker in Israel has to take care of *three hundred* people. It's an impossible and thankless job.

On one of his very first visits to Israel, Yechiel accompanied a social worker during their home visits. He wanted to understand the role of the social worker, and what the limitations of their care were. In one home, a little girl didn't have boots. Yechiel asked why they couldn't get her boots. The worker told him that they did not have a petty cash account, assistance was limited by bureaucratic policies, and their hands were tied. "I don't have a budget to cover small things. Sometimes I can take care of it out of my own pocket, but I can't do that all the time."

This, and the fact that there was no process to quickly provide a little girl with a pair of boots, outraged Yechiel. It became the seed of his vision to create a nationwide network of assistance; a single number to call if a family needed an electric bill paid, or formula for a baby, or a refrigerator, or even a pair of shoes. A network that also allowed social workers a number to call to cover the smaller immediate needs that would not be taken care of quickly through bureaucracy.

Too many needs were urgent and immediate. Yechiel knew this and despite push back from his executives, I knew the center was integral to his plans for the future. I trusted him, as always, but now I was stymied by the fact that he had not left anything in writing. The only thing in writing was a damning report from an outside company stating it did not fit his organization. I can still hear Yechiel as he said to me many times "if you want something, you are going to have to fight for it, I mean really fight for it." When the organization's remaining leadership decided to close down the call center one month after Yechiel's passing, I wanted to do something. I was appalled that his organization moved away from his last passion project, seemingly overnight.

I could not let Yechiel's dream die with him. His organization would continue to do the work it does, but his personal dream for helping vulnerable individuals one by one in Israel was not met. The call center that he started, enabling people to call directly and ask for help, had to continue. They had nowhere else to turn, whom would they call? Closing the call center meant that when someone's electricity was cut off, when a child was sleeping on the floor or the washing machine of a family of nine children broke down, these people would not get an answer. Nobody was dealing with these kinds of emergencies. I told Hadas we had to do something. Like everyone else at the call center, she had also been let go and was looking for her next challenge.

Together Hadas and I met with heads of nonprofits trying to figure out how to start from scratch and put together a new organization. She arranged to fill my days with advisors, lawyers, nonprofits, accountants, and we asked a ton of questions: who is the best lawyer, how do you register, how do you write bylaws, can family be on the board, how is it is done, how much does it cost, what did we need. We wrote lists of potential supporters, board members, and then chose the seven who would become our new board.

Meetings. More meetings. We needed to learn, ask and find answers. Some were afraid to meet. Some just did not know how to react around a new widow. In the beginning I had tried to act normal, when I was still too numb to understand exactly what I was doing. I was clinging to the past, and I wanted the call center back. We put it all together and filed the request to open a new organization, in order to continue helping individuals in need and find some kind of normalcy in my life. We had little time to think of a name and in a momentary lapse of creativity, we called it the Eckstein Fund, figuring we could always change it in the future.

With the call center's number disconnected, we started getting calls from social workers directly on Hadas' and my personal phones. The community was confused, "Wasn't direct, one-on-one assistance to the less fortunate in Israel the entire point of Yechiel's organization? Why did the organization suddenly disband the nerve center of the operation?" I could not think about it and honestly had no answers. I focused forward. Yechiel would want this legacy to continue. But it was rough. We were now working without staff, without an office, and on a shoestring budget.

> *'How are you?' I'm shattered, thanks, how are you? I walk aimlessly through the rooms of my house, what have you been up to?*
>
> **– Christine Silverstein**

It becomes clear to me that society really does not understand that a woman can still be grieving her husband three months later. I was not allowed to say I was having a bad day. Invariably people would ask, "Why, what happened?" Some days it was all I could do not to scream back, "*What do you mean, what happened?? My husband died, my life ended, that's what happened!*" I never thought I would have to explain myself a mere three months after and every time was a shock. People saw me outside my home and just assumed I was doing fine, that I was over "it." Life was moving on without me. I was barely holding it together.

No one but a rare few realized the strength it took for me to go out, even just for staples. The first few times grocery shopping was reduced to me purchasing just one item at a time, because frankly, I would not last more than ten minutes inside a supermarket. I lost it when I passed the corn. Corn. *Yechiel loved corn* and would always ask me to get some. He loved to snack on corn at night, and I would find it in the cracks of his recliner the next day. When he ate corn, it went everywhere. Or when I passed the deodorant section, my eyes would search for his favorite, Old Spice. I was able to save Yechiel's Old Spice when my brother was getting rid of everything, and I still opened it for the scent.

Honestly, I thought I was crazy and would have never admitted to doing that until I heard from other widows doing the same. I recently found out they made laundry softeners with Old Spice so now we can have our sheets smelling like them…

'*Wonderful*,' I thought, '*Can I cry any harder in bed?*'… or would it become comforting like everything else?

We had two single beds pushed together, and his sheets still smelled like him – I did not want to wash them. Looking at his empty bed each night was a constant pouring of salt in my open wound. Would I ever get used to it? I tried filling it up with pillows so it wouldn't look empty, not sure that was any help. When it was time to change my sheets, I left his on, but then I would have different sheets on each bed. Another minor every day task that would be a nightly visual reminder that he was not here. That my time was moving on without him in it. The first time I changed the sheets on my side only left me with a hollow feeling in my chest. I still could not bring myself to wash his… and because the beds did not match, I covered it with a single bedspread.

Months passed before I could bring myself to change his sheets. Eventually I would take them off, and wash both sheets, but then I felt silly washing clean sheets.

When the heat of summer started, I realized the switch to the ceiling fan was on his side… and I found myself moving over into his bed. The mattress felt softer, I tried not to think about it. Eventually I would switch beds, sleeping on my side, then his, back to mine again. Some time later, I would go back to only sleeping in mine. Eventually, I didn't make his bed anymore and I used a bedspread that covered both beds. One could not see that his bed did not have sheets. But it took me a long time to realize I did not have to put sheets on his bed because he was never coming back. Of course it made sense to not put sheets on his bed,… but it was a process to get there. And in those early months, I could not bring myself to make such a seemingly small change.

Some widows never go back to their beds.

The night Yechiel passed away, all the other rooms and beds in our house were occupied, and our couch was not big enough to sleep on, so I went back to my own bed. There literally was no other place to sleep and I had not given it much thought. I was not thinking about anything that night; I was just in a state of shock. Looking back, I am glad I did since most women are not able to go back into the bedroom they shared with their spouse. Some sleep on the couch for months, some get a new bed and some change the room around. They all felt they had to change something. The last time I saw Yechiel alive was in his bed, so one would think that it would be the most traumatic for me. Instead, it became the place where I would cry freely, with his picture on the wall, his bathrobe hanging where he left it, his shoes by his bed. I suddenly longed for the sound of his CPap machine that used to bother me so much. I used to have such trouble falling asleep with that noise that sometimes I would have to go into another room. Today I need some noise to fall asleep and miss it terribly. Months went by before I finally took it off his night table and donated it.

Friends – or those who I thought were friends – were wonderful during the first month. They bought me food, called and checked on me. One day I mentioned how I would love a bowl of couscous and hot vegetables and the same evening, a friend rang the doorbell and bought some for me. A cooked warm meal felt so good in those days when I could not cook anything. Honestly most days would go by before I realized I had not eaten anything. After all the food from *Shiva* was gone, I would open the empty fridge looking for something, I would end up just having a cup of tea with a cracker or cookie. My couscous friend disappeared; she did not even take my calls after that offering. Weird. It felt like some thought once one good deed was done for the grieving, their role was over.

I went back to searching for more widows to talk to. I started feeling the need to talk to someone who could understand. I searched for grief counseling, and spoke to whomever I could. I connected with some who were easy to speak to, but it's hard to make a real connection when you are not at the same stage of grief. At the two-month marker, my sister-in-law had taken me to a grief group. I was 51 and the other women were in their 70s and 80s. I didn't feel connected and did not go back. I kept looking and waiting for a support group to open.

One day, I found a private Facebook group for widows. It was absolution, deliverance, liberation, and grace. I would urge everyone in grief to find such a group as soon as possible. I only wish I had found it sooner. I am not the type to comment or post much, but reading the questions and comments from the over 10,000 members worldwide was an immediate relief. First, the group confirmed that I was not crazy, that my feelings were legitimate and normal. Second, I found a place where I felt understood. Really understood. Finally.

It is the club nobody wants to join, where we are all experiencing the same blinding pain. It is not a grief group for anyone – it is a specific group solely for grieving widows. People suggested books on grief, but such reading was too intense and difficult. Concentrating on more than one page at a time was still hard. I tried reading a page only to realize nothing registered, and I would find myself reading it over and over like in the first weeks. The social media page was snippets of solace in short sentences and quick paragraphs.

I wish people knew more about widowhood. People who got divorced would compare their pain to mine. So the idea that I would be doing okay in three months, made a certain morbid sense. I was not, this pain was not comparable. People who lost parents, grandparents, aunts, uncles, tried to relate. I have lost close friends, family, and the pain is different. Life as I knew it ended the day

Yechiel died. I am panicking, full of fear and anxiety of what the future holds. I have to adjust to a new life I did not choose.

People attend the funeral without realizing that for a widow it is just the beginning. All of us can feel awkward around grief so I can understand how it is easier to just stay away. While it is true I have pushed people away in the first year because I did not want to feel pitied, I had hoped that those who considered Yechiel a friend would check on me once in a while. I had made similar mistakes years ago myself when I knew friends were grieving; I have since learned to call them and keep in touch, and I know I will not be bothering them by calling to check in. Even if the conversations were brief, knowing someone cares is a bit of weight lifted. I really appreciated those calls. Some were once a month, some every week, but it was a real eye opener - I learned who my real friends were, old and new. They just wanted me to know they were thinking of me, and it validated my feelings. They were not trying to fix me because there was nothing to fix. I was broken but they understood I could not be fixed; the pieces could not be put back together.

I was feeling a slow transformation in me, but I was not aware at the time that I would have to find the new me, a new life for myself. Life for a widow does not just go on because the life you had does not exist anymore. You have to create a new one. A new life that becomes your new normal.

The hardest part is that there is no time to reconcile with it. There is a "before" and an "after" Yechiel died. I cannot put them together. My entire perspective of time and the way I talk is in relation to before Yechiel died or after Yechiel died. I am not the same person. It is not the same life. This is an unwanted rebirth.

I could not deal with the "How are you?" or any other generic question to my state of being. It was really starting to get on my nerves. How does one answer that? Because my truth will always be, "I'm devastated, my husband died." I realize nobody wants to hear that and the reactions I would get if I answered truthfully would not be pleasant. I continued to fake it. "I will be ok" was usually my answer.

I needed proactively positive people around me, ones who would say, "We're going for a walk at six," rather than, "You should walk more, you'll feel better." What I needed was decisive action since I had none of my own. "Call me if there's anything I can do," did not help.

A woman walked into my house one day with a pot of soup. It was perfect. I had food for days. Had she asked if she could bring over soup, I would have declined. If someone asked if I wanted to go for a walk, I often did not. When a friend said "I'm picking you up", it felt like a lifeline I could hold onto with my mind. With precise directives, I could opt in or out when the time came, but the decision for setting time and direction was taken out of my hands. It was the only way to reach through the numbness of my grief.

We all have our trigger words or phrases, and "*How are you*?" was definitely one of mine.

I was the type never to confront someone. Never in my right mind would I have confronted someone to say stop. Normally, I just smiled and moved on. Mentally blocked them out. But grief was starting to change me. I stood up for myself. I finally told someone today not to ask me those words anymore. I surprised myself. I suddenly had the confidence to stand up and tell someone what I felt. Where did that come from? I did not recognize myself.

What we once enjoyed and deeply loved we can never lose, for all that we love deeply becomes part of us.

– Helen Keller

May 6, 2019

Ohmygodohmigodohmigod!

Three months to the day after Yechiel's death, we received the document of registration for our new organization. Authorities have approved The Eckstein Fund and we are – as of today – a registered Israeli nonprofit!

I am excited and terrified.

This new project gave me purpose and a reason to wake up in the morning. Yechiel's passion and vision became my passion and vision. And what do I know about starting a nonprofit – nothing! But I had to try.

What was the worst that could happen?

I met with anyone who answered my calls. I had missteps, but I kept plowing forward. A few might have tried to take advantage but Hadas was vigilant when offered grand promises. We led the call center for three years and we knew how to rebuild it. It was challenging to work and plan without a budget, but one meeting led to another, opening door after door. Some days it felt like insanity. I was still grieving. Most of the time I felt like a robot. Some days I still could not get out of bed, wanting to just stay under the covers and cry. It was one baby step at a time. Even though she filled my time with meetings, Hadas knew I was only good for an hour before I crumbled. It was exhausting to focus even for forty-five minutes;

Hadas often had to take over, when she felt I was losing my train of thought. I did my best. Barely functioning, but making it work.

At first, we worked from my home until we had enough funds to hire our first staff person and connect the hotline. We looked for a small office in Jerusalem and decided on a shared office space walking distance from my house. When we went to see it for the first time, there was a surprise at the entrance. There stood a striking couch made of varying colorful cubes, and it took my breath away. The same couch had been in Yechiel's office many years ago. I had a photo of him sitting on that couch, and I picture him right in front of me. Am I hallucinating? I felt my voice tremble a bit when I asked how it had gotten here. It turned out that the new office space we were visiting and Yechiel's old office belonged to the same owner. Destiny perhaps.

There was a lot of work to do in the months leading to the opening of the call center. Computer systems, telephone system, website, bank and credit card approvals... It was just the two of us, Hadas and me. I was just a half a person; I hoped for some relief of my pain with all the action, but it was uncontrollable. PTSD? I am not a doctor but I understand the meaning, now more than ever. Why is it that we cannot take control of our actions? There were still too many days when I could not get out, days when I would break down in the middle of the day, and meetings where I had to step out suddenly because I would choke up with tears. I am normally a private, do it myself person, but I accepted help from whoever offered. I knew I needed help.

Having the organization registration galvanized me. Where do we start? We needed a real logo to brand our new organization, business cards and marketing material. Hadas had a childhood friend who was a graphic designer. When we arrived at her home office, the

strong and peculiar scent of eggs was somewhat uncomfortable. That is when I noticed the kitchen was full of meringues in all shapes and colors. My brain moved on. The kitchen, after all, is not my strength.

We spend hours with Ortal, designing, thinking and planning. We had some optional designs that she sent us by email, explaining why she could not use her printer.

"My printer is loaded with edible ink," she said.

I had never heard of such a thing. She explained that her business focused on designing personalized edible sheets to make meringues. She called them "transfer sheets". She also managed a network of workshops all over Israel. I got curious, and as we were heading out, she invited me to join her one evening the following week. I accepted despite my reservations about baking. Evening activities were always distracting and very welcome.

I went to the workshop the following week and was surprised how fast three hours went by. I returned home with two platters of fresh meringues in varying sizes and colors, ready for the oven.

Meringues turned out to be a *great* distraction. I started making them all the time. I found myself obsessed with experimenting: different colors, combining hues, flavors, shapes, sizes. I obsessed over packaging, scouring shops and dollar stores looking for jars, ribbons, boxes in all sizes, every possible container idea, and I piled it all in stacks around my kitchen. The amount of eggs and sugar I was buying was absurd to the point of comedy. But the response I received was, "*Wow, you made these?!*" felt good. I celebrated each as a small victory: *I was able to get in the kitchen and complete something*! The idea came to me that we could market meringues to all different companies in Israel, creating edible sheets of company logos, from airlines to insurance companies. To cover all of Israel with branded meringues. It would be the income we were searching for in the Eckstein Fund. We started with a few clients – a university and other nonprofits that offered them to staff and volunteers. It filled up my evenings and I loved making them. I made so many, I was giving them away as gifts.

Gradually, I was becoming interested in myself again and I was encouraged by it.

Although Yechiel was much younger than I am when he started his organization, he did not give up. When he first started he was alone, frequently ridiculed, and too few in his community believed in him. He did not get the love or support he needed from his family. He would tell me how even his parents did not believe in him. Friends he thought would stand by him, lashed out. However, Yechiel was a pioneer. There are rabbis and organizations that now capitalize on the path he blazed. Back then, he was ostracized in the community. He doubted himself many times, yet was certain he had to keep going. By the time I met him, he had learned to hide his feelings and show the world only what they wanted to see.

I understand that in my bones now.

I didn't want to wake up. I was having a much better time asleep. And that's really sad. It was almost like a reverse nightmare, like when you wake up from a nightmare you're so relieved. I woke up into a nightmare.

– Ned Vizzini, *It's Kind of a Funny Story*

My dreams are so real.

I wake up in the morning after dreaming of Yechiel and for a split second, have a sense of relief – *thank God it was all just a nightmare.* It does not last. It never lasts. It just feels so good even if just for less than a second. In my dream, he is there with me, telling me that his death was all a lie, that he did not go anywhere. "Why did they tell you I left?" He kept repeating that he is here, here with me.

In my dreams, he is always reassuring me that everything will be "all right." I seek out sleep in order to talk to him again. To be near him, to feel his arms around me. I hear of so many other women that have not had a dream about their husbands. I feel fortunate.

A month before Yechiel died, I had the strangest dream. I dreamt that I was getting ready for work. In real life, this was my private time. In my dream, I found a live camera. I was shocked. I searched for the source, and discovered a hidden back room. There was Yechiel, sitting in that secret room, watching me through the camera. I woke up unsettled. Later that day, when I got to the office, I told Hadas about the dream.

I laughed it off, because there was no way Yechiel would even conceive of violating my privacy.

A few days after he died, I could not shake off the feeling that Yechiel was there. In our bedroom. In my bathroom. There, more than any other room, I felt his presence. I shared my anxiety with Hadas, "he's in there."

"Please get out of here." I said out loud.

"Please move to a different room." It still ranks up there as one of the stranger moments I experienced in grief.

I was not the only one dreaming about him. Others would call me to share when Yechiel showed up in their dreams.

Dvora called me unexpectedly early in the morning. She just had to share her dream with me. She said it was a very long, very involved dream.

"Everyone was searching for Yechiel. Not just friends, family, and coworkers, but the entire city came out for the search. We looked everywhere. Called his phone several times to no avail."

She and I were together, running to every place he would normally visit, searching buildings, and every room in those buildings, calling out his name repeatedly. Emails, texts, phone calls, all went unanswered. Nobody could find him - he had disappeared. When suddenly I call him yet again and he answers in his rushed typical voice.

"I have to leave, I have to hurry, and I have to get my luggage. I need to get my luggage."

He told me he was carrying his luggage 'upstairs' because they were waiting for him. He said goodbye and he had to go. Dvora and I kept asking him, "Where are you going?"

"Upstairs. I have to go with them upstairs." – He said.

I feel strange. It is a surreal feeling. In my dreams he is always with me, this is the first time I get a message through someone else that he is leaving, and in a way, he comes to say goodbye and tell me that he is fine.

Many widows shared their story with me in my first year. Of

husbands saying hello or goodbye in dreams. A widow friend had told me that she never dreamt of her late husband. Five years later, she made the decision to move to a new home in a different neighborhood. On the morning of the move, while the movers were still unloading the truck at her new house, a friend she had not seen in years surprised her on the street. He was equally startled to see her. "You don't understand," he said. "I had a dream about your late husband last night. I dreamed that I met him here and I asked him what he was doing in my neighborhood. He said that he had moved. That he lived in the neighborhood now." Seeing her now gave a completely new meaning to the dream.

This does not make any sense, and yet I start to believe in signs and hidden messages.

Widows do not often share their dreams with others. I don't either. I cannot tell anyone these stories, afraid no one will understand. Would I get pity or worse, thought of as crazy? It is enough that it feels crazy making. For me, as for other widows, these are encouraging messages that bring us some measure of comfort.

Courage is not having the strength to go on, it's going on when you don't have the strength.

– Theodore Roosevelt

Four months. I am still numb. My brain is still not working, but I have started trying to keep my grief private. Hidden. After the initial shock of Yechiel's death, I started to make a conscious decision to focus on my blessings.

It did not always work, and I could not always control the sudden outburst of tears. Whenever I went out, I tried putting on an imaginary mask. "Fake it till you make it," as the saying goes.

I got into a small argument with my son over this. I could not get the message through that I was faking to myself. I was forcing myself to smile until it came naturally.

"You have to be real, and whoever sticks by your side is your true friend," he said. If you sit with a friend and do not express the truth about how you are feeling, it has no meaning. You have to be honest."

Honesty. I reflected on that. I saw how even good friends kept a distance or stopped calling altogether. Is it dishonest to keep my feelings to myself and pretend I am ok?

I am learning to walk on an unknown path while figuring out my new identity.

Four months is very raw in widowhood. Only another widow can understand the depth of loss I was struggling with. That void was a pit I needed to navigate without turning people off around me.

I figured out the question of who needs whom quite quickly. I needed people around me – friends, yes, but often strangers. I could not be a puddle every time. Even a close friend would get tired of it eventually.

I needed a group that shared the same pain. I was not looking for new friendships; I started to look for a place where I could break down.

Hadas was still bearing with me, and that meant the world to me.

Part of growing stronger was learning how to fall and get up. Just like a baby will hold onto things before it can walk on its own, it is a stage of development. My son did not understand, but is it the idealism of youth to believe you only need true friends in life? Or that people will stick around you when you are a sobbing mess every time they visit? Ultimately, people want to be around people who make them feel good. You can cry a few times, but if every conversation devolves into a depressing turn, eventually people will stay away from you.

The question is who needs whom? I need caring people around me, I have to learn how to keep them near.

I was trying to build an organization. It is hard enough to get people to invest time and energy on companies built by women, even harder if they think one of them is an emotional wreck. So yes, I faked it. I did all I could to look presentable even though I wore the same two or three outfits for months. Wash and wear, did not even care to put them away.

The amount of energy it would take me to get out, prepare and concentrate was sometimes too overwhelming and exhausting. I remember the shocked looks from people after their usual polite, "How are you?" to which I would respond "*Al hapanim,*" – Hebrew for horrible. Sometimes I just did not even have the will to fake it. I

would try to catch myself after and say something like, "But I am going to be ok, someday."

Grief will fester inside, and I had to show something other than my pain. Getting used to smiling again took time. But it made people more comfortable than the image of a widow in pain. People have such an expectation of others to be positive, to see that you are okay and looking to move forward. I kept my pain private, only sharing with a few people in those first months. For the rest of the world, I had to look 'normal'. I had to *practice* smiling. The days I did not were the worst. I would sink and dissolve into the void.

I realized that I constantly needed the approval or validation of my feelings. Perhaps I always have and just was not aware before of how much Yechiel did that for me daily. Now I was at a loss. I leaned more and more on social media groups for widows. A post in our group today said, "Grief is love that has nowhere to go." This resonated with me so much it was nearly crippling. The intense love that I had for Yechiel suddenly had nowhere to go. I cannot stand it; I am going out of my mind. If I am not busy with appointments during the day, I have blinding moments of panic. My Facebook widows group becomes my go-to safe space, at any time of day or night. I am not posting anything yet, but reading other experiences remind me that I am not alone. I commented a lot, found a voice, and discovered a supportive community there. It was comforting to hear their stories. The more I read, the more I was relieved to realize what I was going through, experiencing, was part of the universal process of grief. *This is a normal process. I am not insane.*

At home, I had his candle; I had his life-sized cutouts. I must have sounded crazy coming back to say, *"Hello Yechiel,"* as if it was really him standing there. I knew those were representations, but I truly felt like he was in the house, and I could talk to him. Wished him good night as I did every night. *"Good night my love. I love you."* Every day. Even when traveling without me, he called to wish me a good night. I could not have openly admitted to acting that way for fear they would insist on me seeing a specialist for delusion. My support group understood these idiosyncrasies, and it was healing to read their admissions of steps they took in their own healing which would not seem normal to the outside world.

You cannot prevent the birds of sorrow from flying over your head, but you can prevent them from building nests in your hair.

– Chinese proverb

I arranged to meet a friend today for my daily evening walk. Sometimes I go alone; sometimes it's good to talk to someone. Today, I regret setting up in advance – I am not in the mood to talk to anyone. I really have to push myself to leave the house.

I love Jerusalem spring evenings because there is a sense of hope. Summer evenings are even better because there is always a nice breeze. After about an hour with my friend, it starts to get dark and we say goodbye. We split up, she goes in one direction towards her house, and I turn towards mine. Suddenly, out of nowhere, an empty chasm of sadness opens up. I teeter.

I am aware of the looming dark of an empty house. The weight of it bears down on my chest. I struggle to find air, and at the same time, I speed up to make it home. I do not want to break down on the street. I am trying to hold it in, just a few more minutes until I'm home. The neighbor is sitting on her balcony and waves at me. I barely wave back and rush into the house. The weight crushes me. I collapse into sobbing. My chest burns. In the distance, the phone rings, but I don't answer. I cannot answer. I am done for today. Despite all that I have left to do, I am done.

Tomorrow will be another day. I survived. I will start over tomorrow.

I begin to notice a pattern of deep sadness when I get home around the time that Yechiel and I used to arrive home. We would call each other around six or 7pm to check in, see where we were, who had how much work left, and determine who would pick up whom since

we only had one car. Inevitably, he would be stuck at work and I would use the time to get in some exercise and walk back home.

It is a constant struggle. I struggle to hold onto the routines I had with Yechiel. Doing so brings him to me, keeps him close. However, breaking those routines pushes the sadness away, if only for a moment. It is a rollercoaster. How can I stop doing what I did every day? We are out of orange juice; Yechiel drinks a glass of orange juice every morning. We are also out of dark chocolate; Yechiel eats a square of chocolate every night, right before going to bed. I will stop by the grocery store on my way home. "Wait – for who"?

It was an exhausting push-pull war within me.

Now, in the past few weeks I was finding it difficult to head home around my usual routine times set with Yechiel. It probably does not make any logical sense to the outside world. I find myself cutting out to get home much earlier; if I get home around 4pm, I can relax and busy myself with writing emails or returning phone calls, and barely notice when it gets dark outside. Or, preferably, I make plans to keep me away from the house until it is so late that when I get home I'm too exhausted to do anything but go straight to bed.

However, some days, like today, the day gets away from me. That moment when I realized I am not home yet but I had no evening plans. Dreading walking into the empty house. I finished a meeting at five and was startled to discover I had no more meetings for the day, no agenda, so I decided to go home. On the way home, I started choking up. The urge to call Yechiel and tell him I was driving and could pick him up on the way was intense. Knowing he would not pick up the phone, that he never would again. The idea of spending another evening without him is nearly too much to bear. I try to stay rational, try to tell myself I will be ok, I'm tired anyway so this is a chance to just stay home and rest.

I cannot negotiate with my mind and the pain takes over.

I should have planned. I called a friend. She was not available. I called my daughter; she is not available either. I start to panic and tears spill over. I finally make it home and walk into the house completely broken and crying. Hours later when I am numb and cried out, I slowly make a note to avoid these situations. I admonish myself to make sure I have plans *and* a back-up plan.

You will survive and you will find purpose in the chaos. Moving on does not mean letting go.

– Mary VanHaute

As the firsts of summer approach, I finally felt ready to make the house feel more pleasant and cover up the humidity marks and some of the painting and marks on the walls that we had neglected because we had been moving. Now that I was staying put, my constant shifting of furniture was not enough. I found myself in a flurry of activity. I decluttered the living room – took down the old curtains that had faded from the sun. Changed around the furniture. I was delighted at how much light suddenly spread in the living room.

Small moments of somewhat happiness.

I bought the dining room table I had in mind for the new apartment and set it up in the old home. It was a bittersweet moment; the house was starting to feel like 'my' house as I emptied my old boxes from the basement. I had boxes there since I had moved in when we got married; we had not had much storage or space in the house, so I left several unopened down there. Now, I was opening them and finding my school report cards, postcards my father had sent me from his travels around the world, and my children's baby shoes… I felt transported to another lifetime, and spent time in the memories from my parents' house in Spain.

Summer days brought long pleasant evenings and the turn of season would lessen some of the pain. That summer, my house was going to be full of guests. My daughter had regaled me with detail about her travels to South America. Backpackers like her used the website Couchsurfing.com; unlike other similar sites, strangers on Couchsurfing.com were willing to house a traveler at no charge. She was enthusiastic, said it was a lot of fun; she met many different people from all walks of life. Since I was alone so much and had spare rooms, she thought I should try it. Every potential couch surfer had to register with verifiable ID, and got a special code; she assured me it was all very safe and legit.

I checked it out and liked the fact that I could decide about what days I could make my house available. I chose to host only female guests and occasionally young couples. In addition, every guest had to send a message describing something about themselves, why they wanted to stay with you and for how long. It was easy to set expectations for strangers. It helped, having other women in the house, from all over the world. Women who had stories to share, they eased the passage of time. Once I had three women staying at my house who had so much fun they asked if they could stay an extra week. I still keep in touch with them. I had a couple from Argentina where the husband was an excellent cook; we ate well that week. During that week, an American girl arrived to spend a week at the house. She could not cook, so we all ate together. I was going to an event one night, and I was relieved when the Argentinian couple was staying in and so would keep the American company. When I got back, I found out there had been a bit of drama. Apparently, the American was an evangelical Christian, and my other guest was a Catholic priest. A heated discussion had ensued. I laughed about it later but I was glad I missed it.

For the rest of that summer and into the holidays, it was nice to have the company. It was a relief knowing there was someone at home; the planning, the shopping, the activities around taking care of guests took care of me. Opening up my home and hosting *Shabbat* meals also helped fill the emptiness. Coming home at night and finding my guests outside on the terrace, joining them with a bottle of wine, made my time a bit easier. Yes, I would still cry with them and miss our nights with Yechiel. Yes, it felt surreal sometimes. "What are these people doing in my house?" Nevertheless, in the long run it helped me. I was able to explain that even if it looks like I am functioning and getting out, the inside part of me is dead. I can smile but that does not mean I am feeling happy. Sometimes I just look strong because I do not want to cry in front of people or mess up someone's happy event, although I cannot always control it. Grief hits at random times and you never know when it will strike. Things that were triggers one day are not so hard the next, so I never knew what to expect.

I bumped into the young paramedic that was at the house the day Yechiel died. I had not seen her since that day and it took me totally by surprise. I had been having a good day, until seeing her again took me right back to the moment of finding him on the floor. I have that image in my mind and I see it every day, not only when I go into the kitchen where I found him. It does not fade away, but just seeing her took me back to the same emotions and shock of that day. I was not ready for that and could not control the crying.

Friends will tell you it will get better over time and that time heals everything. Right now, time is just making it worse. I feel that some creature pulled my heart out of my body, and time cannot heal this pain. I just slowly have to learn how to live with it. It does not get better, but seeing the person I love more than anything lying dead by my side is *changing* who I am. You can never be the same again. Even places where we went together or were familiar to both of us, now felt different. Everything is changing.

The fear of forgetting some of our moments together makes me want to start writing. The fear of losing the memories, which are all I have now. If I forget anything, there is no one to fill in the gaps. Although, realistically he would not fill in any gaps if he were alive, since he forgot something right after it happened. He compartmentalized everything. He deleted everything after he dealt with it, even his emails or to-do lists. He did not save anything.

It is also a constant surprise (and bit of a disappointment) to me when someone assumes how I'm feeling based on how I look. It is a major effort to get out of bed, shower and get dressed. It does not make any sense and yet, I feel hurt. Is it because they don't know what I am really going through? Or because nobody sees my pain? I have not bothered to go through my closet for the past year. I had a few outfits, and now 4-5 shirts that I wear, wash, and wear again. I continue to wear mostly black, rarely any colors, just feels the most comfortable. Wigs came in handy; they allowed me to avoid having to take care of my hair.

In addition to the excruciating pain that I was feeling, I started feeling physical pain. Difficulty breathing, joint pains, extreme headaches and so much more. Waking up in the middle of the night with shortness of breath was the scariest. I felt alone in the house even if I had guests. I was scared and not sure of what to do. I am not one to run to doctors over every little ache, but when this continued for several nights and I could not breathe, I panicked and went to the emergency room. They kept me for the night, running all kinds of tests, and could not find anything. When I told the nurse my husband had recently passed away, the doctors were quick to attribute my pain or discomfort to that fact. I felt helpless. Not sleeping at nights was taking everything out of me. I needed eight hours of sleep before Yechiel died and now I am barely getting five. I could not function, and on top of the confusion, difficulty concentrating and memory loss, not sleeping well was destroying me. I had to learn to breathe again, even if doctors told me my pain is due to my grief. My virtual friends in my support group told me otherwise; the pain is real, it is physical, and you cannot hide it. Relearn to breathe. Meditate.

My son Jonathan was big into meditation in those days, going out on the Tel Aviv beach in the early morning to meditate. He tried to get me into it but it did not work. Every time I closed my eyes, I saw the image of Yechiel lying on the kitchen floor. I could not concentrate on anything.

Oddly, I could already feel the creeping anxiety of the coming long, dark winter months. I needed to start planning now. I had to create a cozy warm space for myself. The heating system was not good enough and the house did not warm up easily, and the humidity issues were not entirely resolved. Given my sensitivity to cold, another winter with the house in poor condition would be a nightmare. Moving was not an option, I could not leave Yechiel behind. I was also sticking to the advice not to make any major decisions the first year.

I converted one of the upstairs bedrooms into an office/bedroom/TV room. It was the perfect spot for Yechiel's recliner, a desk and a chair. I covered the bed there with throw pillows, and added a strong heater for the room. Seemingly small changes, but it was huge for me. Before I knew it, it was the middle of summer, and I was heartened to realize that I would be ready to face the winter.

In the middle of all this, I started feeling the next big first coming up like a tsunami: Yechiel's birthday, just five months after he died.

I was still so raw and in the early stages of my grief, even if it seemed a vast majority of people thought I should already be over it and ok. I experienced deep anxiety every time I had to consider which holiday/anniversary/milestone was the next one I had to get through. His birthday raised a lot of different questions and worries for me. How do you mark a birthday of a dead beloved? What was I supposed to do? What would be acceptable? Was I not supposed to mark? How could I not?

The one thing I knew for sure, I did not want to be alone on that day. I had to figure out a way to be busy the entire day. Distraction and friends. Maybe Yechiel's friends also. I imagined the noise around me would just blur out the pain.

It was odd to consider celebrating a birthday because we never really put great emphasis on them. We had spent Yechiel's last birthday at a spa hotel right outside Jerusalem. We got a couples massage and took a room for the evening. I have a vivid memory of him dictating a Facebook post that day, overlooking the Jerusalem mountains. "Today I'm 67 years old..." He wrote once again that he felt luckier than Moses, that Moses only got to see the Promised Land, but he got to live in it. It would be his last birthday post. This birthday, I wanted people to talk about him. I did not want it to be a sad day; I wanted it to be a warm event. I wanted people to share anecdotes. My son looked at me in total surprise when I mentioned it to him. He seemed shocked and asked, "You're having a party?" No, it was a friendly gathering.

I needed to listen to my heart and follow my feelings. It was a personal decision of what I wanted the day to look like. I had to take care of myself, realizing that there was nobody else to take care of me now. What happens during such a celebration? I had a bunch of ideas, like maybe it could be the launching of the Eckstein Fund. It seemed fitting to celebrate his birthday by publicly announcing that the hotline that he dreamed about would carry on in his name.

When his birthday arrived, I had meticulously planned a gathering of about fifty people in our home. I had set up standing tables on the deck, an open bar, and hired a waiter to pass hors d'oeuvres. There were flowers everywhere, meringues I had made with the Fund's new logo, and gift bags I had stuffed for everyone who came – with meringues, of course. It was lovely, low key, but definitely celebratory. Some were surprised that the atmosphere was happier than they expected, and more than a few shared their fondest memories of Yechiel. All who came were supportive of me, and I think I made it through the evening without crying.

However, it was surreal. I felt like he would walk through the front door at any moment and say, "What are all these people doing here? My birthday? Is that today?" Looking back, I am not sure I would do it again, but it felt right and what I needed that day. It was the first birthday without him, and I did not know how to handle firsts. I was not making the right decisions; I was just following my feelings. I wanted to celebrate him on my own terms and I did.

He would have been 68.

Grief can't be shared. Everyone carries it alone; his own burden in his own way.

– Anne Morrow Lindbergh

It was strange to receive criticism on the choices I made to survive, but I stopped apologizing for the way I was grieving, for the intensity of my pain.

I posted once that I felt I got a sign from Yechiel, and a 'friend' posted that "you can see whatever you want." It struck me. Why be mean spirited? I started to let go, not taking it personally. They must be having a tough day, and it is not about me. You do not believe in signs, I choose to believe in signs – and that's ok. I can choose to live in a wondrous, unknowable universe, and signs are comforting. Signs help me get through and I see in my group that other widows find comfort in them as well.

Unfortunately, my experience is that modern society does not know how to deal with grief and most people ignore it. They say platitudes because we think that should comfort a widow. There are days when *nothing* makes things better. In the days where I need friends to surround me, I find that some are just no longer there for me. It's not that they don't care; they just don't know what to say or what to do, so it is easier to do nothing. This lack of reaching out, compassion, becomes a harder gap to bridge the more time passes. It is often said that we get to see the true side of people in our darkest moments, and that was so true for me.

Today, I strongly advocate for widows to grieve how they choose.

Some widows have their children around and are able to discuss and make decisions as a family. I lived by myself now, and had to learn to make decisions on my own. My husband had been my person to turn to, my person to discuss life decisions with and now he was gone. I leaned heavily on Hadas, but often I felt I did not have anyone to

consult with and sometimes I was just unable to make any decisions. The reality of being completely alone was, and still is, agonizing. I am half the person I was before, and the pain is indescribable. Sometimes all I needed was a hug, just a hug to give me the confidence I needed.

Coming to terms with my aloneness, that I needed to take care of myself, was paramount. I was thankful that I was starting to recognize and identify what I needed. I took the time to analyze my feelings. My feelings. I did not have the space or capacity to worry about others right now.

I learned not to let anyone tell me how to grieve. I was the only one who knew what I needed to do to heal. What is right for one person was not necessarily good and right for me. Some will mistake a widow's actions with selfishness. I believe we should brush it off. In that sense, my son was right: true friends *will* understand. At this point, I needed to protect myself because it was clear no one else would. Yes, I was thinking of myself first, it was pure survival.

Little by little, making a conscious choice to be around people who made me feel good and to read inspirational stories, helped in my healing. I stopped answering calls from those who kept repeating, "Oh, you poor thing…" or gave me that pitiful look every time I saw them. It was grating, depressing, and I removed them from my life. There were also those who asked too many questions, "Why do you still wear your wedding band?"

I removed those as well.

I did what I needed to do to stitch my life and myself back together again. That meant moving forward without some people, and holding space for new friends that were slowly coming into my life.

When we are no longer able to change a situation, we are challenged to change ourselves

– Viktor E. Frankel

It's dark out and someone is ringing my doorbell. The bell rings again, and from the security camera, I see a friend. I am about to open the door, when a voice in my head says, "Wait - It's way too late in the evening for him to be at the door." I fear that not for any respectful reason from a married man. I freeze. I have no guests tonight. My eyes glued to the camera watching him. Silently screaming at him to go away. A thousand thoughts jumble in my mind – the broken lock on the front gate, wondering how far he will go, images of me forgetting to have locked the gate. The knowledge that I am alone in the house. *Does he know I'm alone in the house?*

Panic is too mild a word. I freak out. The front gate had been broken for a few years. "Please don't slam the gate, it's delicate." I would admonish Yechiel repeatedly, but it did not help. The gate was old and we tried fixing it a few times, but the lock kept breaking. I gave up and we learned to live with it. I did not really care since we were in the process of moving. It stayed broken. As long as I could lock the gate at night, I felt safe. Someone could still open it by pushing on it strongly.

He walks to the front door and rings the bell. I don't know what to do. I freeze. No way am I going to let him in late at night. I try to ignore it. He rings the bell again as if he thinks I might be sleeping and he is determined to wake me up. I don't move.

I cannot reach my phone but realize I will bolt for it if he smashes his way in.

I am just imagining things; he would not break in like that. I know him after all, or think I know him. I'm scared, I am conscious of how

unsafe the house really is. Anyone can break in; the large kitchen window does not lock since that dreadful day when I got in through the window. After what seems like hours, he moves to the exit and out of the view of the camera. There is no relief. I wait in the dark to see if he comes back. Or tries a different approach. I make a mental note to call a locksmith in the morning and get the gate fixed. I am awake for the rest of the night.

A broken lock on the gate, chipped and dingy paint on the walls, appliances in the kitchen… There are so many other things to fix around the house, but I am scared to let a man into my house. He will realize I live alone, with no husband in the house as a deterrent. I cannot handle that. I took a pair of Yechiel's shoes and left them near the door. I hung one of his jackets on the back of a chair and left other items around that gave the impression of a man living here.

A few days later, the locksmith arrives. The cylinder and the intercom system cannot be repaired and have to be changed. It triggered me. *His gate key will not work then, Yechiel will need a new key. I have to change the key on his keychain that is still on the door.* I am not being logical, I know this, and it's not as if he will be using his keys. His key is still in the door. Yechiel put it there, and I have not removed it since. I use it every night to lock up, just like he did. It was always, and would always be, his set of keys in the front door.

The locksmith installs a new system for the front gate and gives me the new code when he is done. – *no no no nononono!* –Is the code on the keypad changed??. My heart starts pounding erratically.

"Can't you leave the same code?"

I am struggling to breathe. I feel tears welling. I want the small things to stay the same. The locksmith looked at me. I try to explain,

"The code is meaningful." I'm not sure I get the words right. The code was always the year of his birth. 1951. How could I possibly get used to a different code?

These seemingly small things sucker punched me.

I need the small things to stay the same. It gives me some kind of normalcy in this craziness. I need to keep doing things the way Yechiel did. Even if I did not do them when he was alive, now I live with all his rituals. Even the small things. *Especially* the small things. Like the way he would ask that when I wash dishes, I put the knives facing down. I did it for him, but occasionally I would forget and do it my way, a little more haphazardly. Now, it comes automatically – and each time I wash a knife, it goes facing down to dry, and I think of him.

The locksmith leaves me the instructions on how to change the code to any number I want. Relieved, I breathe again.

Triggers are like little psychic explosions that crash through avoidance and bring the dissociated, avoided trauma suddenly, unexpectedly, back into consciousness.

– Carolyn Spring

Triggers change over the months.

Eventually, I become accustomed to certain situations. I still think of Yechiel when passing the corn on the cob or the cans of cranberry at the supermarket and it fills me with sadness. Maybe one day I will be able to smile when I pass those. Other moments that were becoming somewhat easier are now resurfacing. Emotions are a rollercoaster I cannot get off. The ups and downs are constant and inconsistent.

I see a photo of a can of diet Dr. Pepper. The emotions and flashbacks are so real; I feel transported back to a time when I was happy. It's hard to find Dr. Pepper in Israel, and it was Yechiel's favorite. It was always the first thing I stocked when grocery shopping upon arrival in the US. Will these memories ever become comforting? It feels like I just got stabbed in the stomach. The pain is here all over again. There are still so many of his products in the kitchen, but I just cannot throw them away. Bottles of diet sprite, his half eaten dark chocolate bar that he kept in the freezer, cans of chickpeas and beans, jellied cranberry – I can hear him say - "I need something red." He always wanted something red on his plate.

For months after his death, I just went to the small grocery shop right next to the house. I was not really buying any food or cooking much. One day I decided to do a larger shopping and went to the supermarket. I don't know what I was thinking; I did not realize how painful it would be. I grabbed a cart and memories started to flow through my mind. Everything was still so automatic, I was used to always buying the same items, and the sudden realization that this part also changed, was too painful. Every item I picked up was for Yechiel. His snacks, his drinks, his crackers, his cheese, his cereal... The tears started... and they got stronger as I went through the aisles. I lost it; I could not control myself any longer and did not make it to the checkout. I just left the cart, ran out to my car and screamed. It was a while until I got the strength to retry.

Every trip to get groceries continues to be painful. Out of habit, I still reach for cans of cranberry at the supermarket and it's so hard to just put them back on the shelf. I avoid it as much as I can, trying to shop at a different supermarket to avoid those sudden swamping reminders that he would never be with me again. Nevertheless, something always catches me by surprise.

I stopped explaining myself to others, and slowly I'm learning to live with the pain.

I try to make the people I like feel comfortable, but I am distancing myself from others more and more. I just want to be around friends who understand without me having to explain myself. I am tired of the looks, the silent and not-so-silent judgment. In a way, it is a natural force compelling me to pretend. Pull on the mask to hide pain and move through the storm on my own. That is exactly what it feels like sometimes. A terrible storm, heavy rain and wind pelting down on you as you try to walk against it.

I call it the wave. I feel it coming today. It took me a long time to recognize an impending crash. It takes time to realize that the body can sense it like a low drone of anxiety. Too often, the wave sneaks up behind me and smashes into all my defenses. Pummeled without warning. When I least expected it. In the middle of the mundane, like grocery shopping.

He would be so happy to know we finally can get sweet corn in Jerusalem. The thought I won't experience his joy at the little things still makes me weep. People are so scared sometimes of my reactions, why would talking about sweet corn make me cry?

Mental confusion and a sort of brain-fog feeling are extremely common in grief. [...] There is an uncomfortable truth here: you are not like other people. Not right now.

– Megan Devine, *It's OK That You're Not OK*

What month is this?

Five months?

Six months?

Seven?

I lose track, until I feel the sixth day of the month approaching. Yechiel died on the sixth, and from the beginning of each month until the sixth, my anxiety builds to near breaking point.

Another month.

Yechiel is gone.

And another month has passed.

How is this even possible? How did I survive another month? Not only was I losing track of time but also I am thrown back into mourning every month.

Rinse, repeat.

Every time I move forward a bit, I tumble back again around the sixth day of every month.

Inexorable.

Embrace your grief, for there your soul will grow.

- Carl Jung

My breath leaves me and adrenaline spikes my gut. It was a simple envelope, but it was the first wedding invitation that did not include Yechiel. Being invited on my own hits me harder than I thought it would. It was a forceful reminder that there is no more 'us.' It is just me now. Every fiber of my being screamed at me to decline, but I forced myself to attend.

The day of the wedding arrived and I did not know how I would find strength. I am filled with self-recrimination. *Why did I say yes? Just pretend... I can't.* I had been to events by myself before, technically there is no difference, right? It is just challenging to pull up the zipper in the back of my dress alone. I can drive myself there. "Switch it on," I hear Yechiel say to me. Pretend. Fake it. Put a smile on and just get yourself there.

Once again, I take refuge under my wig.

Orthodox Jewish married women cover their heads in different ways, depending on their background. Yechiel did not care one way or another; when he grew up, his parents' generation did not necessarily wear head coverings on a daily basis. Consequently, Yechiel never suggested I cover my head. In fact, he always suggested I decide what is meaningful to me regarding religion.

It became more and more popular in Israel to follow orthodox dress codes. He never dictated what I wore, but in certain situations he would offer, "You might want to wear a hat to feel more comfortable." So, for our first year of marriage, I would cover in a religious skirt and hat, and then I would go back to my regular self for the everyday, pants and no hat.

One particular time, I wore my religious outfit to an event one day, and my usual clothes to work the next day. I looked, of course, very different. One of the rabbis I had met at the event the previous day came into my workplace for a meeting. I accidently crossed his path. I was mortified. I felt naked, exposed. I knew I was turning several shades of red, but he was very polite. I went home and vowed it would never happen again. From that day forward, I wore a hat.

Two years into our marriage, I was still wearing caps and hats. We were attending a conference in Paris, which would have a black tie event at night. That meant gowns and definitely no hats. I mulled over scarves, every option, but nothing seemed appropriate for my European standards.

A wig seemed like the only alternative. However, Yechiel did not see wigs as a head covering, and while I agreed with him, it would be just for this one event in Paris.

That first wig was horrible. I think of it now and I cringe. I cannot believe I wore it. Thankfully, I only wore it at events outside Israel, when I felt I had no other choice. I bought a better one a few years later.

I loved that they were so easy and comfortable to wear. Wearing wigs made travel easier for me. I did not need to worry about finding a hairdresser who could handle my unmanageable curly hair nor attempt to style it myself. I soon preferred wearing a wig; it was quicker, easier, and it offered a bit of camouflage. Then came another wig. And another. One with bangs, one without, curlier, straighter. I appreciated that I could 'send' my wig to the hairdresser, instead of sitting there for hours. Soon, I began wearing them every day.

Once you are "not married," you are not required to cover your hair. Technically, I was to some, "not married." Some of us follow a different custom: once you cover your hair, you always cover your hair. Uncovered hair tells the world that you are available. Like a wedding ring.

I was still wearing my wigs. They had become part of my escape, of not showing the real "me". I feel protected under it and it keeps me connected to Yechiel.

I made it to the wedding. It took all the strength I had to pick myself up. It would be so easy to just stay in bed and cry. I beeline for a glass of red wine. Numb the feeling. Try not to think. But also out of habit. Holding my purse in one hand and a glass in the other so that I can easily avoid shaking hands with anyone. Physical touch right now is an anathema to me.

Despite the wine, my mind betrays me. Memories of my own wedding day with Yechiel flood me.

Yechiel and I chose to have a very small wedding. It was the second marriage for both of us and we did not feel the need to have a huge party with hundreds of guests. We did not even send invitations. We also did not want to trouble anyone to travel to Israel for the wedding. We decided to have a very intimate celebration, just the two of us with the two required witnesses and a rabbi. As it is custom, since my children were younger and from a previous wedding, they were not in attendance, but they arrived for the reception and joined us in a small party following the *chuppah*. Our parents lived in Spain and the United States at the time, so they were not there. We insisted it was not necessary; we would have a quiet toast when we saw them next.

Jewish custom also requires the bride and groom to have a week of absence before the wedding. It was challenging not to meet or talk for a week; my butterflies rioted but we followed the rules. One week.

The night before the wedding Yechiel called me. I saw his name on the screen of my cell phone and hesitated. Or panicked. Probably both. *Why is he calling me*? Every possibility ran through my mind. This was not protocol. I did not answer, *maybe it's a mistake*. The phone rang again. I realized it was not a mistake. I picked it up.

"We have a small problem,'" Yechiel said. I stopped breathing. This is not what anyone wants to hear from your future spouse the night before the wedding. "I spoke to the rabbi, and he insists on having a *minyan* (a quorum of ten men)." This is not necessary for a Jewish wedding, but since usually there are hundreds of people attending, this question generally does not come up. "I'll ask a few people, can you also call some friends?" *Relief.* I told him I could. I called my cousins and two friends, and asked them to come earlier. It was a bit awkward, this last minute invitation. Fortunately, they understood and were happy to join us. I called Yechiel back, "We have ten men!"

The next morning I got together with three close friends for my own wedding preparations. Hair, make-up and some pampering, and light refreshments at a lovely Jerusalem venue. When visiting and choosing the place, I had very few requests. I insisted on only one: please make sure the room is warm. It was a stone structure, not in use every day, and therefore not heated on a regular basis. It had been dreadfully cold when I had visited, and the manager assured me several times that it would be preheated before our get-together. But, you probably guessed it, the morning of my wedding, the event room was freezing – they had not turned on the heat. I felt a flash of fury, disappointment; *this was not how I wanted to start my day.* My friends were with me and soon such a trivial thing became unimportant.

I learned an important lesson that day: when something matters to you, double and triple check – especially here in Israel where the answer is always "*no problem.*" Whenever I hear "no problem" in Israel, I know this means there will be a problem.

That morning, we laughed, we prayed, we sang and we joked together. It was a beautiful and emotional day. It was all very low key; one of the girls noticed I didn't even have a bouquet. She turned some of the flowers in the room into a makeshift bouquet for me, and headed out to the ceremony.

I will never forget the look on Yechiel's face when he saw me walk into the room.

Our evening was magical, the silence in the room overlooking the walls of the Old City, as the sun was setting in Jerusalem, the rabbi pronounced the prayers. The other ten men that the rabbi had insisted on were apparently there, but I did not notice them. I could only see Yechiel. The love radiating out of Yechiel held me captive. My dream came true. I was in love. It was just the two of us under the *chuppah*, just as we wanted it. Then Yechiel started to sing.

"*Joelle*?"

I am suddenly back at my friend's son's wedding... by myself. Someone was saying hello. The *chuppah* is about to start. The wave is coming - I know this feeling. I am not going to make it. I know by now that I can fake it for about an hour or so, after that I cannot control the tears. I look at the beautiful white *chuppah*, decorated with fresh white flowers all around. I smile at the thought of our *chuppah*. "I'll take care of it," Yechiel said. I thought I could trust him. Jewish couples usually put much thought into it since the *chuppah* is the one wedding must-have. For our wedding, Yechiel took care of the details of the rabbi, *chuppah*, and technical aspects of the ceremony, while I took care of the room and the caterer. "Make sure it's beautiful." I had asked. Truthfully, I only had eyes for Yechiel. I could not remember our *chuppah*.

In our wedding photos, the *chuppah's* four poles stand out. They were red, and looked like... broom poles. Yechiel and I would laugh about it later, and I do remember it was not what I expected. I am almost positive that I must have a disk somewhere. I went through the house, and could not find it. Where could it be? I have not seen it in years. Some videos I can watch repeatedly, albeit crying through them. I guess it is better I don't find that particular one just yet, I am not ready and afraid to watch our wedding. I looked at the photos and the top of the *chuppah* might have been beautiful, but all I could see were the red poles. I asked Yechiel once, "And who's the guy holding one of the poles?" "Oh, that's the rabbi's driver." We laugh. The memories ache. I smile. The wave pulls, threatens. I squeeze my eyes shut and focus on my breathing.

I left my friend's wedding right after the *chuppah*. That is all I could endure that night. There is a limit to how much I can fake. Dancing? No, not tonight.

Yet again, the hardest part is returning home alone, walking into the empty house. Especially tonight. The wave crashes. Does this ever get any easier? It is draining everything out of me.

He who has a why to live can bear almost any how.

- Friedrich Nietzsche

Because Yechiel's organization had been headquartered in Chicago, we split our time between the US and Israel. Sundays in Chicago were special, an extra day of togetherness that prolonged *Shabbat.* In Israel, Sunday is the start of the workweek, like the US Monday. After all these years in Israel, I still am not used to Sunday being the first day of the workweek. I missed the weekends that included Sunday. In Chicago, Yechiel and I would look forward to our Sundays off. We had a one-bedroom apartment in Old Town, near Lake Shore Drive. We would go for a run together along the beach, go out to brunch or just a movie when the weather was too cruel for Lake walks. Yechiel loved his gym membership at the East Bank Club, and we would often meet there at the end of the day or go together on Sundays.

Sundays now are usually a struggle for me, more than every other day of the week. I try to have a full schedule planned from the week before. I panic if by Thursday I don't have something planned for Sunday. Some go by "let's play it by ear" – right now, I just cannot count on it, and I need definite plans. I need the certainty that my Sunday will be full. The truth is, I like to plan every day like that, and know what my day looks like when I wake up.

I woke up early. Once upon a time, I was able to wake up, shower, and get dressed in 20 minutes, taking my coffee at the office.

Yechiel always needed two hours in the morning, and even then, I would find him suddenly rushing to get out the door. It was especially challenging if he had to leave the house earlier than 7am. Two cups of black coffee (his second cup with a cookie), reading all the newspapers, morning prayers and shower, all these habits meant he was usually late and sweating when he got out the door. He would never give up on any of those steps or change the order. Newspapers were usually all over the floor by the right side of the recliner. The left pile he had not read yet, the right ones... "Make sure, Pedro knows, the right one to throw away." With time, he started to put the throwaways in a bag, so he saved the bigger bags for newspapers. He would be positively gleeful when he had a large plastic bag. Like a child collecting stones, he would 'collect' these larger bags and announce aloud "Yay! Another bag for newspapers!"

Yechiel always placed his used coffee cup in the dairy sink on the left. The right sink was for meat dishes. I appreciated how neat he was about certain things. He never left dishes around. He always folded his *tallit* (prayer shawl) and put it back in its bag.

In all the years, only twice did I see him leave his *tallit* unfolded on the table, meaning he had to run out of the house. Usually, no matter how late he was, he always took the time to fold it. And never ever did he miss a day of prayers. On some occasions, if we had to leave the house before sunrise, it would result in having to *daven* on a plane or in an airport, where people who had never seen a Jew praying would stare. He would not care; it was unthinkable to go a day without praying.

Writing these words, I suddenly realize that he only had one cup of coffee on the morning he collapsed. His cup of coffee was almost empty but not in the sink, and the cookies were not out. It hits me with the force of a car wreck. My knees fold. I cannot process this information. I do not want to process this information. *He never had his second cup of coffee.*

I copy his routine and rituals. I wake up early now and take my time. Two hours in his honor. Read the morning paper. His office canceled his subscription but even if I did not usually read the printed paper, I renewed it for myself. I normally read the news online, but somehow found pleasure in reading the paper, and enjoyed opening the door in the morning and waiting for me. I am up early enough and I hear the delivery boy throw it over the fence.

And I think of him; and somehow, that gives me strength to get out of bed and make the choice to face the world and be grateful, all over again every day.

Later that morning, I got a message canceling my first meeting. It was not an important meeting, but important enough for me since it's my reason to get out of the house. I am crushed. Why does this affect me so much? I lose my balance so easily. I have to fill in the next couple of hours now, and I don't know how. Again, I forgot to set up a plan B. I have to recalculate and slowly, I get better at it.

After some time of pretending, I started to find some hidden strength. I felt Yechiel around me, always sending me strength. I know it might sound irrational, but I needed to believe in that to keep me going. He had taught me to see the positive in everything, and over the years, it changed who I was. I found myself basking in his encouragement whenever I could. Dreams I had of him at night would energize me the next morning; notes he had written in the margins of books seemed to be written just for me.

Grief can be the garden of compassion. If you keep your heart open through everything, your pain can become your greatest ally in your life's search for love and wisdom.

– Rumi

We are entering the three weeks, a period mid-summer that starts with a day of fast to commemorate the destruction of the walls of Jerusalem and culminates with the fast on the ninth day of the Hebrew month of Av, the saddest day in the Jewish calendar. This is a time of mourning for the Jewish people over the destruction of the first and second Temples. It is also on this day that other disasters occurred in history, like the decree for the expulsion of the Jews of Spain in 1492, or more recently, the start of WW1, or the 1994 bombing at the Jewish community in Buenos Aires. A time where there are no celebrations in Israel. No weddings, no playing music, no enjoying ourselves – some do not even eat meat for three weeks, and especially not during the last nine days. In Jerusalem, we can feel the mourning in the air, and this is especially tough for me these days.

The fast of the ninth of Av – *Tisha B'Av* - starts tonight. Besides the fast, Jews also observe some laws of mourning, like sitting close to the floor and wearing non-leather shoes.

I am having a tough day. I try to think of what a "good" day would look like. I have so many memories with Yechiel from *Tisha b'Av* every year. He did not mind so much the fact of not eating or drinking for

25 hours; the only part that was truly hard for him was not having his morning coffee. However, in the last few years, his doctor had ordered him to drink some sips of water, but he ignored it and insisted on fasting.

We had many options on where to go for the evening reading of the Book of Lamentations – *Eicha*. Yechiel and I had a favorite spot in our neighborhood that overlooks the old city, a place where our synagogue gathers and sits on the grass of the promenade. It is a very emotional location, with a breathtaking view. A must stop for all visiting Jerusalem, and tour buses line up there all year round for taking photos. I once took a video of Yechiel on one Friday morning, with the background view and him playing the guitar and singing Shabbat songs. I regret deleting it after I posted it on his Facebook page, and I no longer have access to it.

Yechiel and I had a tradition to join our synagogue on that promenade on the evening of *Tisha b'Av*. The last time we joined them, Yechiel's hearing had started to decline and that night he kept moving to get closer. He became aggravated and uncomfortable because he could not follow the reading. So, the following year, we decided to stay at home. We sat on the floor of our balcony with the cool Jerusalem breeze, and he read *Eicha* in the traditional melody with his beautiful voice. It was so intensely beautiful that I started to weep. I feel the tears again remembering those moments that will never return.

The national mood of mourning and the anticipation of tonight and tomorrow are especially difficult this year. The kitchen taunts me with memories of preparing a meal for us before the fast and sitting down together before going to the Promenade. Even in the summer heat, Jerusalem gets chilly at night and I could still hear Yechiel, "Do you have a sweater?" He was always conscious of my cold sensitivity. When I would say yes, he would continue, "Do you have a blanket to sit on? Your flashlight?" I would smile; it never occurred to him that hardly anyone used a flashlight today when our phones have one. I say nothing but, "Yes, I have my flashlight."

How do I get through this by myself now? The agony of each "first" was difficult enough but added to having to observe laws of mourning was too much right now. The Jewish people have been mourning for 1951 years; yes, we count the years since the destruction of the Temple. That number – 1951 – is a physical blow. Yechiel's year of birth.

I sob before going out. I do not prepare a real meal just for myself and scrounge whatever I find. Thankfully, the anticipation was worse than the actual experience. Yes, the memories were hard. Watching everyone sitting on the grass, I expected to see Yechiel next to me. It did not seem real that he was not there. I can hear the voice and the mournful tune of Lamentations, but I am not really listening. I am following the words without paying attention. I can only see Yechiel sitting on the balcony.

How much pain can we endure? I have heard of dying of heartbreak. Elderly couples who pass away months, days, minutes, apart. I understand that now.

I tried to identify the kind of pain in that moment. Is it dangerous? I know the signs of the dangerous moments. Moments when I would totally lose control and risk hurting myself. I have been close to that line many times over the past months. I cannot prevent them. I cannot control them. I can only try to stay around people. And especially avoid driving. Driving is the most dangerous. I could imagine going off the road or driving into a wall.

This is not a dangerous moment sitting on the grass. Painful, yes. Dangerous, no. I would be able to drive back home by myself.

There is a double message on *Tisha b'Av*: we mourn and remember the destruction but we also have hope and spread love and understanding in order to merit the *reconstruction* of the Temple.

I did it. There is hope. I got through this one. One more small victory.

Yes, I start celebrating my small victories.

It always seems impossible until it is done.

– Nelson Mandela

I had many memories from traveling with Yechiel that it was unfathomable to think about traveling without him. I cannot think of a major airport I have not traveled through with Yechiel. In Israel, the international airport has large posters with him and his foundational works along the boarding bridges. His larger-than-life joyous smile greets every passenger.

The first flight I took after Yechiel's death was with my daughter Amanda. She was moving for a semester abroad in Italy, and I had promised I would help her out and spend a few days with her in Rome. I tried hard to be strong. I picked her up and drove to the airport, but I started feeling the pressure of tears as we approached the parking lot. I was unable to control it. I was nauseous and could not breathe. I wanted to look strong in front of my daughter, but I could not help it, I could not make it stop.

Sometimes the anxiety leading up to a specific date would turn out to be worse than the day itself. Of course, sometimes, the pain was just as bad or worse. In the days leading up to my trip to Italy with my daughter, I thought I would not be able to handle all the memories. I felt like I might drown in the sensory overload of the past, my current, and the anguish of what-ifs and could-have-been.

Somehow, I made it past the posters, walked through the memories and boarded the plane. We ended up having a great time together in

Rome even if the memories of my time in Italy with Yechiel were acutely painful and the nights were particularly hard.

Italy has always been special to me. I went to Italy for the first time with my parents and my brother, and it was our last vacation together as a family. We stayed in a beautiful hotel overlooking the

Villa Borghese gardens; we toured the city and tasted our first authentic Alfredo pasta. Italy was also the last trip I took with Eli before our divorce, just the two of us without the children, our own friendly goodbye trip. Eli and I had been friends above all else, and decided to take that last trip together. Italy was poignant, and memory filled.

The next time I went to Italy was with Yechiel, and an entirely different experience. Where Eli would take care of all the travel arrangements and knew his way around by just looking at a map, I had to handle everything when traveling with Yechiel.

We had decided to start our Italy visit with a few days in Florence. When I look back at the photos, it is hard to place the trip and I find it hard to believe. Did all this really happen? It all seems like a dream. We spent a very special *Shabbat* with the local Chabad of Florence. We often relied on the local Chabad house for our observances. Every Chabad community made us feel at home and always welcomed us with so much more than a smile. Chabad houses around the world are awe-inspiring in their welcoming, and Chabad families were always inviting and friendly. Yechiel was always especially amazed at the women, their strength, intellect and beauty blew him away. He publicly acknowledged the women's hard work, and always joked that he must have been a woman in a past life.

Visiting Chabad houses around the world changed my perspective on life. Before Chabad, I had trouble understanding some aspects of Orthodox Judaism. Even though I grew up in an orthodox community, where men and women did sit separately – even on separate floors – I had never seen separation elsewhere. During those first few years with Yechiel, I was uncomfortable with separate seating at some events that kept the men and women apart. It seemed archaic, not progressive until one Friday night, at the home of the chief rabbi of Russia. I was shy, out of my element, uncomfortable without Yechiel by my side.

At first, I regretted being there, but as the evening progressed, the conversation was an eye opener. In a room with only women, the conversation turned quickly to private issues, intense discussions that I had never heard in front of men. I was thunderstruck. That evening, I started to realize the power of women.

The thought of those trips is much harder today; my memories jumble up between them. Eli with his maps that he constantly carried around, (in the days before Google maps), and he made a point to be well versed in everywhere we went. 'The smartest man I know' is the way my daughter described her father. It was irritating to watch a game show or play any game that required general knowledge – Eli always knew all the answers. He was also a travel expert and he took care of everything, down to the last detail. He had an unerring sense of direction, quickly figured out cities in minutes, picked the best hotels and found the most delightful restaurants. Eli was a consummate travel guide and partner.

My first experiences traveling with Yechiel outside the United States were quite the opposite. Europeans regularly cross over into neighboring countries, speak many languages, and experience many cultures. Yechiel grew up in a closed religious environment and despite his degrees in Christianity and Buddhism, for him, all had to be the American way. Anything different from the American way was bizarre or eccentric. Table manners were irrelevant to him and proper etiquette was not necessary. He said what he wanted, behaved as he wanted, and with his charm, he usually got away with it.

One of our first trips was to Spain to visit my parents for my father's 80th birthday, together with a few days to visit the south of France. 'Is it near?' Yechiel asked me. Geography was not his strength either, let alone geography of Europe. I did not enjoy having to plan every detail of the trip, but it slowly built my self-confidence after all those years where Eli had done everything for me. Yechiel was very appreciative and encouraging, and praised my ability to handle all the reservations. He did not take it for granted. I booked hotels, rented a car and we were off. We arrived at the rental car pick up. He enjoyed hearing me speak different languages, and would usually have me handle check-ins. It was really to give him time to be on his phone, catch up on his work and answer emails. We headed to the parking lot to pick up the car; I was done with my part, now he would drive.

Yechiel got the luggage in the trunk, got into the driver's seat, inserted the key and looked down at the shift. "What's that?" he said pointing at the shift. I honestly thought he was joking. In Europe, a majority of cars are stick shift, especially at that time. I tried explaining to him how to use it. I learned to drive in Spain, where the only option was a shift car. He practiced inside the parking lot, but it was no use. I soon realized this was not going to work. I could not teach him to drive a manual in five minutes. I was disappointed. We had a planned vacation in the south of France and it meant that I would have to drive the whole way. And I don't particularly enjoy driving. The drive through the Pyrenees between Spain and France is stunning, but it was not as romantic as I had expected. Not just because I was driving so cautiously focused on the road, but also because Yechiel spent the entire drive on a board meeting conference call.

I avoided renting a car after that.

So, no car for Florence. Once again, I organized the entire trip, hotels, guides, and flights. Sometimes it felt like too much. Yechiel had grown used to having a secretary do everything for him. He struggled even to connect the Wi-Fi in the hotel. I did all the talking, including ordering food even if my Italian was not great. *'Ask the waiter if...'* Or *'Please call the front desk for extra towels'*. I would remind him that they were used to tourists and nearly everyone spoke English. It did not help; when in Europe, I did all the talking.

We had a wonderful guide and so armed, Yechiel and I walked all over Florence, visited museums and historic sites, took photos by the famous bridges, taking in all the beauty of that wonderful city. Yechiel loved history; he asked the guide a hundred questions. We looked around for a meaningful souvenir and some gifts. We had a habit of getting a painting or print from any new city we visited; something to hang up at home but lightweight. Sometimes it was just a postcard at the last minute. I would frame some and place them around the house.

I look around our bedroom walls today, full of those memories – I see Australia, Rio de Janeiro, Amsterdam and Venice. Moscow and Mexico are in the next room, together with Korea. Chicago in another room. Greece in the bathroom. Yechiel loved the Hong Kong pieces he had chosen himself. Those were in the living room.

The Uffizi gallery in Florence was crowded with tourists and painters of all mediums and genres. We chose and paid for two beautiful watercolors, took a photo with the artist, and he scammed us. When we opened the package at home, there was only one.

'I'm sure it was a mistake,' Yechiel had said. He always gave others the benefit of the doubt; trusting that people are inherently good and kind until proved otherwise. I am not sure if he was right about the artist, but in the end, we got our painting back thanks to his photo and the guide.

From Florence, we traveled to Venice to meet up with Nancy and Harry. We had met them for the first time a few years prior at a conference in Paris. Harry is one of the few who could get Yechiel to go out. He would call every time they were in Israel, and never gave Yechiel a choice. Harry did not take no for an answer. "Why does he want to be my friend? I don't know how to keep a friendship." He did not need to. Harry was always there, keeping the relationship alive.

It did not stop when Yechiel died. They have remained friends and are always there for an evening out, a dinner or just conversation over a glass of wine. Once *Shiva* was over, they were the friends of Yechiel who remained true. All others paid lip service, and disappeared.

At first, I did not want to believe it. I needed to hold on to the people who were close to him. I needed to talk to friends who knew him. I needed to share memories with them.

It became painfully true that most people do not stay in touch. With time, other people come into your life and others leave. I was beginning to understand that the old 'me' did not exist anymore. I was slowly becoming the 'new me'.

New identity, new relationships.

It was wonderful to see Yechiel laughing and enjoying himself with Nancy and Harry. This was the only time in all the years that we ever went away on vacation with friends. It was always just the two of us and I admit it felt lonely sometimes. We had each other, but Yechiel needed the quiet time in between events, conferences, dozens of church visits or meetings. I would visit the city on my own while he rested or occasionally went to a meeting by himself. I also had a handmade jewelry business at the time, and would be busy with orders for gold crochet pieces. I carried a book and a small crochet

hook with me on every flight and everywhere I went. After having one confiscated at airport security, I realized that the crochet hook passed if disguised as a bookmark. Long flights were more bearable having an order to finish. Reading and making jewelry filled up most of my time in those days.

Yechiel always mentioned that he only had two friends. The only ones he had weekly conversation with; occasionally we went out to dinner with other couples, but nothing on a regular basis. Yechiel saw his life as a mission and work was his priority. He admitted it was not the right choice, but as much as he tried to make time for friends and family, work always took over. Even if he missed an important event, everyone always assumed he was at work. Sometimes, I made excuses for him; the truth is he was in the hospital many times in the past couple of years and often did not want anyone to know what kept him away.

Travel always coincided with his work, so after Florence and Venice, we attended a conference in Rome.

With all these memories vying for space in my brain, my anxiety grew as my mother/daughter trip to Rome approached. The reality was far different from the expectation. I loved that week with Amanda. We stayed at an Airbnb in the heart of the city center and we walked everywhere. We attempted a photo sitting on the famous and extremely crowded Spanish stairs before the police whistled loudly for us to stand up, (they strictly enforce the prohibition to sit due to the crowds). A flash of Yechiel in that moment, as he would always point out someone's out of the ordinary job. I imagined him musing, "This guy stands here all day to blow whistles at tourists who sit down for a second." Just as Yechiel's father did before him, he would always make sure to say a good word to these people with jobs that seemed hard to him. He would have gone up to him and said "Thank you for being so attentive and keeping order." He would have also told taxi drivers what good drivers they were.

Amanda and I found a spot for a quick photo at the Fontana di Trevi, and I found myself enjoying a little boutique shopping for the first time in almost a year. We played tourist, which is something I did not get to do with Yechiel in Rome. I had a unique and memorable time at that conference, including a private visit to the Sistine Chapel, an outdoor event by the arch of Titus, and dinner with Prime Minister Berlusconi. Yechiel was always too busy with his phone to enjoy any of it. He felt such trappings took him away from the heart of his mission.

As my short time in Rome ended, I dreaded leaving my daughter alone in a strange city where she still did not have any friends. I also could not imagine getting back on an airplane by myself. I would be completely alone on the flight back, and I was terrified. Amanda stayed in Rome for four months on a student exchange program; fortunately, she left days before the outbreak of Covid19.

If the flight to Rome had been difficult, the trip back to Israel was worse. It's not like I had never taken a plane by myself. It was the bombardment of flashbacks. Upon boarding, I became terribly nauseous, and nearly fainted. I had the crew all around me making sure I was fit to travel. I still had to make it through the posters inside the airport sleeve after landing. I waited until everyone got off the plane and slowly walked by them, caressing every one while hopelessly crying. How do I still have tears left? I did not know it was even possible to cry as much.

The next trip was just as hard.

The beginning is always today.

– Mary Wollstonecraft Shelley

I am a little bit stronger every day. Some days I feel like my brain is crawling through quicksand, but I am making it.

One day or day one, my choice. I have to *choose* to get stronger. And I have to choose again, every day.

I hurt for the widows in my group who were not finding any comfort. I hurt for those stuck in their anger instead of moving forward. I hurt for those who are not capable of choosing happiness. There are days when I am not capable either, but I am trying as best as I can.

Anger is one of the stages of grief, but I believe it should be just that, a stage. I am not sure whom I am supposed to be angry with, I certainly was not angry with Yechiel. Stages of grief are not set in stone, and I am not convinced we need to go through them all in order to heal. What worked for others might not work for me; I have to discover my healing path on my own.

It was extremely hard to see any blessings at first. I would ask Yechiel to show me the way; I would constantly talk to him and imagine his answers. I pictured him in my mind, and focused to follow his example; I slowly began to heal. I catch myself marveling at the incredibly beautiful fifteen years we had together and all that I learned from him.

Yechiel always pushed me toward strength. Now, I had to push myself.

It took six months to raise the funds to reconnect the call center.

Hadas took care of acquiring all the necessary technologies and we decided to go live on November 1, 2019. Yechiel's dream would be alive, and that gave me hope. It also helped that I dreamed of Yechiel telling me that it would work out. The detail of the dream was comforting– he was dressed in his usual light blue Brooks Brothers shirt and Dockers tan pants. "The hotline is a life-saver for Israel's most vulnerable, you won't need to worry about raising the funds to continue. The money will come". In my dream, he walked away and then turned back. "That's all you need? Not an issue". Dismissed it with his hand and kept walking.

The hotline - the social 911 network - would reopen, this time under the new name of the Eckstein Project *in memory of Rabbi Yechiel Eckstein.*

By the end of August, Hadas and I were busy with connecting the phones and computer systems. I now had something to wake up for every day; a light in the midst of the darkness. Hope for a new beginning.

The thought of a new beginning reminded me of a theme Yechiel spoke about often - the new moon, which also symbolizes a new beginning. He loved the message of the new moon and felt a spiritual connection between its cycles and life itself. In his speeches around the world, he would relate the importance of the phases of the moon to everyday life. Each month, we see the wax and wane of the moon correlated with our levels of energy. Our energy grows as the moon grows; it is a time to focus on goals and momentum. Even when it starts diminishing, we have confidence that the moon will come back – progress and change. In our darkest time, we know it will get better. From its fullest, brightest, to half and then three quarters, and even invisible, the moon diminishes and then reemerges. So do we, in our darkest times, when we are at our lowest levels of energy, we should have faith that we will one day become strong again. Yechiel would then end with a focus on the meaning of the moon in our lives, coming full circle to say, "Just as the moon has no source of light on its own and so gives on the light that it receives, we also have to give as much as what we receive."

On the new moon – the beginning of the Hebrew month in the lunar calendar, people greet each other with, "*Chodesh tov*." - "Have a good month."

"This month shall be unto you the beginning of the months," (Exodus 12:2) is the first commandment or *mitzvah* of the Torah. We celebrate this mini-holiday by gathering to learn Torah or a special meal in the evening, and adding special blessings and Psalms the next morning. I was always somewhat self-conscious about the neighbors and Yechiel's booming voice as he sang *Hallel* on *Rosh Chodesh*. He would go outside on our balcony overlooking Jerusalem, oblivious to anyone around. It is quite common to hear prayers sung outside in Israel; However, Yechiel did the same on hotel balconies around the world.

He celebrated this holiday with great joy.

On *Rosh Chodesh*, I would bring my colleagues at the hotline a little "happy new month" reminder in the form of cookies, sweets or cake. In fact, I brought a small breakfast every day – a bag of sliced bread and cheese. Ever since I overheard one worker when she commented about not having any money to buy food that day or the next until she got her next pay. We all sat in cubicles, and it was easy to hear each other. It crushed me. I made sure she got help that day and I promised myself that I would bring at least bread and cheese every day. Others also started bringing in leftovers or extra spreads, so there was always food in the small kitchen. The hotline operators had the lowest pay in the organization, making barely US$ 20,000 a year, and so, I felt that they deserved extra small benefits – *Rosh Chodesh* was one of them.

Every new moon is now a holiday to endure on my own. I miss him. I miss seeing the childlike joy it brought him when I reminded him it was *Rosh Chodesh*. I feel empty, but as I read the extra psalms and prayers, I remember that the moon becomes complete again and I try to focus on renewal. The moon miraculously gives light again, and I too, have the hope of a better future ahead.

The extreme ups and downs of this rollercoaster I am on will gradually level out. Through it all, I continue to tell myself that I will be okay. When? I do not know. But I *will* be ok.

Holidays were beautiful with Yechiel and they are a huge part of my memories. It makes me smile; picturing him now, arms wide, singing with joy on our balcony. Now, I need to take the lessons of the past, and move forward.

"Music is the divine way to tell beautiful, poetic things to the heart..."

– Pablo Casals

Ever since I met Yechiel, I listened to his CDs in the car. I loved his voice, and I loved to listen to him sing. After he died, one of the CDs was still in the car. Hearing his voice was a jarring blow. Incredibly painful in the beginning, and yet I could not stop that ritual for myself. I cried and cried, yet continued to play them until I was able to listen… gradually, without tears. To be able to hear Yechiel on CD tickled me when he was alive, and it would bring me comfort again.

On a particularly difficult day, I was driving, letting Yechiel's singing transport me to happier times. It was a CD I had listened to for years, heard thousands of times. This time, my breath caught on one particular song. The song recalls Genesis 12:1, when God commanded Abraham to leave his home and while He does not tell Abraham where He wants him to go, He promises, "I will show you the way." Like many languages, Hebrew is composed of masculine and feminine words. Yechiel sang in the masculine as in the Scripture, yet turned to the feminine in the middle of the song.

After all these years, and only after Yechiel passed, did I realize that Yechiel used the feminine form. Yechiel had transformed the song and God's command and encouragement of, "Go, I will show you the way," as a directive for a *woman*. The lyrics of blessing were directed toward a *woman*.

Suddenly it felt like Yechiel was singing directly to me. Singing a song of moving on, moving forward, and having faith in the path. With every lyric, even God's, '*I will bless you,*' I felt like Yechiel was talking to me. That somehow perhaps he had known this day would come and he made sure I knew he believed in me. There he was again, encouraging me to keep going, no matter what. To not lose

hope. To take a leap of faith. I had been feeling overwhelmed with the enormity of what I was doing, pulling the call center back together; anguished that the help I thought would be forthcoming from his friends never materialized, many pulled away or would not return my calls. Fatigued, I knew at that moment that I had no choice: I had to keep going. Yechiel was telling me to go forward, stay strong, have faith; *he will show me the way.* My breath catches and I *hear* him, I really hear him.

I was going to be ok.

When you see something beautiful in someone, tell them. It may take seconds to say, but for them, it could last a lifetime.

– powerofpositivity.com

These are the first words I see on my phone this morning.

Every morning is still a struggle to get out of bed. For the past couple of months, I feel like I have been hit by a truck. Fighting the pain in my body, I scroll down my different feeds, looking for a positive message while I stretch and do some exercises for my neck and back, hoping to alleviate the aches in my joints.

I make every effort to listen to positive talks, encouraging podcasts, meaningful life quotes… and try to start my day by looking for them. I scroll through, looking for something encouraging, some light to get me through the day. When I look for it, I usually find it. My social media feed this morning shows me not only one, but three posts in a row of positive messages:

"*If you really want something, go make it happen.*"

A young woman started selling handmade bracelets from her bedroom in order to pay for college, and seven years later, she has been speaking at women's conferences and was interviewed on Oprah.

"*Be thankful for the hard times – they can only make you stronger.*"

The man who posted this had almost given up when he moved to Israel six years ago. He was homesick, depressed, and terribly lonely. Reflecting back, he encourages others with his writings on gratitude, and how much stronger he has become. One can hear a message a thousand times, but when one needs it most, it hits differently.

"Don't give up on your dreams."

The importance of repeating positive quotes every day and practicing positivity is slowly helping me feel somewhat stronger. I needed all these messages today, even if I cannot fully believe in them yet. The advice I received is to keep repeating them, even with tears flowing. I can make it out of bed today.

My search for positive quotes continues. Focusing on good thoughts is easier said than done, and takes so much practice. How do I find the strength to even practice? Can I find something beautiful to say to someone today, as the quote suggests? I argue with that inner voice telling me to keep going or to give up. I will do my best to make it through the day. A good deed – a *mitzvah* - usually relieves the pain for a short while. I look forward to answering a few calls at the hotline once we open our new office; Helping others makes me feel grateful for all that I *do* have.

¡Oh, memoria, enemiga mortal de mi descanso!
(Oh, memory, deadly enemy of my rest!)

- Miguel de Cervantes

I hit nine months. How did I survive this long? Suddenly, I felt that I was going backwards.

The one-year anniversary loomed large and I stopped sleeping through the nights again. I started having issues breathing. I would wake up several times during the night short of breath and would stay awake for hours. It scared me. Deeply. The enormity of being home alone, the vulnerability of waking up not being able to catch my breath. After a couple of weeks of sleeplessness, I woke up one night at 2am and again, I struggled to breathe. Panic blossomed as it quickly got worse and I became lightheaded. I could not faint. Whom could I call in the middle of the night? I could not think straight. I stumbled my way downstairs and made it to the car. With no strength to even order a cab, I somehow drove myself to the ER, struggling to breath the whole way. I broke down sobbing when I got there.

Is anyone with you?

I lost my balance and collapsed. I remember being wheeled into an exam room and several doctors running different tests. I was in a total fog, not being able to breathe, terrified, and alone. Someone was asking more and more questions.

Is your husband with you?

No. I could not utter those words. He is not dead. I still could not answer the truth. Lying in the hospital, denial and disbelief kicked in. He was coming back and would take care of me. I just needed to be calm until he got there. He would be there. He promised.

It was not until hours later, after I calmed down a bit, when another nurse came in. She seemed caring, her voice soft and sympathetic. I told her my husband had died. Just like that, released a few hours later. Free to go home. The doctor said it was "just an anxiety attack". With the knowledge that my husband died, the doctors brushed me off, and told me to see a therapist.

I believe anxiety or any kind of depression and mental health are not taken very seriously. I was discharged without substantive diagnosis nor did they give me any medications. For weeks, I continued waking up nightly with shortness of breath. Every day was a struggle because I was so exhausted.

After seeing a series of doctors who could not (or would not) help, I saw a lung specialist and left out that I had lost my husband. He was the first one to take me seriously and ran a different set of tests. Suddenly I had asthma. I was shocked. I had never had asthma in my life and now I had to walk around with an inhaler. However, I finally got help, and I got my sleep back.

At least, back to the kind of sleep I had since Yechiel died. Going to sleep every night by myself is still the hardest part of the day. How do you *ever* get used to the empty side of the bed? Or not kissing your husband a good night? For years, I went to sleep early and woke up early, and now I could not get myself to go into the bedroom by myself. I obsessively leave the lights on in the house, because I just cannot bear the darkness. I did not want to sleep in the dark; I did not want to walk into a dark room. A widowed friend gave me the advice to leave the lights on, especially outside the front door. It made me feel safe. As soon as it starts getting dark, I turn on the lights. Front door, kitchen, bedroom and family room – the only rooms I use. I still spend most nights needing to hear his voice so I would pop in another video. I wait until my eyes close and then sometime during the night, make it straight to bed and crash. I then turn off the bedroom light, but all other lights stay on until morning.

Reality was a sucker punch every morning. It was not just that it was another day, one day further away from then and now. In my dreams, I was with Yechiel most nights and life was normal. Waking was a terrible riptide of awareness, death by a thousand cuts. I still had days when I just could not get out of bed. I wanted to slip back in the unconsciousness where he was still there, vibrant and alive. This was not sustainable. I cannot not live with this much pain, it is too debilitating. I am back on the rollercoaster, this time downwards at full speed. I needed something to lessen the impact, shake the hold it had over me. Nothing really takes it away. Medication can dull it, but it is there, a constant ache. Time heals all wounds seems like a nonsense aphorism. It was not getting easier; I was slowly learning to live with it, like a tree that grows around a steel stake to the heart.

This particular morning, sitting in his chair with my tea, I noticed his Buddha. It was carefully set in the corner of the living room where only he would see it. During our trip to Thailand a few years ago, he had gone into each store to admire the Buddhas. He said he could not buy one, but he clearly wanted one. He said it was not fit for a rabbi to have a Buddha in his house. Finally, on the last day of our trip, he gave in, and decided to buy a small one. Yechiel watched as the shop owner wrapped it carefully for our trip back home; he was like a little boy with a new toy. He was so happy. He very rarely bought anything for himself; this is one of his rare acquisitions.

When we got home, he carefully chose the spot for his Buddha, down where it would not stand out, but he could always look at it when he sat on his recliner. It was a private joy.

Amusingly, the Buddha made Yechiel notice when the cleaner had been in the house. The man who came would always move smaller objects, including the Buddha. He would move it from the floor and put it in a more prominent place, rearrange the pillows, and set up picture frames. It was never the lack of dust or fluffed pillows that Yechiel noticed, it was the Buddha's travels around our living room. When Buddha moved, he would smile: *Pedro was here*. Pedro. This always made me laugh because the man's name was not Pedro, but Yechiel decided it, so Pedro he became. And Pedro always moved the Buddha.

Looking at his Buddha now, I felt the familiar pang and then a brief moment of concern. Was the Buddha out during *Shiva*? When visitors came to the house, Yechiel made sure nobody would see it. Sometimes if someone came over unexpectedly, he would look at me with a smile I loved, and whisper "*Hide the Buddha*."

Hide the Buddha. That smile. My tea was gone. The Buddha remained.

Grief can be a burden, but also an anchor. You get used to the weight, how it holds you in place.

– Sarah Dessen, *The Truth About Forever*

Yechiel's candle was out.

This morning I went down to the kitchen and his candle was out.

A special seven-day *yarzheit* candle.

Out.

They never blow out.

I was shocked. I panicked. I am overreacting. I had been lighting them for months. I knew it had been lit the night before. I had kept this ritual for months. It was my only daily ritual. The only thing I still did for him, checking that the candle was always lit. Hands shaking, I light the candle again. I found myself talking and begging the candle for answers.

"Is this a sign of something?" Am I even supposed to believe in signs?

"What are you trying to tell me?" Am I really talking to a candle?

"Yechiel, talk to me."

I stood there to a silent candle and I struggled to compose myself. I don't know how long I stood over the candle before Pedro arrived. Pedro likes to have a cup of coffee before cleaning, and talk for a few minutes. Yechiel and I enjoyed talking with Pedro. Although he spoke only Spanish, with just a smattering of Hebrew, Pedro and Yechiel would understand each other. Their camaraderie was strong despite only a few shared words, and they would often share a laugh together. Pedro used to be a Christian, and then he immigrated to Israel and became interested in Judaism. It took him four years to convert. The rabbis would not accept him at first, but he went above and beyond to prove himself. He steadfastly goes to nightly rabbi teachings, prayers and attends weekly classes. He would often share what he learned, occasionally opening with, "I attended a very interesting class…"

Without warning, Pedro says, "I heard an interesting parable from the rabbi last night." Rabbis often use parables to express a point, and his rabbi told the story of a man losing his son. He was miserable, and could not get over the pain of losing his son. Years went by, and every single day, he is consumed with grief. One day, the man has a dream. In his dream, he sees his son in heaven. The son is with many other little boys, playing and laughing. The man knows that his son is trying to send him a message that he is in a good place. When the boys prepare to leave, they are all carrying a lit candle, except for the boys' candle. The father asks his son in the dream, "Why is your candle not lit?" His son smiles sadly at him, "I keep lighting it, but your tears keep blowing it out."

I got goosebumps.

I stared at Pedro as he finished his coffee. What was I to make of this? Pedro had no way of knowing I found the candle out that morning. Why this morning, of all mornings, did I receive this message? My brain reeled, something clicked even as I struggled to make sense of it at the time. It felt like Yechiel had sent Pedro to tell me, "You are crying too much, and you blew out the candle." It wiped me out for the day, but it was also a tiny step forward.

Messages come when you need them. They are unexpected, surprising – both heartbreaking and heartwarming. I was recounting the story of Pedro and his parable to a friend I had not seen in a couple decades. She had lost her husband around the time we had lost contact and I reached out to her because I was reconnecting with all the widows in my life. The years just vanished as we talked, and we talked about being aware and willing to see and hear the messages. She had been very young when she lost her husband, and through her grief, struggled with the fact she never dreamt about him, saw no sign, and received no messages. Fast-forward many years later, she made the decision to move out of her home, and to a completely new city. During the chaos of move-in day, as she was working to unload the moving truck, she encountered a friend she had not seen in years. He greeted her with, "Oh my god, now I understand my dream!" He had seen this woman's husband in their neighborhood and asked him what brought him to a place so far away from where he lived? The woman's husband said, "Oh, we moved, I live here now!"

Of course, the young woman was stunned. She felt that she had just received a message, and it brought her peace.

I know, and most widows do, that our loved ones are around us, sending us comfort and love through friends, dreams, and yes, even candles.

I imagine it takes an open mind and being open, to be able to receive them.

It is kind of shocking when your world falls to pieces and everything and everyone around you carries on with life. How can the birds continue to sing? How can people carry on loving life? It is like you have become frozen in time and now watching life like a movie.

– Zoe Clark-Coates

Ten months after Yechiel died, I returned to Chicago. I knew I would eventually go back one day, just did not know it would be so early. A couple months earlier, I received a call from Lake Shore Drive Synagogue; they wanted to have a memorial service for Yechiel, put up a plaque in the entrance of the building, and asked if I could be there. I was moved and speechless. I did not feel strong enough to get on a plane again after my first experience. I wanted to be there, but how could I do it?

It took me a few days to decide, my brain warring with me. I really did not know if I was strong enough. I thought about all the life-sized photos of Yechiel at the airport, could I walk past them without breaking down? I thought about Chicago, being in *our* US city without Yechiel, walking into *our* synagogue – with over a decade of High Holy Days memories and sermons. I could not do this alone.

The first time I traveled to Chicago was to join Yechiel for Rosh Hashanah in 2005. He greeted me at the airport himself. I was stunned.

What was he thinking, taking time off on these critical sermon-writing days? It was so unexpected and set the tone for a week that was so different from anything I had experienced from him before. Everything was new, unfamiliar and confusing. I was a stranger in a strange land. Yechiel was *como pez en el agua* – in his element. It was magical.

The second time I traveled alone to Chicago, he wrote to me to say that he could not pick me up at the airport because he was stuck at the office. He was back to his usual pre-holiday self, a time that he described as "running around like a chicken without a head". When I got to our apartment, I laughed aloud. His note said, "Welcome home hon, I'm sorry I didn't have time to get milk for your coffee, but I have plenty of… vodka!" With a huge smiley face at the bottom of his note.

My body shakes. If I traveled to Chicago now, there would be no Yechiel waiting for me. No love notes. Only memories.

I accepted the invitation. Hadas and I take the next few months to plan a larger "tour" of the United States, to fundraise for the new call center. Chicago would be my last stop on this trip. I would visit six cities, and meticulously planned where I would stay. I could not stay alone in hotels yet; I still needed to be around people constantly. I booked meetings, lunches and dinners, and made sure to be with friends at each stop. I will be away from Israel for six weeks.

I steel myself for the trip.

I started to pack my suitcase. The loneliness in packing just one suitcase, when I was so used to packing one for Yechiel, was debilitating. I would look through his closet and always made sure he had everything he needed. At that moment, alone in our bedroom, I felt an urgent need to take something of Yechiel with me. I could not get on the plane and feel alone, I needed to feel him by my side. I looked through his books and came across *Man's Quest for God* by Abraham J. Heschel. A deteriorated and yellowing copy from 1954, this book had a profound impact on Yechiel. Reading it was a personal journey that he took every year during the High Holy Days. Even though it was not Rosh Hashanah, I decided to take it with me. As with all his books, Yechiel had written his name inside. It struck me that even though Yechiel had a big and powerful handwriting, he wrote his name in the book in teeny tiny letters. I had never known him to write so small. I was noticing new things about my husband after his passing, such as his changing handwriting, and his voice becoming deeper through the decades. It had never occurred to me before that our voices age, and it was a revelation to discover the difference after listening to discs and interviews that he had recorded in the early years. I felt closer to him with every little discovery.

As I browsed through the book, I noticed Yechiel had marked up some of the pages, underlined passages, and written notes and reflections on the sides.

"To pray is to take notice of the wonder... to regain a sense of the mystery that animates all beings."

"It is gratefulness which makes the soul great."

"Gratefulness, yes! That is the secret."

Yechiel *lived* gratitude, and yet, felt a need to underline these passages to remind himself. He taught me not to take anything for granted, to start each day with gratitude and acknowledge our blessings. I remember the first time I met my father-in-law, when I answered, "I have two children." He corrected me by saying, "We don't *have*; we are *blessed* with."

I made a mental note to remember to concentrate on blessings and gratefulness. Yechiel underlined this for a reason, and I took it to heart.

Here I was, on my own, now landing in Chicago, feeling like a stranger all over again. Everything around me looks familiar, the long corridor with colored bright lights at O'Hare, and the same one I walked all those many years ago. I feel different, a truly totally different person, but I still don't know who I am.

"Please take North, Sir, and then make a right on Dearborn." Yechiel would direct the cab driver each time to our apartment on West Schiller Street. This time, the cab makes its way towards my friends' apartment on Lakeshore Drive. My heart is aching looking out the cab window at all the familiar buildings, stores, each one bringing back a different memory.

Why am I doing this to myself? I feel the pain in my heart. There is a moment of panic because there was no turning back at this point. I *have to* do this. Staying with friends was the only way I got through it. Thank God for the warmth and invitations every night from the wonderful members of Lakeshore Drive synagogue.

Yet nothing could have prepared me for what I felt walking into the synagogue. During the *Shabbat* before the ceremony on Sunday, I felt Yechiel everywhere; I could *see* him everywhere. When one first approaches the synagogue, there are three steps down, and a guard; Yechiel always took the time to talk to the guard, to ask about his family. Now, every step I take in, the guard, I feel his painful absence. I am bereft. I cannot begin to describe the overwhelming feeling of loss. The excruciating pain.

I mentioned signs earlier, and Yechiel sent me one that day. I was stunned to notice some verses in the *parsha* reading at the synagogue that day. "Surely the Lord is in this place, and I was not aware of it. "(Genesis 28:16). A verse that Yechiel referred to every time he spoke in Christian circles, and when he spoke at churches. Now, I could hear his voice so clearly. I got goosebumps. That verse was so Yechiel, and he touched many lives with it. Christians wanted acceptance from the Jewish people and he opened his arms to them. He became *their* rabbi. This verse resonated with him. He often spoke of how we do not always *see* holiness, and how sometimes, we have to struggle to find God.

The Torah reading this Shabbat also recalls Jacob's vow, "If God will be with me, and guard me on my way, and He will give me bread to eat and clothes to wear..."

Listening to these words feels like an electric shock. I felt as though Yechiel was speaking directly to me.

The lesson continues with making do with little. Israeli journalist

Sivan Rahav-Meir, who I follow every week, wrote about this *parsha*, explaining its hidden message, "There is a redundancy; why say bread to eat or clothes to wear? Isn't bread always to eat as clothes are to wear?" What else would we do with clothes other than wear them? Sivan explains that this is a call to be grateful for the ability to notice and value what we have. Some have too much food around and it goes to waste, others have closets full of clothes that they do not even wear and do not appreciate or even complain, "I have nothing to wear". Yechiel certainly appreciated food and could never throw anything away, and always insisted he had enough clothes – even if they were ratty by years of wear and tear. I smiled at the memory of just replacing his old torn and stained clothes and shoes without asking him.

Frank asked me to prepare a few words for the ceremony a few days later at the synagogue. How could I speak in the main sanctuary? Just the idea of standing in the same place where Yechiel delivered his sermons from each year, was making me shake. Talk to the community? That is insane; I do not have the strength to do that. Besides, what can I possibly say? Let alone say it without choking?

Yechiel was no longer here to speak for me; I had to step up. Frank was about to finish speaking, he ended with a reflection on how Yechiel never compromised his Judaism to secure his objectives, and I found myself walking towards the *bimah*. I had never stood up there before. The sanctuary looked so different from this angle; it had an overview of the entire room, and it was daunting. I could only picture Yechiel standing there. I looked to the left, to my former seat. This was surreal to me. I tried to detach from my thoughts and keep myself together. I spoke about 'my Yechiel' and told some anecdotes, then, I got more serious and spoke about his continuous search for God, mentioned *A Man's Quest for God*, quoting the lines that were underlined in the book.

I did it. I don't know how, but I did it. "Let's go home" – as Yechiel would say, even when we were not even close to the end of a trip.

This trip had been a whirlwind of one city to the next. It was my first time traveling on my own to the States, planning each visit, and finding a place to stay. It was usual for Yechiel and I to travel for his work and to be away for long periods, but this was the first extended trip by myself. With Yechiel, I loved returning home. I would nest for a few days, recharge, we had "us" time, and home was comforting. Now I was anxious. I missed the house, missed seeing his picture in every room, feeling him around me. However, returning to Israel meant coming back to my reality and that he was no longer in the world. Landing in Tel Aviv, I realized for the first time in my life the importance of having someone pick you up at the airport when you are mourning or feeling low. I needed someone there for me now, as I was mentally exhausted.

Thank God that Hadas was at the airport.

The comfort of being together again and walking back into the house with a familiar face, made a huge difference. The difference between being happy or breaking apart. She also had a surprise for me; she knew what I needed. Lately, I have been noticing the amount of cats in Jerusalem, and I am especially attracted to kittens. We discussed the possibility of getting a pet for company, a dog or maybe a cat, but I was afraid of the commitment. While I was away, Hadas had picked up a kitten for me, reasoning that cats were lower maintenance. I instantly fell in love with the tiny creature. I imagined Yechiel saying, "What is *THAT*?" Or, his usual "Why do people have dogs?". No way is that cat sleeping in my bed!" It makes me chuckle a bit. Yes, I feel I am betraying him in a small way, acting as though he still lived here, and wanting to leave things exactly as they were. But then, I have also made some changes around the house, and those small changes – including the kitten – make me feel good.

And so, the cat stays.

Hadas named her Kitty. Well, *Pizzie*, the Hebrew word for tiny. The feeling is strange, as I start to realize peace. It's my house and suddenly I don't have to ask for anyone's opinion – I can just decide. And yet, it issurreal – I want to ask Yechiel and I don't want to decide things on my own, but I'm settling in to working things out for myself. And there is strength in that.

Pizzie took a few weeks to get used to – she was a bundle of energy, wanting to play all the time. She broke things around the house, too many for me to count. I didn't realize how much childproofing one needed for a cat, and she would wreak havoc before I realized I missed a spot. I had a cat and a dog growing up in Barcelona, but I remember our cat being very gentle. I had no idea a cat could be this havoc-wreaking, house-destroying creature. Pizzie threw everything she found on the floor listening to the sounds it made. She was on everything and followed me everywhere. And she became a lifesaver. Having a living creature around the house, especially in the mornings and at night, has saved me. Those mornings when I have no energy and can't function, she forces me out of bed. The nights that feel endless and lonely, she curls up next to me to comfort me. There's life energy in the house when I return, and it makes a huge difference. This tiny beast relies on me for food, water, and warmth. She needs me and it is comforting to be needed. I rub her stomach and get a purr, she makes me smile.

Oddly, what strikes me most is hearing something breathe in my bed again. The first night home, in the quiet of the house, I could hear her breathing. A tiny little sighing. It was a strange feeling, comforting, and poignant. I am not saying that I replaced Yechiel with a cat, but having Pizzie was healing.

Thinking of it now, I pick her up and she leans her head on my neck. I feel her purr. It's the only thing close to a hug that I've gotten in months.

There are always flowers for those who want to see them.

– Henri Matisse

My first birthday without Yechiel. Somehow, it is not as bad as holidays without him. He never gave much importance to birthdays. Honestly, he was never aware of the date unless he looked at a calendar.

If I wanted to plan a celebration, I had to do it myself. I loved planning everything on my own, and anyway, I could not count on him for any organizing of birthdays, or any kind of party. He did not remember any dates anyway, and the only birthdays that stuck in his mind were his parents' and siblings'.

Birthdays for Yechiel were just an opportunity to take the day off, even if we did not always celebrate. Perhaps it was less of a deal because he got me gifts for no reason other than to say 'I love you,' birthday or no. We would sometimes just go out to dinner. Time and Yechiel had a different relationship. He remembered some dates, but he had little notion if a particular date was a few days or a few weeks away.

"I know my birthday is July 11, but I don't know if that is next week or a month from now."

He used an old-fashioned calendar and when I first met him, he would painstakingly transfer over the dates by hand, every year. Eventually, I transferred the dates to my computer's calendar and reminded him of each one.

In all the years, I only organized two birthday parties. One for my 40th birthday, where I had a blowout. Tons of friends, karaoke, and a full house. The second was many years later, for Yechiel's 60th. Somehow, as I approached my 50th, I enjoyed more intimate

celebrations; I felt different. I felt like I was starting a new chapter. I wanted to pursue my passions, grow the call center and explore new ideas.

In those days, Yechiel was consumed by thoughts of retirement. I was starting to feel the difference in the future of what we wanted. Conversations of the future turned more and more into all the things he wanted to do in retirement. He dreamed of a place in the Jordan valley in northern Israel, growing cucumbers and making pickles. He actually looked into a few places, visited some houses with plots of land and lived in utopia for some time during the year before he died. It was clear to me that he was already tired, and he had enough.

Perhaps his influence shaped the fact that while I looked forward to my fifties, I only wanted to have an intimate reunion. Yechiel asked if he could get me something special, and I recalled that on a trip to Chicago several months earlier, I had gone window-shopping with Tonya, his former Chief of Staff, and admired a pair of boots. She had encouraged me to treat myself for my birthday, but they were too expensive and I did not want to spend the money.

Yechiel did not have a head for personal details so he had no idea my boot size, or the specific boots I had even talked about. He tried searching for them online but recognized that was an exercise in futility. A few weeks later, he was back in Chicago by himself. He recruited Tonya to help track those boots down. She went back to the store, but only to put the boots on hold and get the details for him. He wanted to pick them up himself. When he returned to Israel, he managed to hide the boots. To this day, I remain impressed that he succeeded in keeping them a secret from me. I usually opened his suitcase and did the laundry, but did not suspect anything when he took his laundry out and emptied his suitcase.

The night of my birthday, I invited five close friends, my children and parents for a quiet evening at home. We all burst out laughing when Yechiel burst into the room singing "*Ho!Ho!HO!*" as if he were Santa with his big white bag slung over his shoulder. He was so proud of his surprise, grinning like a kid in a candy shop.

One year later, I turned 51 - one month before Yechiel died. He walked into my office at a time when we were all gathered in the conference room, with a big fruit basket and an old box that I recognized instantly. I had ordered a new watch that had not arrived yet (I would order my own birthday gifts, and showed him what 'he' had gotten me), so he took an old one that I had at home to remind me that I had a new watch on the way. We both started laughing at the sight of the old box with the old watch. Everyone wanted to see the 'gift' and did not understand why it was funny to receive a watch. While the rest of the departments in the organization were intimidated when the president walked in, my staff saw him in a different light. They were used to him popping in to joke with them, bellowing, "Give me back my wife!" or "She spends so much time here at the call center, I don't get dinner!" He made everyone laugh each time. Everyone smiled as he hugged me. While I often shied away from public displays of affections, my colleagues were like family.

There would be no more birthdays with Yechiel. That was my last birthday one with him.

I remember that day, as my first birthday without him was coming up. I did not want to celebrate. I did not want anyone calling to wish me a happy birthday. I was not happy and I had to make it through the day as best as I could. I decided to turn my phone off. I tried to ignore it was my birthday. This was becoming my coping mechanism, my pattern throughout the year. I shut off my phone for the day in case anyone called to wish me a happy birthday, shut it off so I would not have to think about it. Or deal with it. Ignore and push aside.

Tears are words that need to be written.

– Paulo Coelho

New Year's Eve.

I am gutted.

It could not be a new year. I could not go into 2020 without Yechiel.

Even though I knew it was coming up, even though I had braced myself against it, it hit me harder than I thought possible. I could not take it in. Swamping panic, I *could not* go into 2020. It sounds crazy, irrational, but there was no fathoming surviving the turn of a year. A new year. One that would have no memories of Yechiel. My insides were screaming. It made it so concrete. This was my life now. Endless days without him.

Yechiel would stay forever in 2019.

The world was moving on, turning a page, leaving a year behind meant leaving Yechiel all over again. I could not fathom that. It also meant that the anniversary of his death was coming up. It would be an excruciating month to that incomprehensible anniversary. I sequestered myself in the house. I could not function. I shook. I cried. I saw him on the kitchen floor again and again. I relived his death, and tumbled back into the first stage of grief. I went through that initial shock all over again. I prayed the world would slow down, and would stop. It was just not possible for life to continue without Yechiel.

I continued to host private group meals at my home throughout the year. A large group from China was booked for January 1, 2020; I confirmed the reservation before I could think about it. As the New Year approached, I thought it would be the easiest way to get through it. I focused on preparations. I had 20 Chinese tourists in my home as the New Year came and went. The conversation turned to a spreading virus and there were pandemic speculations. I remember thinking, "Oh, come on, that's ridiculous." Their visit kept me busy, occupied my mind. They were very curious, but could not speak English except through their translator. They seemed more interested in the house and the Jewish lifestyle than the food, and I could tell they were completely fascinated and humbled to be in a Jewish home. When the food was served, the translator repeated to me that they liked very spicy food. Over and over "More spicy! Spicy! Spicy!" Their visit delighted me; they would be the last group I had in my home before the outbreak of Covid19.

Say not in grief 'he is no more' but live in thankfulness that he was.

– Hebrew proverb

It is the first anniversary of Yechiel's death.

We decided on a small gathering of close family to meet at the cemetery followed by a larger memorial. It turned out to be one of the hardest moments I had to endure; standing alone at the cemetery for his *yahrzeit*. I had been to the cemetery almost every other week during the year, always alone and sitting down to talk to him. However, that day, even with the family there, I felt lonelier than ever. All other family members had their spouses to hug. I had not anticipated that. I was fully aware that I was alone, but seeing them in pairs made me realize how lonely I really was. I had no one to hold on to, let alone to protect me anymore. My legs were shaking, my tears were uncontrollable, and all I had was the stone on the grave to hold me up. I just leaned against it wanting to die with him, which I was very close to doing that day. I stayed at the cemetery for hours after everyone left. I had planned to attend the memorial. I even wrote a few words for it, but time lapsed at the cemetery. I could not face talking or seeing anyone that day. I missed my children; they were out of the country with their father. I was happy for them, but I felt left behind, set aside. I slipped into a spiral of thinking they preferred to be on vacation with their father than to be by my side when I needed them.

I stayed at Yechiel's grave and lost track of time. Everyone else left. I was scared to get on the highway by myself and drive back to Jerusalem.

Death ends a life, not a relationship.

– Mitch Albom, *Tuesdays with Morrie*

"What? Still? You're not over him yet?" *Over him?* This is not a teenage breakup. Consider yourself fortunate that you do not understand.

I had been close with my neighbor when her husband passed away. We knew each other from the time our children were two years old and went to kindergarten together.

"What a tragedy!" I thought to myself. Her daughter was the one to find her father in the bedroom, scarred probably for life. It took months before any of them were able to go into that bedroom. I spent endless hours with her every day after that; I realized the shock that she was in, and thought I could understand her grief. She would share her thoughts, cry and ask me how to live without him from now on. Eventually, she made some changes around the house, but could not get herself to donate his clothes. Just sitting with her seemed to help, but she was always sad. I did not know what else I could do for her, or how to bring her some happiness. I would sit with her, let her share her story, repeatedly. I let her grieve as she wanted, and did not judge her.

How could I have imagined back then that nine years later, our roles would be reversed? Suddenly, I saw her in a very different light. She told me to grieve just as I want, to try to survive the day. There is no right or wrong, you just have to do what feels right – for you. I got the stamp of approval that I needed. She did not judge me. She understood.

Then I lost my best friend Deborah. She had been in a coma for the past ten years, but it was still a blow. We remained friends from our teenage years through living in Israel, talking every week on the phone. She drowned in a swimming pool full of people. Nobody noticed and by the time her young son alerted the lifeguard, it was too late. She lay in a bed unresponsive. She was 39 at the time of the accident and left two small children. I cried as I visited her every week in the first years, talked to her even if she did not answer, and imagined that some of her involuntary face spasms were actual responses. I missed her terribly; I was devastated.

I thought I knew what grief was. I was never able to laugh again with anyone as I laughed with Deborah, a true friend with whom I confided everything. My memories of the first dates with Yechiel connect with her, as I would call her to share every detail. Years later, we still recalled the fun Jerusalem nights we had spent with her, as she was the first one of my friends to meet him. The night of her accident, I went back to her apartment, not knowing at the time that she would never wake up. She was in an induced coma to alleviate the stress on her. For weeks, all her friends were waiting by her side, waiting for her to wake up until the diagnosis came that it seemed that the damage to the brain was too severe. I helped with packing up her rental apartment and donating her clothes. Saying goodbye to my best friend was the most painful experience I had ever gone through, but luckily, I had Yechiel to go back to, my husband to talk to and comfort me, to hug me and tell me I would be ok.

Looking back, I now realize how clueless I was, thinking I understood the pain of others.

I understand today when others offer me help and yet do not realize they cannot. I want to imagine most of them mean well, but just do not know what to say. I don't think people are deliberately saying hurtful things; I want to still believe in the goodness of people without being naïve. My widowed friends opened my eyes on many things throughout the first year. While common sense told me not to open the door to a close friend of Yechiel who kept ringing my gate bell at 10pm, there were men who still tried, calling themselves friends. Widows are often vulnerable and believed to make bad decisions, which can open a crack for some to take advantage. People, men and women, I had not heard from in years, suddenly wanted attention. I ignored them.

My source of strength, comfort, and support was gone, and I learned that one of the ways to face the world was to pretend. Pretend I am doing fine. Put on my imaginary mask and fake it. However, by faking being ok or simply being out and around, some assumed I was not mourning and doing fine.

I was surprised the first time I did not cry for an entire day. My windows slowly started to get longer, but I still choked up often. There were days I still had to pretend I was okay. I made it through all the first holidays without Yechiel, the first birthdays and other important dates, but I was scared about Year Two. Some widows recalled how the second year was worse, the shock having passed, the reality sinks in and the pain is even more brutal. I could not imagine a pain more acute than what I already went through. I would not survive it. Jewish belief is that God only sends you what you can endure, and yet, I was terrified.

YEAR TWO

In the end, Tipping Points are a reaffirmation of the potential for change and the power of intelligent action. Look at the world around you. It may seem like an immovable, implacable place. It is not. With the slightest push—in just the right place—it can be tipped.

– Malcolm Gladwell, *The Tipping Point: How Little Things Can Make a Big Difference*

This house was our home. The sanctuary we made for just the two of us.

The subject of our home – *my home* – keeps coming up. I feel like I cannot get away from it, it's everywhere. It is the first question that people ask, "Are you staying in the house? Are you going to move?" I have heard the same question repeatedly in the past year. Why does everyone ask the same question, this question? It seemed irrelevant. Nosy. Gossip in the face in my grief.

I want to stay right here. This was our home, and it was my home now. I moved into Yechiel's place when we got married, and we made it ours. We had originally explored the idea of buying a new house, but eventually decided to remodel and make his house our home. He did not really care about colors or details; I had to insist he come along and help decide on floor tiles, kitchen cabinets and such. He did not have much patience for it, but he endured it with me. We remodeled the entire house: floors, kitchen, bathrooms, and from the first day I moved in, he made sure I never felt it was just *his* house, but *ours*.

A couple of years ago, we realized that the day would come when it would become harder for Yechiel to go up the stairs. It seemed that the day would come sooner than later. New construction was starting in our neighborhood, and we signed for a new apartment on plan. The kitchen counter installation was scheduled for that Thursday afternoon, just as I returned home after the funeral. We were excited about moving into the new apartment, but when my phone rang that day, the first day of *Shiva*, I did not care. I had no desire to go ahead and move by myself. The kitchen counter, as the rest of the kitchen, would never be installed. I had been meeting with architects, designers, contractors, meticulously planning the new home, and suddenly, I had no interest. "You had an appointment today and you didn't show." I handed the phone to the first person next to me: "Handle this please." The apartment was almost finished, the move scheduled, my house in boxes… but all that excitement disappeared in one instant.

I could feel Yechiel everywhere around the house, but the day he died, I knew I was not going anywhere, and I was no longer moving. Yechiel is still here, even now. I see him everywhere around the house. I have images in my head of him standing or sitting in every inch of the house. The thought of leaving him and those memories behind is not even an option. I knew at that moment that I would not be moving alone. Instinctually, I knew I was not going to make any sudden moves; later on, other widows gave me the same advice: do not make any major decisions in the first year, do not even think about it.

Everyone who is further down the path of her widowhood journey tells me that the feeling changes, that I will feel differently in a few years. I am told that eventually the memories hurt you, keep you stationary and you will want to move forward. They say you cannot live in peace while surrounded by, and living in, memories. That eventually a house will suffocate you. I do not see it that way today, but I suspect that widows, who have been through it, know. In any case, I have decided that when I know, I will know. Right now, I am feeling the need for some minor changes, to paint, maybe some new furniture. But moving? No. I need the comfort of my home.

After the first year anniversary, the same question started popping up again. Israelis tend to be much more direct and ask very personal questions – even strangers will ask the most direct inappropriate questions – I'm still not used to that. I still have no desire to move. Why do people keep asking? Why do they even care? Why do I have to decide anyway? I have decided to stay. If I'm comfortable here, there is no need to move anywhere else. Some people are even more intrusive in their questions. "Have you cleared out his closet yet?" "Have you sorted out his clothes?" I lost track of the number of times I have been asked that question. No, I have not touched anything, but what is it to them?

I asked my sister-in-law for advice on how to deal with such personal questions and she suggested a response that I have adopted: "Why is that important to you?"

Yechiel's clothes are still where he left them, his bathrobe is still on the hook and his slippers by his side of the bed. I mostly keep these details to myself – my bedroom is my private space. People are quick to make suggestions around me. "You would feel more comfortable in a smaller house". My thoughts are "Is your husband underground? No? So why do you even feel like you can make that suggestion? Instead, I keep quiet and give an awkward smile. I have to reach these decisions on my own, and for now it is not about the space, this is our home and I am not ready to part with it. It is such a personal decision, when to remove or not to remove my husband's things. When people offer help to come clear his closet, I politely reply, "I'll let you know when I'm ready. Thank you so much."

I may not be in the majority though. Every widow I know has moved to a new home, or is getting ready to move around the second anniversary, unless there are children still living at home. They cannot take it anymore, the memories are too painful. Most widows feel that in order to heal, they need a fresh start in a new environment. Of course, everyone handles grief and moving forward differently – there is no right answer.

I am going to do what feels right for me. Will it turn out to be a mistake? Maybe, but don't we grow from our mistakes?

She is clothed with strength and dignity;
she can laugh at the days to come.

– Proverbs 31:25

I had been dreading the winter.

This one more than others. My first full winter without Yechiel. The first anniversary of his death right in the middle of it. It was cold, dark, and lonely. My children were visiting their father's home in Uruguay. Eli had a house by the lake with a small private vineyard, where friends and family came out every year for the harvest. My children would join their cousins to harvest grapes, sort and crush them, making about 200-300 bottles of wine, and they were excited for this reunion every year. This year was especially festive for them. Eli had been diagnosed with cancer a couple years earlier, but he was in remission and feeling better.

Right after the first anniversary of Yechiel's death, I felt different. The pall of winter did not have the sting it used to, and something seemed to shift in my mind. I started noticing the change in the little things. I had created some different small routines. My mornings did not look quite the same as with Yechiel, part of it because Pizzie now woke me up for food. My evenings looked much different, not rushing to get home or going to sleep much later. I wanted to understand and try to analyze what was happening to me. Introspection. Awareness. Reflection. I am not who I used to be. I have not become a different person yet, but I definitely feel a change.

The healing process takes a long time. Losing the stability Yechiel and I had, having that ripped out from under me was shattering. I can see the changes, but cannot figure out who I am yet. I have to slowly find that out. Decide whom I want to be, make the right choices. I have to learn to live with this new person building inside me. I feel more aware than ever. Also aware that I have already made mistakes.

I cling to Yechiel's values to guide me and try to follow his example. For the past year, I have thought about how he would examine different issues and always had the right response. I recalled the advice he would give me and tried to imagine what he would do in my situation. He was excellent at analyzing a situation and reviewing facts without emotion. *Never answer on emotion, listen and try to understand the other side.* If there is emotion, wait – "sleep on it", and do not react. I became a better listener thanks to him, and learned not to respond on impulse. He would sometimes "sleep on" a thorny issue, which often meant that he did not sleep at all, think it over and then respond. I followed suit, but during that first year, I found that silence worked better for me. My attempts to respond to certain issues, together with my lack of communication skills, did not turn out very well.

Yechiel taught me to rely on my instincts and not put stock in opinions and gossip. He was judged and criticized during his life while pursuing his vision, and eventually learned to brush it off and not dwell in the negative. He admired intelligence, loved to listen, and wanted to learn from those smarter than him. His Jewish education taught him to question everything. Every conversation with him would include him asking several times, "How do you know?" He would grin and say, "I like to scratch and kick the tires." He liked concise, direct answers, and would ask, "Is that a yes or a no?" If someone hedged, he would repeat, "No, I asked you a yes or no question, I don't want any excuses." It was the foundation of his management style, and how he walked in his world.

Occasionally he would speak like that at home, "It was a simple question…" I would smile. My natural instinct is different, but I learned with Yechiel to have proof for even the seemingly obvious things. Proof my answer was accurate. Just like with his own staff, it was not until they had proof that Yechiel would accept the answers or suggestions. Even then, "Are you sure? How do you know?" He was a voracious learner, a sponge, wanting a reason and an explanation for everything. When he felt strongly about an issue, he was hard to convince otherwise. To work with Yechiel meant doing the homework; to persuade him to think differently, one had to be extremely well prepared and articulate.

Fortunately – and frankly, surprising – arguments were not a part of our marriage. Mostly because I recognized Yechiel's drive for explanation came from boundless genuine curiosity. There was never shouting, raised voices, or one-upmanship. We spoke about everything, and when we disagreed, we told each other gently how we felt. I loved talking with Yechiel. The long conversations we had while dating continued into our marriage. We did not have children at home so our nights were spent talking, just the two of us. Friday nights were especially lovely, our own private universe with no phone or electronic devices to distract us. We developed a custom of "vodka night" right after lighting *Shabbat* candles; an island of time to talk, meditate and pray together. It was magical.

I miss those Friday nights most of all.

Silence is the most beautiful of all sounds.

– The Lubavitcher Rebbe

And then the world stopped.

It was surreal. I wanted this when Yechiel died. I wanted the world to stop; it did not seem possible that the world was moving on without him. The first time in a long time I felt at peace was when the lockdown started. All of the sudden, the streets were quiet and nobody was out.

Finally, it happened. This is what I expected the world to look like without Yechiel.

A dreamlike hush fell over the country. Planes grounded, stores closed as they do on *Shabbat*. There were no cars in the streets, people stayed indoors. My heartbreak, my anxiety, my loneliness, eased for a moment. A different malaise set in. Coupled with the illogical guilt. I did not leave the house for six weeks, I barely moved and I ate whatever I had at home. I did not care that I had no fruit or vegetables. Deliveries took over a week so I did not bother. I was grieving again. For him, for me, for us, for the world. However, there was a relief knowing I was not alone.

Six weeks. Not for anything. I was hearing madness on the news, of people washing all their groceries, including bottles and milk cartons, removing and washing all outside clothes, showering directly upon returning to the house, and disinfecting everything. I could not deal with all of that. And truth be told, I was scared. If I got sick, who would know? I thought a lot about how Yechiel would handle this extended lockdown.

Can I say I was glad Yechiel did not have to live through this madness? A world torn apart by a pandemic, by polarizing politics, and mass protests? Despite myself, I spend time wondering what he would have done, what he would have said.

I picked up one of the books Yechiel was reading. It is still on the table together with his reading glasses. *Meditations* by Marcus Aurelius. The bookmark is on page 60. I start to read, my heart starts to beat heavily and tears sting my eyes. *"Nothing happens to anyone that he can't endure."*

Not today, I set the book down. Closing my eyes, I ask Yechiel to send me strength.

None of us knows what might happen even the next minute, yet still we go forward. Because we trust. Because we have Faith.

– Paulo Coelho, *Brida*

My second Passover *Seder* without Yechiel occurred during the first lockdown.

People had been saying that we had not seen the last of Covid, and they were right, but at the end of March, confirmed cases were spiking and there was a run on hospitals. Israel issued a lockdown mandate just a few days before *Pesach*, Passover. People were confused, how could the state possibly tell the elderly that they could not see family during one of the biggest holidays? No one wanted to be alone for *Seder* night, and there were many who strategized how to get around the lockdown.

People rallied around those who would be alone, with no festive table. However, when the lockdown started, I was fine. When the world stopped, there was suddenly no stress or pressure around the *Seder.* There was an outpouring of caring, and community outreach. A message went viral on social media, that at 8-9pm, everyone should go out on their terrace and outdoors, and sing together *Mah Nishtanah* - the main song of the *Seder*: the child asking why tonight was different than any other night.

They held *Seder* on TV so everyone could leave their TVs on, and be a part of a national *Seder.* At the appointed time, I walked outside that night, and felt like the world joined us in singing. During what would be recognized as the beginning of the pandemic, it was poignant, chilling, and incredibly humbling and beautiful to hear so many voices asking why this night was different from any other night.

A friend had sent me a recording earlier that day, of the *Haggadah* set with Moroccan instrumentation and music. Like on *Shabbat*, we are to refrain from using electricity and electronics. I started the *Haggadah*, lit the festive candles and sat in the quiet to listen. Last year, my first *Seder* without Yechiel was different and far from family. This one… I don't know what it would have felt like if there had not been a lockdown. I was at peace. I was by myself, and yet did not feel lonely – I felt everyone was on the same boat.

*A journey of a thousand miles
begins with a single step.*

– Lao Tzu

I had an epiphany of sorts today. Death. Birth. What if I said that in order to deal with Yechiel's death, I was subconsciously trying to give birth to something? When I look back at the year following his death, I identify some key dates: March, I contact a non-profit lawyer who can advise on registering a new organization. May 6 – I received the certificate for the newly registered "Eckstein Fund." Exactly 3 months after his death. I made it through the first trimester. The "baby" is safe. We start helping some people in need in Jerusalem.

April through October – we put together a board, raise our seed money, build the infrastructure, computers and phone systems, and rent an office.

November – we reopened the hotline – exactly nine months after Yechiel died. We gave birth. Let me focus now on growth and renewal. Whatever energy I could gather on the days I could somewhat function – I would save for this. Nothing else mattered. The hotline had to grow. I was in denial and this was my way of keeping Yechiel alive. I had yet to learn how to grow stronger, learn ways to boost my energy, and heal.

My emotional journey felt like a painful rebirth. Life as I knew it ended with Yechiel's death. It is and will always be the demarcation line of my two lives. One month before, one month after, they are separate lives. One with Yechiel. One without. In those initial moments of grief, I had to learn to breathe and live again. As one cannot expect a newborn to run, one cannot expect a widow to function. It is a process. Every small detail of living is a muscle you have to relearn to use, to strengthen. You cannot expect to run, you cannot even walk, and you are not even crawling. That whole year, my emotional "baby" was learning to turn over, to stand up, and to crawl. I honestly could not think of that muscle until after the first year. Only after the beginning of the second year could I begin to analyze situations and understand what I read.

I started writing after the first year. That entire first year was *survival.* I just needed to survive. Most days I felt like I had to teach myself to breathe again. Everything felt outside the body. Raw. Painful. Robotic. You brush your teeth, you take a shower, you eat. Not necessarily in that order. I felt like one day I would be on the path to some small semblance of normalcy, and then I would lose my way, find myself back on the original path, bereft and lost. Whenever I could robot myself into clothes, a wig, maybe a little makeup, and push myself outside, I knew people looked at me and thought, "Oh, she's doing great." No one could see that I was in survival mode.

When life shows you painful and difficult moments, it is only normal to feel like part of you is dying as well. For one year, I could not see how I could ever smile again. Sure, I was fake smiling. But a real smile, a natural smile that lights up the eyes, and radiates joy? I was not there. My "fake it until I make it" became "fake it until I feel it." I lost a little faith and it was so hard to find courage and strength. There is no way I could find anything positive during that first year.

Hadas would keep repeating to me, "You are going to be ok." I did not want to be ok. *How could I be ok if Yechiel was dead*? She insisted. She asked me to repeat after her. "I am going to be ok, one day." Slowly, I started saying those words to myself and using them as an answer.

"How are you?"

"I will be ok."

I did not believe them at first, but I kept repeating, to myself and to others, until they became part of me. What do I want my life to look like? I have to decide how I want to live. Do I want to suffer?

I did not know how to get out of it. I thought suffering was not a choice, it just happens. The pain was there, I could not control it. I could not make it go away. I felt like I could not change that. I had to decide what tape I wanted to play in my mind. Years ago, I might have just said, "Well, that's how I am." Now I know better. We can all change our mindset. I was just learning how. Baby steps.

They are brought to their knees and fall, but we rise up and stand firm.

– Psalm 20:8

R*esilience.*

Building *resilience.*

I remember when I was young and broke my arm, I noticed all the people who also had a cast. It felt like suddenly there were more people around with broken limbs. Now, as I was trying to find a way to get stronger, I started hearing the word resilience everywhere. English is my second or third language, and I could not entirely capture the meaning of this word. It was hard to wrap my brain around it. The first year, I was in survival mode, and honestly, could not relate to or absorb anything I read about resilience. I was just trying to get out of bed and take a shower, and reading was extremely difficult. I was trying to read about grief and building resilience, but would find myself rereading every line and not able to remember anything.

I had never even heard of resilience until I met Yechiel. So many books on how to build resilience, connecting grief with resilience. What exactly is *resilience*? Is it within you or can you build it? I was ready to start finding some answers.

A part of me wants to feel the pain, does not want grief to go away. If the pain goes away, would that mean growing distant from Yechiel? Would I feel like I was betraying our time together? My grief and love are still one, totally connected at this point. I am afraid that if the grief eases, I will not feel the love. I started to feel the waves were further apart. The pain was starting to become more bearable. Like my love and grief were still one. Once the pain fades away, is my grief over? Is it even possible for grief to end? I could not make any sense of it. If I did not hurt, I was not grieving, and if I were not grieving then, ... what did that mean? It was illogical, but since he was not present anymore, the love turned into grief. Grief was my way of loving him. As time progressed, and I felt less grief, I was so confused. I did not want to let go. I still wanted the closeness.

The second year feels different. Resilience now makes sense to me. I am starting to connect to myself; I have space to think instead of shuffling in a fog. Now that the waves are further apart, I can build my strength. I do not feel in survival mode any more. But how do I express my love for him? How do you love someone without being able to hug him, laugh together and care for him?

When I was finally able to concentrate on more than a paragraph, I started reading more on grief lumped life experiences as one and on building resilience. I personally found it unhelpful at the time. I wanted to read something that related more. I did not want to read that my grief was the same as other traumatic life experiences, nor was I focused on building myself up. I still focused on the small things, one day at a time. A shower and getting dressed was an accomplishment. If I remembered to eat, it was a step forward. I found myself gravitating to social media, and to the widows support group I found there. It was strange to me that I felt more comfortable talking to total strangers; but I found that other widows were the only ones who could really understand what I was going through. It validated my feelings.

I could mention something that I was doing or going through, and widows would relate. I could talk about having life-sized cutouts of Yechiel in my house and they got it. I read of the strange things other widows did, and to be able to laugh at our oddness, to share in a special dark humor was a lifesaver.

I was in a fog most of the time, but even living my pain, I knew that the only way up for me, was to first hit rock bottom. Somewhere in my consciousness, I knew once I hit bottom, I would figure out how to pull myself up. I got through all the 'firsts', I made it this far.

In my 20s, I saw a therapist for depression who described a landscape of me at the bottom of a pit and said, "I can throw you a rope, but ultimately, you will have to climb up by yourself." I do not remember much from those years in therapy. I was totally lost, but my therapist explained what help looked like. It was not sitting and crying with me, it was to show me the light, and give me hope.

After Yechiel died, the fact that there would eventually be a path up for me, was reinforced as I listened to other widows who were further along in their journey. Witnessing their strength, reading their stories and seeing that they were ok. I noticed they spoke of their late spouses with a smile and humor; those were the stories that gave me strength. They showed me light, a path to hope.

Does living in Israel give one a different perspective? Did living in Jerusalem have an influence on me? Wars, terror attacks, armed soldiers – we have been conditioned to live with these as a part of our daily lives. I have lived in Israel since I was 15. I have lived here many more years now than I lived in Spain. I raised my children in Israel and felt the pride and terror of seeing them in army uniforms. From the first Lebanon war, the Gulf war in 1991, I have seen much fighting since moving to Israel in 1983. Israelis have been through many wars and each time our nation recovered.

When a bus exploded at the bus stop in front of our house in Jerusalem in 1999, I was traumatized. I did not step on a bus for ten years, and as a young mother, refused to let my children get on a bus. I drove them everywhere. Just when it started feeling safe again, my colleague's daughter was killed on her way to school on a bus by a suicide bomber posing as a passenger. Her son was still finishing his breakfast and getting dressed; she did not want them both to be late for school, so she told her daughter to go ahead and catch the bus by herself. Her son took the next bus and lived. I think of her, and the horror of it nearly undoes me. Yet, today I take the bus almost every day. Driving into downtown Jerusalem is an exercise in frustration and madness, and there is rarely parking available. The bus is convenient, easy; it takes me door-to-door in 15 minutes, while by car it takes at least double that time.

Still, for years, the parents and families of the murdered kept the bus stop as a memorial. They put a table in the stop, candles and vases of flowers were refreshed daily. Every day, driving past that bus stop, was a reminder. The trauma was intensified because I saw it every day. A bus stop covered in photos of the children, the teenagers, everyone killed there. The bus stop was renovated recently, and a plaque with the names of the victims lay instead. The plaques are all over the city, at every bus stop and every location in Jerusalem where Israelis were killed in terrorist attacks. Every time I pass one, I have such a vivid image of the old bus stop.

Now, the image of Yechiel on the kitchen floor is one that will never leave my mind. It is carved in my mind. This is part of my struggle, my pain. My mind keeps returning the memory of him on the floor. I struggle against it – I want to see him alive, smiling, and kissing me. I *do not want* to see him on the floor, this is why I watch the videos so much, to try to re-image my thoughts. I want to see him *alive* and vibrant.

I feel smothered by *Shiva* notices. In Jerusalem, they are black and white paper notices for the outside of houses in mourning, and I saw them everywhere. I could not pass one without stopping to read the names. So many names. The lettering of each name always seemed huge. Yechiel's name written in huge letters. I think of all the widows, and the weight of their loss crushes me. Before Yechiel's death, a *Shiva* notice barely registered other than feeling poorly that someone died. Now I know the pain of the living. I have a compulsion to visit each one, to reach out. It is not possible with Covid lockdown, but the urge is strong.

During the subsequent lockdowns, I gravitated even more to positivity, inspirational videos, and motivational speakers. Like meringues, or rearranging the house, it became my obsession. As I was figuring out who I was, my brain would become manic with different activities. Making meringues, long walks, social media, TED talks, YouTube, Sudoku… I felt like a teenager with ADD. Interests changed suddenly and randomly. I would follow a compulsion and a month later, I would lose interest in it. One day my daughter suggested a Netflix show. I watched the first episode and ten hours later, I was still in front of the TV. I called my daughter in panic, "What is this??" I watched four seasons in two days. I switched Netflix for motivational speakers and learning more on widows, and it became my new obsession, I felt drawn to it like a calling.

I think of the mothers who have lost their children in the terror attacks. I listen to some amazing speakers and I take in their strength. Not only in Israel, but through social media, TED talks, or podcasts, I sought out messages that inspired me. I discovered people I had never heard of, all ages, from all over the world. I think of Yechiel repeating the words of the Sages, "From all people I learn." (Psalm 119) Yechiel lived by this, learning from all. Every person has a story and everyone can teach us something. Yechiel would ask questions every chance he could, and he waited for answers. Now, I find myself asking women how they did it. If they can do it, I can do it. As Eli would always tell me years ago, "Pick yourself up, brush it off and get out, you have work to do." I wanted to be happy; I did not want to live a life of sadness. I had to learn how.

It does not matter how long you are spending on the earth, how much money you have gathered or how much attention you have received. It is the amount of positive vibration you have radiated in life that matters.

– Amit Ray, *Meditation: Insights and Inspirations*

How do I find meaning?

How do I find purpose?

I believe what I was learning about positivity - we can learn to become positive. I can learn to rewire myself. For that purpose, I feel that first, I need to clean out anything negative in my life. Anything that affects me in a negative way. Just walk away and brush it off.

My first husband was skilled in the art of deflecting a fight. He was extremely rational, focused, and calm in business and in life. There was no arguing with Eli because he would not rise to it. I joined Eli in his business too, and watching him move through the world was fascinating. At work, I watched him calmly listen to rants and complaints and at the end he would just say, "If you are not happy here, you are welcome to leave." It just did not ruffle him; he was not going to fight with his staff. What did not merit a reply did not get a reply. He believed not everything needs to be a fight.

It strikes me that my father shares similar traits but comes about them differently. He listens, truly listens, and is always soft spoken and calm. People like talking to him and he can find common ground with anyone. He, too, does not fight.

I am learning to choose my fights with more deliberation today. I did not know any better back then. I am learning now about life skills that many people learn in their youth. I am learning what I wanted to fight for, what to let go. It is odd to say that as an adult, I am just beginning to mature now, but I was. I learned a lot with Eli, and I grew with Yechiel. I regressed after he died. My world was out of control so I was out of control. My compass was gone and my ability to make the right choices left with it. I remember calling a close family member and asking to meet as soon as possible. I make a note to myself now to call and ask what his suggestions were because for the life of me, I cannot remember. I remember feeling it was important, and feeling the need for guidance, but I cannot remember the actual conversation.

Everything felt like a fight. A struggle. I registered a new organization without even understanding what I was doing. I felt under siege by Yechiel's organization. I was coping with loss. *Not everything needs to be a fight.* It felt like there was grace in letting go. I remember those painful moments when I discovered that I was not invited to events in his memory. The only way to get past that pain, to cope, was to ignore it. Sometimes I wish I had functioned differently – ignoring and not responding may not seem mature, and to outsiders it may have seemed childish, but I have to admit that was the only coping mechanism that helped me at the time. I had not realized what a buffer Yechiel had been for me. No one is there to pick up the pieces. If I did not respond to an email, it was left unanswered. I had a mental block against the mail. I could not pick it up; so much was in his name. I was afraid to open it. There were sharks there.

Memory loss is one way of coping with damage.

– Jeanette Winterson, *Why Be Happy When You Could Be Normal?*

The memory loss is terrifying.

I discover more and more gaps that I cannot remember. I realized very early on that I could not remember my day to day. I had to write everything down. Literally everything, including what time I woke up and what I ate. Memories come up of Yechiel writing everything down, although he would record it on his voice-it. It amused me at the time. The first time we were at a hotel together, upon walking out of the room, he took out his voice-it and recorded "I'm in room 1215." I burst out laughing.

Today, while I am dimly aware of all those moments that I could not handle and the situations that I chose not to take care of. I have some flashes of clarity. I cannot even remember some people's names. In a conversation with a close family member, I apparently said hurtful things. He reminds me. I apologize. I cannot remember what I said or why I said it. I can remember moments and certain situations but I cannot remember the conversations. I can understand someone not believing me when I said I could not remember, since apparently I repeated the same comments on different occasions. I try to think of other moments, meetings, car rides. I cannot remember any of the words. I remember pain, sadness, and tears. I am quite shaken tonight as I struggle to remember. It feels like someone pressed 'delete' on my brain. Hadas confirms my concerns – I have memory loss. Every day, I ask her questions like:

"Did I know this person?"

"What time did you say the meeting is?"

"When did we decide to do this?"

"What did we agree on?"

Yechiel did not remember faces. As sharp as he could be with his work hat on, other things would totally elude him. He would lean over to me and ask, "How do I know this person?" or, "Do I like this food?" I constantly reminded him of names and people, even at family events.

I never had an issue with memory... How could it be that I was struggling for these answers and asking these kinds of questions?

Thankfully, I have Hadas as my right hand, and I can count on her for everything. More than ever, she is my reminder for everything.

At first, I thought I was perhaps only being a little forgetful, having to write everything down. However, when I try to think of specific events of the first year, I can barely remember words. I am suddenly terrified. What kind of a fog was I in, and what kind of things did I say that did not make any sense. Did anyone realize how much of a state of shock I was in? Can anyone see that? My husband was the only person who would notice panic or shock in my eyes. Nobody else could have possibly seen it, let alone help me. Hadas was the next closest person, and she took over.

I ask my widow's club. Am I losing my mind? They assured me memory loss is normal. Do not worry, all the symptoms are normal, but do not try explaining that to anyone who has not lost a beloved spouse.

Outsiders saw a different me. People are quick to assume. Again, they did not see the struggling terrified woman that could not get out of bed in the morning. The broken woman looked for some light through an encouraging message and gathered all her strength to get up and get out of the house. People see that woman already outside, driving, dressed up with make-up and all, ready for her meeting at the nearby coffee shop or grocery shopping. Understandably, they figure all is normal. Assumptions. It is human nature to assume, we are usually not conscious of the fact that we never know what someone else might be going through. Most people create their own imaginary story around a situation, even distorting the facts to fit their assumptions.

I am in pain again and feel betrayed by my brain. How can I fill my memory holes? Is it my body automatically activating a defense system?

I am exhausted. Drained. I need time to refill my energy. I felt that I was in the right direction, and now feel back at square one again.

I disconnect from the world for days and lose track of time.

An abnormal reaction to an abnormal situation is normal behavior.

– Viktor E. Frankl, *Man's Search for Meaning*

I am struggling to find a sense of normal, although I believe there is no normal in grief. Part of the issue is due mostly to not being able to communicate effectively with the outside world. Most of all, the energy to find the right words and trying to explain anything these days is wearing me out and debilitating. How do I relearn processes and communication again?

Sometimes, it is a blessing to speak many languages. However, I never mastered the skill to speak one at a time. Growing up, I used all the languages in the same sentence. Switched constantly between them. I spoke mainly Spanish with my father, English with my mother, French and Hebrew in school, and some Catalan outside. I mixed them around since everyone around me understood all the languages. It was extremely difficult to speak English by itself with my limited vocabulary. I did not have enough words to express feelings or to make my point accurately. It did not help that I was extremely shy, well into my forties. I was still learning to articulate my thoughts and feelings. I feel I am getting worse at expressing myself. Confusion, fog and disappointment is causing misunderstandings with people around me. I struggle to express any kind of feeling, causing misunderstandings around me.

I have said that I believe widows are entitled to grieve in their own way, but I was not aware of the consequences of how I handle and deal with my grief. The world moves on after death. Too often, it is easy to overlook someone else's pain when consumed by our own. There were times I was so caught up in my own pain that I could not sense it in others, but I *expected* them to understand me, and was bewildered and hurt when they did not.

Too often, I was reeling because of a perceived insensitivity. My pain was so visceral it created a powerful sense for survival, a fight that I had a right to grieve any way I wanted. I did, but it was easy to get mired there. I was so fragile, I would kick and claw to protect my wounded self.

Words like trust, betrayal or pain started taking a different meaning. I feel like a child learning new words and learning how to talk.

I was deeply hurt when people close to me could not feel my pain, until I understood that I needed to be more specific and clear with my use of words.

Hurt and betrayal led me to push some away. In my pain, I wounded others with my own retreat. It caused a whip crack across our friendship, until I changed my language. I learned to use I-statements such as, "I was hurt, because when you said you would be here for me, I thought you would call me every day to check in", instead of accusing messages such as "You told me you would be here for me and I haven't heard from you in two weeks."

This set a very specific expectation: It took more time than I would like to admit until I realized that people could not guess or even see what I was feeling.

My pain felt too intense to ask others to be aware of it. Honestly, for me, it just felt like they should *know.*

As difficult as it was, I tried to remember that others are grieving too, and that everyone grieves differently. In their grief, they are also wounded, confused and hurt. My brain fog is real; I do not always remember words spoken in haste, in anger. I needed to be precise, and started spending time scripting exactly so when my brain was not vigilant, I had a roadmap. At this point, I also started practicing more and more compassion – I was healing slowly.

Setting expectations around trust is a paramount place to start. A friend had shared personal experiences of my grief to others, which to me, was a serious breach of trust. The words I used were "I don't trust you anymore." However, I did not talk about the specific incident and could not articulate it. In my grief, I felt the cut of betrayal too deeply. She was left not knowing where my attack came from.

Candidly, I do not even remember saying anything to her about it. I remember feeling betrayed, but I do not remember confronting her about it. It was nearly a year later when I asked why she pulled away, when she brought the moment up. Suddenly everything fell into place. I realized what I said, how I had not been specific, how she felt, why she pulled away. I was able to articulate it. "I shared my personal feelings with you, and I thought you would hold them safe. I no longer felt safe with you when I felt like I needed you most."

I soon realized I could not trust my brains to behave or think rationally under the weight of grief. The primal coping mechanisms for shock made me think I was losing my mind. The emotional anguish expressed itself in bodily pain. The toll of grief is consuming, and lasts longer than what I thought my brain and body could endure. It seems impossibly shortsighted to me now that as a society, we do not prepare ourselves more, that society has not made it a priority to train us, have structures in place, to deal with death. Most everyone on this planet is going to experience the death of several loved ones. Even when surrounded by friends and family, grief becomes a solitary journey. Although some customs and beliefs teach to avoid speaking about death, it is a requisite for surviving grief and healing.

We should prepare for grief, we should learn about it. I personally never wanted to talk about death with Yechiel, and every time he brought up the subject of his Will and Testament, or even burial plots – I pushed away.

Thankfully, he left me everything in writing, yet, how many women are in the dark after the loss of their husband – just because they believed the myth that not talking about death will delay it.

In grief, at a time when I wanted most to curl under the covers and not think, I had to learn communication skills.

Like many others of my gender and generation, I do not know how to ask for help. After losing Yechiel, the lack of support felt like death by a thousand cuts. It was a slow awareness to realize people did not know when I needed them

I hope to revisit those I may have hurt and let them know I care too much about them for our relationship to go downhill like this. I am not convinced it is possible, but I will certainly try rebuilding some of those relationships. My journey through grief has given me a keener sense of the healing power of words, and the potent destructive power they can hold.

The happiness of your life depends upon the quality of your thoughts.

– Marcus Aurelius

I adopted the "speak good – it will be good" method. No matter what the circumstance, I turned it around and I looked for the positive side of things, and reflected on all that I was grateful for in my day.

I developed my own formula to achieve this. Decide, practice and visualize. Repeat.

Every day, I had to make the same decision again. Be grateful. I tried, but some days I just was not able. How can I be grateful if my husband died? The following day, I would try over again and remind myself that there is always something to be grateful for. Keep practicing and use the power of words:

-I choose life, and I will be ok.

-Use language that is more positive.

Standing in front of the mirror and making an announcement to myself, "I am going to be okay" made it sound real, and I was determined to make it real. Some of the words I was accustomed to using did not match the positive language I had decided to speak. I changed some of my vocabulary. For instance, "Problems" become "issues" or "obstacles to overcome" and "I don't like that" became "I prefer this."

I am not going to lie; initially it felt ridiculous, silly, and crazy even. I noticed how many people use negative language. Slowly, it became empowering. Practice. More practice. Yechiel's words resonate in my head;

he was the embodiment of positive and encouraging speech, praise and compassion. I had had the best teacher, and I already had it inside me, now it was time to bring it out.

I think back to those first few months when Hadas would tell me I was going to be okay and make me repeat it to myself. If anyone embodies the power of positive manifestation, it is Hadas. Even something as minor as finding a parking space in Jerusalem, she remains positive, "There will be a spot waiting for us." Amazingly, there always is.

At Dale Carnegie workshops, they teach that, "If you say it out loud, it will be true six months from now." Professional athletes and coaches use this method. Visualization creates a mental image for an intended outcome. Sending that energy and words out into the world, programs the mind and body for success. We have to believe that words have power. Pronouncing words aloud and writing them down, creates the environment and motivation to our goals. Like everything though, it is like a muscle. It needs to build up. Slowly, it becomes stronger. *I* will become stronger.

I also started practicing by 'inviting' positive energy through my words and thoughts. I went on a two-day retreat that focused on visualization, "If you want to be xxx, act like xxx." Visualize it as though you are already there. Visualize the details of how you are dressed and what the surroundings look like. Speak with determination, and believe it. Before Hadas and I went into a meeting, we visualized the positive outcome, what we wanted the end of the meeting to look like. Whether the handshake at the end, or the partnership we expect, we still go into each meeting with that image and expectation.

I focused on reminding myself that being angry at the world is not going to advance me anywhere. Life is unfair. Yes. Yechiel is gone. I hate it. I did not ask for this new life. I have no control over what was. I cannot sit, wait, and expect a different outcome. Yes, I want the world to be more sensitive to me. Maybe I need to be more sensitive to the world.

The pandemic has brought a new awareness in our everyday lives.

Knowledge that we are not in control of our world, and not fully in control of our own spheres. It is not just me anymore; everyone is trying to cope with his or her new reality. Everyone is struggling with and realizing how important a routine is when getting through a difficult time. As the lockdown continues, suddenly others start to understand the need for a healthy lifestyle, sleep, and self-care. These terms were much harder for me to explain when Yechiel died.

Terms used in grief seem easier for others to relate to during the lockdown. There is global recognition of the pain of isolation, the primal *critical* human need for connection, how vital it is to be a part of a community, part of something greater than our individual selves. Protecting our loved ones, caring for others, survival, is creating a universal language.

A seed grows with no sound, but a tree falls with a huge noise. Destruction has noise but creation is quiet.

- Elin Peer, Yellow

Yechiel and I visited South Korea several times to expand his organization there, and I was amazed by the Koreans' curiosity about the Jewish people. Wherever we went, we were asked about our customs, lifestyle, and rituals. Yechiel spoke more and more about family values and how important the *Shabbat* and the family were to preserving Jewish continuity. He spoke about how this "magic ingredient" could benefit other countries like Korea. Yechiel explained that we have all the answers in the Bible, but it was not enough to learn this in school. The *Shabbat* table served as the weekly platform to inspire friends and family through talks and songs about the Bible. It was only by bringing it to life in the family, that we could ensure the continuity of Jewish life. The *Shabbat* table, the closeness of family, the sense of community had to be made exciting and attractive to every Jew, not just religious Jews. The Korean people were fascinated about this.

Today, I realize the deeper meaning and appreciate even more the words that I heard him say so many times. The importance of the community is essential to our survival. I would not have survived if not for my community, who cared that I was always taken care of on *Shabbat*. At first, it was the hardest thing to do. I couldn't stand hearing someone else make *Kiddush*. My tears would flow uncontrollably, but eventually,

I learned to hide them. I admit I was sometimes inclined not to keep *Shabbat*, thinking, "What's the point?" Yechiel never questioned it; you do what you have to do. It was never ever a question because *Shabbat* was holy.

In grief, for me, *Shabbat* was a double-edged sword. I missed Yechiel most on Friday nights. I missed his scramble to get everything done before sundown, the weight lifted as I lit the candles, his voice, and the rumble of his chest as he said the prayers. But as much as I struggled through each *Shabbat* without him, it was because of *Shabbat* I felt the rally of my community around me. *Shabbat was* holy, sacrosanct, and kept me sane even when I thought it wouldn't. I read how lonely my widow group members are on the weekends and I hurt for them. The expectation that friends and family will always be there, and the realization that they leave after a few weeks even in the best-case scenario, is painful. In Israel, being a part of the Jewish community meant never really being alone. Even at my lowest, when I felt like I was smothered by emptiness, I knew there would always be a member or even a stranger who would gladly and with open arms, welcome me on *Shabbat.*

During the pandemic, everybody is realizing the incredible importance of community. We are encouraged to reach out to one another, check in to see how someone is really doing. I see strangers posting that they've made soup and it's free to anyone in need. I see posts of people going to the grocery store and putting the word out, asking if they can pick up anything for shut-ins. The pandemic has finally raised the awareness we so desperately needed in the world today. That a social 911 network should be our way of being. That calling, support, and care, needs to happen all the time. The isolation felt by the pandemic is the isolation felt by too many widows. It's not enough to call once or twice after a person dies; keeping in touch on a regular basis is crucial to someone who has been cut off, set adrift, to those drowning in loss.

At first, I could only talk to other widows, only they understood. Now more than before, I needed to hear pain that mirrored my own, I needed to witness those who went through it and came out the other side – those who reached a point where they could be positive and embrace life again. I need it because it helps me visualize a world where I can too. I had to find more widows.

April 27, 2020

Eli passed away today.

Eli, my first husband. Eli, the father of my children.

Even though he had been sick, it is a shock. I just lost Yechiel one year ago. Now my children have lost their father. I reel. I cannot bear to see them in pain.

I met Eli in the summer of 1990 in Jerusalem. Eli was older than I was, 17 years older. I was reluctant to go out with him, because he was much older than I was - 17 years older. Nevertheless, I had tumbled head-over-heels in love after our first date. I was working at Iberia, the Spanish airlines ticketing office, and Eli owned a travel and tours agency focused on Christian tourism from South America and Spain. We met when his office needed to issue airline tickets. At a time before current technology, electronic ticketing, before instant payments, and the speed of computers, the airline had to issue the tickets for the travel agencies. Every month, the agent paid the airline for all the tickets issued the previous month. By asking us to wait one day to issue tickets, meant Eli would have an extra month to pay for them. The only issue was that the first of the month was a Friday, and we did not work on Fridays. Eli came to the office and played his charm on us. My boss said if I wanted to do this man a favor, I could do it, but I would not get paid extra for it. Even though it was my first time meeting him, I agreed to issue the tickets early for him.

That Friday, Eli came into the office and brought me cherries–the first cherries of the season. Unlike the US, but like most places in

Europe, our produce in Israel is only offered seasonally. Cherries are only available for about two weeks out of the year. I loved cherries, they also reminded me of my childhood. We all loved cherries at home. His thoughtfulness touched me. He picked up his tickets, and I closed the office after he left.

To this day, I think of Eli every time I eat cherries.

A few minutes later, I saw him sitting at a nearby café talking with his sister, and I waved from a distance. Months later he revealed to me what he was telling her - "That's the girl I'm going to marry."

The next week he called and said he was checking to see if we were open so he could bring us the voucher for more tickets. I found it strange; everyone else just sent vouchers with delivery services. He owned the company, surely he had someone on staff that could take care of a minor errand for him. I was already saying to my boss, "Don't leave me alone with him." On some level, I must have felt an attraction to Eli and was rebelling against it. He called right before closing to say that he sent his delivery person who would be there shortly.

"Please issue the tickets and give them to him" My response was immediate, "I thought *you* were coming in with the voucher. " He chuckled,"did you want me to come in?" I was suddenly tongue-tied. In the silence he said, "If you want to see me, I can meet you at 7."

I froze, I could not say anything but yes.

We met in a lovely outdoor restaurant and we ended up talking for hours. I was utterly smitten by the end of the dinner. When he finally walked me to my car, he asked when he could see me again. I had final exams the following week, and I did not know what to say. Eli thought I was blowing him off by not answering. Very quickly, a whirlwind romance evolved; we moved in together one month later.

Eli proposed very quickly, he was a man who knew what he wanted and went after it. Married in seven months and our son was born the same year.

During the Gulf War, tourism crashed in Israel and we moved Eli's business to New York City. In just a couple of weeks, we packed up the house, rented an office on Madison Avenue and started working. Eli and I worked well together and soon we were opening another office and hiring a couple more employees.

Eli flew regularly back and forth to Israel. He visited the Jerusalem office, hoping tourism would pick up there. I managed the New York office while he was away. We specialized in what we called the Triangular tour – New York, Niagara Falls, Washington DC. A weekly charter flight from Spain meant that we booked hotel rooms months in advance. The summer months were stressful, with more flights coming in. Once I was securing a series of room blocks at a hotel, and they were confirming only part of the dates I requested, and not others. I balked. I needed those rooms and the passengers already had their flight confirmations. We were out of time. I called Eli in a panic. He was unfazed.

"Call them back and cancel the dates that they confirmed".

I was stunned. I could not imagine what we would do. Eli repeated what he had just said. Call them, they either confirm all of our bookings or we book a different hotel. He knew business, and he was correct. The next day, the hotel confirmed every single one of our blocks.

Two years later, when tourism picked up again in Israel, we moved back home, keeping our New York office open. I had no idea how it was going to work. Eli wanted me to work in the Israel office now. I did not see how that was going to work, since I was used to working with Eli in the same office, just the two of us. I was not sure how I would feel with the staff around. We agreed that I would try it for a year. Give it a real chance.

"You cannot give up, if you try, you have to commit for a year. After that, you can make an informed decision, not one based on emotion. So I committed for a year. With Eli, I learned to think things through, and to take chances. To roll up the shirtsleeves and do what you have to do. He built a travel empire on these principles.

Like Yechiel, Eli was not a big birthday person either. When we were settling in as newlyweds, Eli and I bought a new sofa and coffee table, and by coincidence, delivered it on my birthday. Eli used them as my birthday present. I was young, I was idealistic, and I was insulted. *Really*? You have to be kidding! He never went out of his way to buy me a birthday present, but enjoyed surprising me for no reason. When we moved back to Israel after living in the US for two years, we arrived home to Jerusalem and a new red car with a big ribbon was parked in front of our neighbor's house. I thought to myself, "Wow, the neighbor just got my dream car! "As soon as we got into the house, Eli handed me the keys to that car.

Shortly after, I slipped into depression. I had just given birth to my daughter in the US, when we uprooted and moved back to Israel. A combination of postpartum depression and readjusting to Israel following a couple years of easy living in the US took a huge toll on me. I became apathetic and felt purposeless. I was seeing a therapist with no results. I felt like I was sleepwalking through life, until he prescribed medication. I got a little better over time, but walked away from my marriage after 10 years. I asked Eli for a divorce. He did not fight. There was no arguing and I felt a certain relief at the time; he just asked me what I wanted. We agreed and had a lawyer write up the terms. In Israel, you have to go through rabbinical court. There is usually a long waiting period. However, when you have a signed agreement in place, it can happen faster. I did not expect to be divorced in a couple of days. In fact, receiving a *get* (Jewish divorce)

in just a few days was unheard of. The lawyer presented our case for us and since we agreed, it was over quickly.

Fastest divorce *ever.*

I was ecstatic. I went out that night and celebrated my freedom with friends. It hit me a few days later. "Oh my god, what have I done?" It was too late. I realized that Eli did not fight for me, and it hurt terribly. He did not ask me to stay; he did not suggest we go to therapy. He just let me go.

"I knew one day you would grow up and leave. But I promised to always take care of you and our children." And he did. He gave them everything and he made sure I also had everything I needed. He kept his promise.

I thought I wanted to meet someone my age and grow together. Once I had my independence and started feeling better, I regretted my decision. Eli moved on and was already in a relationship. We remained friends, and continued to have Friday night dinners together with the children for three years.

Two years ago, Eli started feeling fatigued. A frequent acute pain plagued his stomach. He went in for a series of tests and the results came back - rare liver cancer. I was devastated, but the children were optimistic. They would fly to the States, to Spain, in search of the best care, the latest treatments. Their father's positivity was infectious and he was doing well with the treatments.

I was encouraged when he pulled through. He loved spending time in his home in Uruguay, his country of birth. Eli loved design, he had a fantastic eye, and he would design and build his second home there. He was enjoying himself again., We met for coffee one afternoon in Jerusalem. I was surprised at how frail he looked. So thin, just skin over bone. He had trouble with his balance, and I fought against going to him to help him as he stood to walk. But he was Eli, optimistic and calm. I thought that it would be the last time I saw him.

I jumped from my chair in surprise when I saw him walking unto my house during the *Shiva*. Customs kept me seated through *Shiva*, but when I saw him walk in, I had to get up to greet him. We hugged. He did not talk much, just, "The children will take care of you, lean on them." I sobbed.

That was the last time I saw him alive. My children spent that following summer In Uruguay with him, and when they arrived back to Israel, Eli's health turned and his decline was rapid.

He went home for one last *Shabbat* and returned to the hospital.

During the first lockdown, hospitals were very strict about visitors. Only direct family, and only one at a time. I was afraid to leave the house; I had not stepped outside for over a month and a half. I put on my mask for the first time, and I drove to the hospital to be with our children. I kept relieving Yechiel's death, but I needed to hold it in for my children. The doctor called time of death. At that moment, the siren commemorating the fallen heroes of Israel went off. It was surreal. The siren sounded just as Eli died. We stood there crying and I watched my children's pain with anguish, not being able to say a word.

"The children will take care of you, lean on them." I sobbed.

You can't stop the waves, but you can learn how to surf.

- Jon Kabat-Zinn

Triggers continue to appear unexpectedly; they take me by surprise and I never know where the next one is going to come from. I was driving back from Tel Aviv to Jerusalem, and the sun was starting to set. A man stands still praying by his car on the side of the road. I suddenly have an image of Yechiel. The flashback is so real, I nearly slam on the brakes. So many memories of Yechiel standing there himself. I can hear him say "I need to *daven mincha*". Every day as the sun was setting he would stop whatever he was doing – be it in the middle of a visit, on a plane, or meeting – and he would take those ten minutes to pray. He never missed a day. Wherever we were. Another car stopped by the side of the road. It is a common scene in Israel, and yet, it takes me by surprise.

I started to feel it in my throat. The tightening. The ache. The wave swelling, tears building up. Would I be able to control it? I'm driving, my vision blurs. I'm in the middle of a highway. *I can't break down now.* Another man standing by his car on the side of the road. Yechiel's memory pushes at me harder. His eyes are closed, standing still and praying to God. Every day. So many places, so many memories of watching him in his concentration, in meditation, just moving his lips in intense concentration. He never used a prayer book; he didn't need one, as he knew all the prayers by heart. It is a physical blow and it winds me. It hurts. I miss the comfort of his praying. I keep driving but I can't stand the thought of walking into the house alone. Not tonight. I can't do it. I can't be alone tonight. Who do I call? I can't call anyone; I'm in the middle of the highway. I don't want to stop on the side of the road, it doesn't feel safe. It's not safe to continue driving either. What should I do? My mind is wandering.

Yechiel's voice is playing on the CD in the car. I try to just concentrate on his words, his soft voice. I make it safely to the first traffic light at the entrance to Jerusalem. I gathered the strength to call a friend, to ask for help when I needed it. "Can I come over? I need company." My voice is broken. I'll survive this day too. One day at a time.

Caminante, no hay camino, se hace camino al andar. (Walker, there is no path, the path is made by walking")

– Antonio Machado

I walked back home. By the generosity of a donor who is covering the cost, my fledgling organization rented a small office in downtown Jerusalem. I am encouraged to see how people are connecting to us, wanting to become part of our network. We are saving lives, one person at a time; volunteering my time and staying busy is healing. I also discovered the convenience of the bus and started to change some habits. I left the car at home. I don't remember ever taking the bus in Jerusalem with Yechiel, and it is actually quite comforting to do something with no connections or memories attached. Something new. Although it took me a long time to overcome the horrible flashbacks of the suicide bombings on the buses, today I can handle the anxiety. However, I walk whenever I can. I smile thinking of Yechiel always taking the car to work even if it was just a 10-minute walk.

But today something was different. I felt a terrible emptiness. There is nobody waiting at home. Why do some days feel so different? I don't understand. Yesterday, and the day before, and the day before that there was nobody waiting at the house either, and yet, I made it home ok. Every step today my nerves become more exposed. Raw. I don't feel like facing the house. The empty rooms. I don't feel like making dinner just for myself. There are many people walking outside, why do I feel so lonely? I am accustomed to walking, I walk almost every day. Friends in the neighborhood are always up to a walking date. It has been healing and wonderful to see families out on the streets, people just walking at the end of the day, so what is wrong today? What is wrong with me? I cannot figure it out.

A friend who lost her husband recently suggested journaling, it had helped her heal. I gave it a try even though I was never a writer. At first, it felt strange writing my thoughts down. Reliving my memories of Yechiel. Connecting to my changing self. Nobody would ever read this. I tried to fill the gaps from last year. This is all I could do some days, just to put all these feelings down on paper. I don't know when I'm writing what I'm going to make of it, but it feels good to get it down on paper. I could not even read a paragraph during the first year, let alone *write* one. Now that I have started, I understand. Once I wrote my feelings down, those feelings were out and dealt with.

Why then, are some days just not as easy as that ? I cannot figure out why some days everything just makes me feel sad, having to hold my tears and feeling overwhelmed. Instead of the usual energizing feeling that comes with walking, today I felt drained. A feeling that nothing means anything anymore, and nothing is exciting anymore; nothing is worth doing because the love of my life is not with me to share it.

I am numb.

I don't feel like being a burden on anyone. Today, I feel the weight of another approaching milestone. Like a millstone. How can it be a year and a half? How did I survive this long? What difference is there between eighteen months or nineteen months? And yet, it is ripping me apart.

How long can I survive on this rollercoaster? I can imagine getting so dizzy that I would fall off. Can I just "fall off" of life? Drop out? I don't feel like I can take this pain much longer. One day I think I am doing ok because I did not cry, the next moment I walk into a supermarket and I see the Bosc pears Yechiel craved so much or the Grape Nuts cereal he always ate… and I lose it, again.

I reach the house, and the mailbox is full. It has been full for a few days now. I still cannot open the mail, I dread it. I admit sometimes telling Pedro to throw it away because I could not deal with it. Yechiel was obsessed with mail; many years ago, his first large donation had arrived by check in the mail, and since then he always made sure to check the mailbox. It is still raw for me, the mailbox is painful in that it is filled with memories.

The entrance has many small trees and plants. Yechiel would tease me constantly saying I could not keep a plant alive. I am not sure they did much better in his care, but he tried to water them once in a while.

My son, who has a green thumb, was visiting one day and encouraged me to plant some herbs. True to the new me, I became obsessed. It was life changing. I started with herbs, and then flowers, tomatoes, and all kinds of garden decorations. They were my morning putter, my evening welcome. I was in awe of all the life that was taking root around me. And I cooed over every new leaf, every budding flower.

"What a caterpillar calls the end of the world we call a butterfly."

– Eckhart Tolle, The Power of Now

Yechiel struggled with finding peace for years. It was always about "when I find a good director, I'll be able to relax" or "when I get x" or "when y happens."

Ironically, coincidentally, when I first met Yechiel, he introduced me to "The Power of Now" by Eckhart Tolle. He kept the book near him and read different parts repeatedly, trying to internalize it.

This carried into his work and everyday life. He struggled to find the right person to help him with his burgeoning organization. He wanted to pursue even larger ideas and longed to find that one executive he trusted to take over the day-to-day, so he could transition to the projects he was passionate about. The turn over rate was staggering. Every time he hired someone new, he threw all his hopes there, and every time he would proclaim, "I think I found the right person!" But with such high expectations came great disappointments, and some only lasted a few months before the hiring process would begin.

I was not consciously aware of this but I realize now that the skills found in the book helped me endure the first year.

There was a brief respite when one of his executives hired a temporary executive assistant who took over the impending project of building-out and moving the US headquarters into a top floor suite in downtown Chicago. She didn't stay long with the organization as an

EA, but because the move was a project she led, she volunteered her nights and weekends to finish it. To his astonishment, she did, on time and under budget. And then she disappeared into a financial firm. He told his executives to find her and two months later, hired her back as his chief of staff.

Like Hadas, Tonya was not intimated by Yechiel. She had worked for founders before and understood the mindset. She was meticulous, driven, and knew how to "kick the tires." At her first board meeting, Yechiel introduced her as his new Chief of Staff and because he knew she was liberal and nonreligious he added, "And our token heathen." As the Christians and Jews around the boardroom gasped in shock, Tonya and Yechiel burst out laughing. Corporate personality tests given by an outside firm would find that Yechiel and Tonya had similar leadership, vision, and working styles. She understood the big picture, and she dug into the details. It made sense to Yechiel – for the two years she worked there, Yechiel saw progress in his organization that he felt had been stagnant. He finally felt comfortable enough to stay in Israel for longer and longer periods.

We sold our Chicago apartment and spent longer periods of time in our home in Israel. Meanwhile, there was drama in the States. The extent of which we would only find out later. Yechiel offered Tonya the VP of International Relations, a position that would be based in Korea. But Tonya was an artist and her work was starting to see success in Chicago; she took our move to Israel as an opportunity to exit gracefully. Yechiel lamented the loss, but Tonya remained one of our dear friends. Whenever her name came up, he would say she was the best hire he ever made in his thirty-plus years as a founder.

It seemed like whenever Yechiel had reached a moment of peace and contentment, like finally finding the right executive to take some of the weight off his shoulders; there was another who sought to undermine it. After another exhausting work trip he would say, "When we get back to Israel, I'll feel better." As much as he wanted to just enjoy the moment, it wouldn't last. He was always hoping that moment would come. His organization now had offices and staff in five countries and there were issues with each. It was a constant demand, a race, a struggle, and it took a huge toll on his health. He was always torn between wanting to be in a future situation without fully accepting where he was at the moment. "I want to smell the roses." He found it hard to accept that his *Now* was surrounded in roses, he had made it. Like any true visionary, he was always dreaming bigger, more ground to break, more projects to start. Yechiel was extremely grateful and aware of what he had, but he pushed for more and was driven to pursue his next dream.

And Yechiel *was* a visionary. The future he saw for Israel was breathtaking in scope. A beautiful future, and he could see the path to achieve it. It aggravated him that he could not do it all, and he was stymied by time, money, resources, connections, and bureaucracy. But he continued pushing himself harder. He even entertained running for President of Israel so he could move the wheels of progress faster. Everything he could to make that beautiful future a reality.

In the spring of 2005 he had his first heart episode. We were walking up a hill in Eilat, in southern Israel, and he stopped half way. He could not make it to the top. He went to the hospital for a checkup a few days later and had his first stent put in. For effect, he told everyone he had a heart attack.

Perhaps it was prescience, for that would come years later.

One of the things that happens to people in grief is they secretly think they're crazy, because they realize they are thinking things that don't make sense.

– Joan Didion

I am often bewildered by the randomness of my thoughts during mourning. Out of the blue one day, I thought about Yechiel's therapist. It had been years since we last spoke of her; but in 2012-2013 she was very present in our lives.

Family, strangers, acquaintances, friends, all suggested I needed a therapist to get over Yechiel's death, but while I'm sure it can be helpful to others, I know it's not what I need right now. I had therapy in my 20s to treat depression but grief is not depression, and too many confuse the two. I didn't feel like I needed a therapist, but a support group. I need a surrounding of women who shared a similar loss, were struggling with similar feelings. I had a grief coach, I found one in Hadas. I found my support group online.

I suddenly realized that Yechiel's therapist probably didn't know that he passed away. I decided to email her. Her email back is loving, kind. It brings me to tears. She tells me how much he loved me, how he would always speak of me, and how much he looked forward to just relaxing with me at the end of a stressful day.

We would have long discussions after his Skype sessions with her. We spoke of her daily while he was still seeing her, her guidance had a great impact on Yechiel, and he tried to live by the messages he had learned with her. Yechiel believed in her, and he took detailed notes that he would then share with me. He practiced in between sessions, but somehow could not fully internalize peace. She introduced him to Byron Katie and The Work, and we practiced the exercise of

self-inquiry together. When he had a particularly tough day at the office, I would gently remind him of the principles we tried to follow. Slowing down enough to be mindful during intense work hours was difficult, and it worked best as self-reflection during the peace and quiet of our home. The process was an eye opener.

I have an unsettling feeling that through all the reflective work we did together, Yechiel was preparing me to live without him. When we were feeling negative, we practiced together those Four Questions: “Is it true? Are you certain that this is the absolute truth? What is your reaction? Can you let go of that thought and be free?”

One year before Yechiel died, a colleague bought me her book. It became an anchor in my working study to help me get through stress at the call center. In retrospect, as ridiculous as it sounds, I feel like I should have regarded it as a prediction of things to come.

As soon as Yechiel was swallowed again in work he forgot everything in the outside world. He was fully absorbed and ‘forgot’ that he was depressed. It would break out, mostly frequently in anger outbursts towards his staff. He would come back home after a day where he screamed at someone, totally devastated and could not forgive himself. Nor could he control it.

In June 2014, three Jewish boys were kidnapped at a bus stop in the West Bank. Yechiel was galvanized; he felt if he raised enough money and awareness, we could get them back unharmed. The US headquarters seemed focused on other priorities besides work and he booked an immediate flight back to stress the urgency of the situation. During a roundtable about fundraising, his new man in charge deferred responsibility because he was moving into a new house; his executive director shrugged it off saying he was not in charge anymore so he was not making decisions; the point vendor brought in the same tired fundraising appeals they did every year in June. Yechiel reached a boiling point. He looked at his chief of staff, "Can you believe this??" He looked at the men he had put in charge, and he was enraged. He slammed his fists against the table and bellowed, "Is NO ONE going to step up? This is our time*! This is our Christmas! THIS IS OUR CHRISTMAS!* Now figure it out and raise me the money!"

The room was shocked. Yechiel got up and left. He was overcome with embarrassment and remorse. He could not believe that had come out of his mouth. He meant to instill on them the urgency of the moment. In fundraising, the window around a major holiday is always a short but crucial time to raise funds that often would carry an organization throughout the year. Christmas, especially for his organization's donor base, was the time they gave the most, their top fundraising month. Yechiel knew that in a kidnapping, time was paramount, and if he was to get the money for the resources needed to bring those boys back, his staff needed to feel the urgency as he did. But he was mortified. Comparing the kidnapping to Christmas was not what he wanted to say. Getting angry to the point of yelling at his staff was not what he wanted to do.

It lit a fire in one, though. His chief of staff stepped up and took charge. In the month that followed, her fundraising campaign raised as much as the top four Christmases in the organization's history. But by then it was too late. The bodies of the boys had been found. Yechiel was devastated.

"'For I know the plans I have for you,' declares the Lord, 'plans to prosper you and not to harm you, plans to give you a hope and a future.'"

– **Jeremiah 29:11**.

I'm reading over Yechiel's handwritten notes from the years in therapy. The first page is the daily mantra:

1. I have everything to be thankful for.
2. Accept God's gift of peace.
3. If God is with me I can do anything
4. I am in God's hands.
5. Attitudes are more important than facts.

How does number 5 fit in with the rest?

Yechiel left me an "operations manual". *Thank you, thank you my love.*

I am overwhelmed with emotion. I have not seen these notes in years, and I find them exactly at the time when I need them most.

"Meditate – focus on breathing." My own breath catches. He really believed in this, and took the time to write it down on a piece of paper.

How is it that he never accomplished actually living by these?

"Choose your actions from a place of love and compassion, rather than fear."

"Push your limits, challenge yourself. You can do it, even if your mind says you can't. Push out of your comfort zone."

I am overcome.

He actually spoke like that to me. He would push me to try different things. I look at all these connections of before and after. It is surreal to look at his notes, the notes we spent hours talking about in those years, and feel how powerfully they resonate in me now. How relevant they are to my new life.

"No expectations," he wrote after one session. He wrote, and I was absorbed. I had already started practicing to live with no expectations. It made sense to me at the time. If you don't have expectations, you don't have disappointment. Being attached emotionally to an outcome causes anxiety, however, when you focus only on what is in your control, there is peace. It is a long process that takes time until they become part of who you are.

De músico, poeta y loco, todos tenemos un poco. (We all have a little bit of musician, poet and crazy person in ourselves, or, we are all a little bit crazy.)

- Spanish proverb

I had not heard it in a year and a half.

Without warning, I am sitting in a meeting when someone's cell phone goes off.

My heart stops.

My body freezes. Time stops. I feel like I am inside a water tank, I cannot hear anything, just distant voices.

That ringtone.

My special ringtone.

That ringtone was reserved on my phone for Yechiel. I want to scream. This is so unfair! I want him back!.

My special music, so I would never miss his calls, even when I left my phone on my desk. I would run to answer it when I heard that special ringtone.

The phone stops ringing and the meeting continues, as if nothing happened. I am shaken to my core. It was too brief, the ring stopped too quickly. I want to hear it again. But it hurts. *Yechiel called.* I want Yechiel to call. It is a desperation that lances through me and takes my breath away. The realization that my phone will never ring with that music again breaks me, again.

Surround yourself only with people who are going to take you higher.

- Oprah Winfrey

I met Amy at a *Shabbat* meal a few months after Yechiel died. We connected immediately and arranged to meet for coffee a few days later. Coffee turned into dinner and we could not stop talking. She captivated me with her positivity and contagious laugh. Many *Shabbat* meals later, evening walks, and countless talks, we went on an inspiring 60-Day Journey together.

I did not know exactly what the 60-day Journey was, or what it would mean for me. When a door opened, I went through it and did not ask many questions, figuring that such introspection could only be positive. I was ready for a spiritual, self-reflective journey that takes place during two powerful and holy months for Jewish people, *Elul* and *Tishrei*. The month of *Elul* is the final month in the Jewish calendar, a month of reflection and introspection, a time where we turn to God with our prayers for the coming year in preparation for the High Holy Days in the month of *Tishrei* starting with the Jewish New Year, through *Yom Kippur* and *Sukkot*.

For the next two months, we started each day with daily meditation that included an inspiring story. Together, we delved into introspection, and spoke about the different ways in which we could practice what we learned. Every day, we focused on a different area of growth: we dove into deep conversations on anger and compassion, acceptance and forgiveness. We were vulnerable in talking about our flaws and the traits we wanted to work on in the coming year. We 'looked in the mirror' to see what we needed to change in our relationship with God, and our relationship with others. We focused on growth and commitment. We reflected on how

to fix past mistakes, what changes in our behavior would we strive to make, or we determined if we needed to let go of past relationships. Whether an unhealthy relationship or judgment, we agreed to just let go of any part of our lives that were harmful.

We prepared for the upcoming holidays, like an emotional and mental marathon training.

I had never really prepared for or thought of the holidays and my part in them, this intensely before. I had never taken such an active participatory role in my own growth before. In the past, these two months (in truth, most holidays) just kind of came around every year; we would prepare the food in advance, or decide where we would spend the holiday, but I never took the time to think and prepare *spiritually.* For fourteen years I spent the high holidays in Chicago with Yechiel. We always discussed if we should do it again the following year. Every year Yechiel would say it would be the last in Chicago, it was always hard on him, but he ended up accepting the job year after year.

The 60-Day journey was an eye-opener. I learned the importance of real, intense preparation for the holidays, the High Holy days. Preparing for Rosh Hashanah, not only on a spiritual level, but also on a deliberate practical level, made the holiday even more impactful.

I have a deeper understanding of what I need now to move forward.

If preparation meant deep dive learning, I needed to learn about grief and be aware of what is normal, and where I need help. Honestly, I did not know what grief was until I experienced it.

I searched out every book on grief I could find.

You can become blind by seeing each day as a similar one. Each day is a different one, each day brings a miracle of its own. It's just a matter of paying attention to this miracle.

– Paulo Coelho

Several years ago, the municipality of Jerusalem placed a piano in a public place for anyone to play. The popularity of the program grew, and the city established more pianos all over the city. There are maps to them, and against the hustle of city life, the oversaturation of online media, the pianos offered a fun break for adventurous passersby.

In the city center there are two or three, and there is always someone sitting at the piano, playing in the middle of the street. I discovered one by the promenade in my neighborhood. The pianos attract all musical levels, sometimes beginners, and sometimes the crowds would be treated to some serious talent. Before Covid, those pianos were nice to have in the city, but now – when the theaters, opera, ballet, orchestras, and all arts were shut down – you can still walk down the street and hear music. In the quiet of the city in lockdown, the distant melodies are enchanting. At any time of day and into the night, there is usually someone playing a piano outside. Before Covid, it was easy to take them for granted, and many walked by like passing a street busker. But after Covid, the music was potent. Magical.

Abraham Heschel wrote, "Our goal should be to live life in radical amazement. ....get up in the morning and look at the world in a way that takes nothing for granted. Everything is phenomenal; everything is incredible; never treat life casually. To be spiritual is to be amazed."

The pianos are a gift for those who choose to see them. Most passers-by rush through, some turn their heads and look for a moment, and a few take a couple of minutes to enjoy the beauty of music. There is a sense of childlike discovery when I hear them. Something new in me opened up, creating a small crack that was letting light in. I was realizing the wonders of magical thinking; I listened to the music in awe.

Keep your tongue from evil and your lips from speaking deceit. Turn away from evil and do good; seek peace and pursue it.

– Psalms 34:13-14

There were many changes happening at the call center back in 2017-18. Strategy and direction were unclear, even if it was clear to Yechiel. Somehow, he was unable to implement his vision. He loved that I spent my days at the call center, and yet, could not handle the confusion that it caused.

Hadas and I looked for ways to handle the situation. She would often come to our house, and together with Yechiel, we would try to find a solution.

Towards the end of 2018, Yechiel knew what the solution was - the call center would have to become a separate entity. He needed time until the following summer and time for the consulting company that was hired to present their strategic plan for the organization. Yechiel's disappointment with the results was palpable. Some may still remember his yelling in the office that day.

This had a ripple effect in the organization; those who were negative about the center took the report and amplified the findings. Yechiel was torn. He always knew the path forward, but struggled with the weeds and brush along the way. When professional opinions offered differing views, he was angry. He loved the call center; it was a huge step toward realizing his dream for Israel. A social 911 network to bring the people together. But he could not convince the executive leadership of the importance of his project, therefore, he decided he would separate it from the rest of the organization under another entity, and he started looking for partners.Meanwhile, Hadas and I turned to *The Four Agreements* by Don Miguel Ruiz, as a coping strategy. We thought about what we could do to help, without waiting for the change to come from the outside, and this practical guide served as our daily exercises.

1. Be impeccable with your words.
2. Don't take anything personally
3. Don't make assumptions
4. Always do your best

We became more mindful, asked more questions and did not make assumptions, even when something seemed obvious. We reminded each other constantly that there are always at least two sides to a situation and tried to get all the facts before making a decision.

It was easier said than done. It was difficult not to take a situation personally and be impeccable with our word when something made us angry. It was easier when only one of us was angry, the other would guide a cool down using The Four Agreements. Hadas was very focused on #2 and #3. And I was becoming more and more aware of #1. Thinking more before I spoke, and stopped criticizing or judging others.

The Agreements did not just apply to the internal stress of the organization, they were universal and we used them to help us be better stewards of the call center.

One of our operators answered a call one day from a woman in Jerusalem desperate for help. The woman had been arrested, confessed to using drugs, and social services had taken her child because she could not pay for rent or food. She was in tears. She needed money in order to keep a roof over her head and get her children back. The call center paid her landlord for the rent before she was evicted.

A few weeks later, our operator recognized the woman and saw her entering an upscale boutique fruit shop here in Jerusalem. She was outraged that this woman would be using her money for luxuries rather than paying rent. A quick discreet inquiry discovered that the woman had gotten a job with a wealthy couple and she had been running an errand for them. This incident was a great teaching example of making assumptions and judgments without knowing the entire story.

Teachable moments using the Four Agreements came up often during the last year of the call center. A staff member personally dropped off an envelope instead of us using a delivery service. The person called to complain, saying it was not received. Rather than accusing or confronting the staff member, we first checked all the facts and quickly discovered that another family member had signed for the envelope.

Sometimes, it was upsetting if a meeting was canceled with last minute notice; I thought it disrespectful; now, such incidents took on less of a personal affront. Putting our feelings aside never came easy, but we continued to practice. Working as a team was much easier than working alone. We developed a mantra of sorts: "Neutralize all judging thoughts, nothing matters, be open-minded."

Yechiel was reading a book titled "Thanks for Being Late" at the time. I still keep it on the coffee table. The core takeaways: do something when people are late, be grateful that you have some extra time. When you look for the positive, you will find it.

The work is constant and never ending. I was used to making assumptions, and it seemed like an impossible habit to break. However, I soon noticed that when I did not make assumptions, I had no expectations, therefore less disappointment - and it started to get easier.

The old habit of making assumptions returned quickly after Yechiel passed away. I believed the obvious, that his so-called friends would be there for me. I never imagined they would move on so fast. I was wrong and deeply hurt. Was it because the widow reminded them of death? or because they thought I was so depressed and could not handle trying to comfort me? I distanced myself and I vowed to have no expectations in the future, I would not be able to handle more pain.

Continuous effort – not strength or intelligence – is the key to unlocking our potential.

– Winston Churchill

My sister-in-law called mid morning, she is on her way to the farmer's market, just a few minutes from our home. The sun is out, it's a gorgeous day. I decided to meet her there. We don't get to see anyone much in these Covid times, so it is great to get together.

She points to the corn.

"You have to try this corn!"

"Oh, how Yechiel loved corn…" I pause. I put it in my basket, albeit wondering if I could even bring myself to make it.

Yechiel could be so annoying with the corn, and yet it brings good memories. I smile. Every time I went shopping, he would ask me to get corn. He loved corn. Or the idea of corn, because Israeli corn had no taste. He was hoping for American corn, sweet corn, the kind you could not find in Israel. Each time, he hoped it would be different. Maybe next time it will be sweet. Again, he would express his disappointment, and repeated himself, but never stopped hoping.

I had not bought corn since Yechiel died. I cried the first few times I passed it at the supermarket, almost picked it up by automatic impulse, and then caught myself. Yechiel is not here. Who am I buying corn for?

I started feeling that already familiar pain growing in my stomach. I drive back home with that extreme sadness; I feel tears on my face. I put the corn and other vegetables away.

"I cannot do this," I tell myself.

It's dinnertime – whatever time it is these days. No specific time, just feeling hungry in the late afternoon, I opened the fridge again, looking for something to eat. The corn is looking at me. *Ok, easy enough*, I do not have the energy to start cooking and looking for the easiest option, so I go for it. Boil the corn.

"*Don't over boil it.*"

I hear him, clear as day. It's funny, he never told me how to cook anything but he was incredibly particular about his corn. "Just boil water and then drop the corn in, cover and leave for 5 minutes."

I feel him next to me. I cook it the way he tells me. Quick, and easy.

That first bite undoes me.

I must be dreaming, how can the corn be *sweet*? I cannot believe it!

Yechiel!?! Why aren't you here to taste this!?

I'm angry, I'm hurting, and I can't stop crying.

To date or not to date?

That seems to be *the* question among widows. My apologies to Shakespeare.

I cannot figure out why widows are asking for advice on dating. I do not understand why they want to date. I have been following posts and comments for a few months now, and there are many expressed thoughts, opinions, and reflections.

There is a range to the queries: *When is it ok to start dating? How do you know you're ready to date? I'm dating someone but my family doesn't approve. When do you take off your wedding ring? I met someone but he is jealous of my late husband.*

I was actually surprised to read many of these questions. I just cannot relate. I am not there at all; I am still very much married. And I had not realized others felt differently than me. I am not envisioning dating anytime soon, if ever. Many other women shared my feelings and shared how they have no interest in a new relationship.

Any decision I make is ok.

I firmly believe there is no right or wrong, if one feels they are ready to start dating, I say go ahead. I started to understand how some widows had been their husband's caregivers for years, and after a long illness, some of them felt the need to meet someone sooner than others who lost their husbands unexpectedly. Although after going out on first dates, some felt a lot of anxiety, and others felt after a few dates that they were not ready for a new relationship after all. Age seems to be a major factor, younger widows hoped to meet someone one day, while older women did not and were scared at the thought. Often I would read, "I don't even know what it's like to go out on a date, we were married for over 30 years."

I was never aware of the difficulties that a widow faced. I was shocked at the stories of men trying to take advantage of a vulnerable widow. I think of the married man who pounded on my door late at night. Not everyone who was nice in public and to my face had my best interest in mind. That is always true when dating, but widows are vulnerable, they are wounded and grieving. This can attract a certain type of man. Unfortunately, age and experience can blind a widow to red flags, and we are often still too under the weight of grief to notice them.

I will know when I am ready to date. *If* I am ever ready to date. That's a big IF. If I am ready to have another person in my life. If I ever feel open enough to allow intimacy. I have lost two great loves of my life, I do not see myself ever letting in a third.

Frankly, I'm pretty content just to have Pizzie around.

When to remove the wedding ring is another question I hear often. I recently met two widows who attended a grief relief program. I was surprised to hear that one of the sessions encouraged all of them to take off their wedding rings together. Sort of a ceremony. Maybe it is easier if you are doing it with a group. Widows in my group shared experiences of when they took their rings off. Some took it off right away; some still wear it years later. Some move it to a different finger, while others wear both theirs and their husband's. Some said that they had melted the rings to create a new one. It is comforting to see the support among widows, even when each one did something different; everyone is encouraged that their decision is fine, normal, accepted. I have been wearing both Yechiel's ring and mine together from the day when the paramedic took it off his finger. Will there come a day when I feel I should take it off?

I was not prepared for what came next.

It started one day when an acquaintance said hello at a coffee shop. I was waiting for my meeting to arrive, and he just said hello and then, "You look great." It caught me by surprise. I smiled uncomfortably and answered with a polite thank you. But my blood boiled. In all the years with Yechiel, a man would have never said that to me. I was Yechiel's wife, and in Israel, men do not just compliment another man's wife in a flirting manner. It is considered rude, forward, and unseemly. I did not fully analyze the situation or my feelings that day, and just tried to ignore it. I wanted to believe that there was only good intention on his side, but I felt invaded and exposed, without my married status as a buffer.

Even while internally seething, I resolved to let it go, reminding myself of the third agreement - do not make assumptions; my meeting arrived and I turned my attention to her. I did not think of that incident again for weeks, until this week. Eighteen months. Every milestone is painful. How can it be a year and a half? I am going through some organization emails to distract myself. Some are from people asking for help, others who want to help or volunteer.

One email is from a man interested in hearing more about volunteering opportunities, with a longer explanation about himself, along with more detail and more praise about me and our work. I hesitate to write back and sit on it for a few days. I am uncomfortable but cannot really place a finger on why his email agitates me. A few days later, I decided to call after some failed attempts at writing a reply. We have a pleasant conversation and on the phone, he seems to be a sensitive, compassionate, and educated person. He shares with me that he is also a widower. We speak a little more and briefly share some of our pain, and that is when it hit me. When I hang up the phone I feel ill at ease. A married woman should not be sharing feelings on the phone with another man.

It strikes me like a slap on the face that the world no longer sees me as a married woman. "*Your husband died, you are not married.*"

This realization is a dark place.

There comes a day when you smile again, and you feel like a traitor. How dare I feel happy?

– Laurell K. Hamilton

I am not married, but I am still very much in love. There is no place in my heart for even the thought of another person. I can understand people thinking that it is irrational to love someone who is not living, but you cannot stop loving someone because he died. The brain and the heart do not work like that. There is no "switch" for this.

"Don't make assumptions". There is nothing wrong with talking on the phone with someone, there was no hidden agenda or any interest on his side, and so I will not assume so. Take the conversation at face value: he just wanted to offer his help. It is a struggle, but I override the odd feeling in my gut.

A few days after our conversation, I received a note confirming my intuition. An invitation for coffee. It is hard to describe the pain and sadness that takes over me. Yechiel is not here to protect me. Being married is no longer a buffer. I cannot just say, 'Sorry, I am married and it is not appropriate." I was never approached while I was married; there was always respect for the rabbi and his wife. And now that I am not considered married, men take liberties without society considering it disrespectful. My pain is acute. I have not cried in weeks, and it overwhelms me now. Yechiel is not here. My true love is not here. I am alone, and I feel like I have to build up a wall around me and protect myself. I cannot let anyone get too close. I am spinning again. I need quiet. I question my reality. Is this my fault? Have I been overly friendly to insinuate that I am open to having coffee with someone?

It feels like a betrayal to my love and I am bereft.

Why is this so disturbing to me? On a deeply primal level, I know I do not want to be considered single. I am married, through and through. I feel like I will be married to Yechiel for the rest of my life. The world is treating me as something that I am not, not yet, maybe not ever. Some move forward faster than others, some of us never will. After 18 months, my mindset has not changed. My life with Yechiel, our plans for the future, the looks and love we shared, is carved in me. Marriage to Yechiel rewired my brain. Those are not bonds that unravel easily after death.

I need to make it crystal clear to this man that I am not interested. I have not reached that point, and do not foresee me ever reaching it. My close friends pray for me to one day have room in my heart for someone else. To be loved again, to love and share happiness. For those who can, I am happy. For now, for me, it seems impossible.

And so, I write back a friendly but clear note, *I cannot meet you.* Simple. Concise.

No room for someday.

I should say, one of the things about being a widow or a widower, you really, really need a sense of humor, because everything's going to fall apart.

– Joyce Carol Oates

I killed my tomatoes.

It's a quiet Friday night and the only plans I had were to stay home and read. I came up with this answer when friends invited me for *Shabbat*, and all I wanted was my quiet space. I also avoided walking back home alone in the dark. I was happy that I was finally enjoying some time alone. I would just relax and read on Friday night. And so, I would say, "I already made plans." I did not want to disclose the entire truth out of fear that friends would pity me or think I was depressed. I was not expecting guests this *Shabbat* yet I did not feel lonely. Slowly, I began to *need* my quiet time by myself without the need of being surrounded constantly. Jonathan surprised me with a visit, he came by himself, and for the first time since Eli passed away almost three months ago, we were able to have a relaxed conversation. His sadness of the initial shock and grief were slowly fading.

Of course Eli's death was still very raw. My son had stayed at his father's house away from the city buzz for about a month after Eli died, but now he was back to living at his home in Tel Aviv. He started gardening and planting. He prepared different varieties for me to replant on my front porch - I think he was a bit astonished that they were thriving.

"The tomatoes have too much water." Jonathan tries to inquire about my watering habits; I will search the Internet after *Shabbat* to learn where I had gone wrong. Tricky, I don't know if I am giving them too much water, or too little. I am not giving up just yet. I planted a second batch of plants and I have managed to keep them alive for a month now. They seem to be doing better.

Watching the growth and taking care of all the plants each morning is very healing.

Does healing mean that I will no longer grieve? I think this might be what I am trying to hold on to. What is grief, and what is grieving? Do they ever end? If so, does that mean the end of a relationship? Is there still a relationship with someone who is not physically present? I have so many questions. Would not grieving be ending my relationship with Yechiel? Is this why we hold on to grief? What is the meaning of feeling better or feeling worse? I cannot be feeling "better" because I am not sick. Although there are still the triggers where I explode and react like a crazy person – but that I unfortunately cannot control yet.

Back to Jonathan. Just the two of us, just talking. Loss and lockdown have amplified my feelings to a razor's edge. He is about the only one who understands me. Everyone grieves in a different way, but Jonathan and I are very similar. We craved peace and quiet, and have pushed away many people that just do not feel right these days. He isolated himself more after his father's death, where I felt the need to talk to everyone in the first months; these days we are going through a similar stage. I find solace in that, contentment. I still need people around me that make me feel good.

I still need to take care of myself right now. There are many people out there trying to teach me how to grieve, how to get you back to being yourself. They cannot understand that I will never be myself again. I am barely starting to realize this now. How can I go back to being myself when the person I was does not exist anymore?

Life stopped for me on February 6, 2019, and yet the world kept going. How was that possible? How can everyone just go on with everyday lives? I had the hardest time accepting that. I did not want to live in a world that did not include my husband. I even had suicidal thoughts. Driving was still difficult because the urge to end it all was still powerful behind the wheel of a moving vehicle. I confess I had to stop driving for a while to protect myself.

The entrance to the house is full of plants; I've collected over 25 pots of all sizes and all my varieties are growing, except the tomatoes. Where once I had only geraniums that stayed alive no matter what, now I had flowers of all different kinds and colors. I saw hope through the growth. I saw sparks of happiness through the colors.

I feel a surge of gratitude toward my son who encouraged this for me.

The warm weather makes all the difference. I am thinking of moving to a warm city next winter. Every morning, I step outside and watch for new leaves and flowers. I have been enjoying the numerous trips to the nursery, buying a new plant or a new pot and obsessively caring for the front entrance. I am surprised to find calm and peace in the simple activities, away from the hectic life of continuous travel without routine. Meetings face to face have almost become a thing of the past and there are new challenges and hardships in our new small organization; around the globe people are realizing how important it is to have small projects around the house, or creating a routine when all we could do was to stay home.

Still, my tomatoes died. I remain optimistic - failure is just part of the journey to success. I will try yet again.

"Where there is love there is life".

– Mahatma Gandhi

One year after my first solo attempt at attending a wedding, I was invited to another friend's wedding. But by August 2020, I am not the only one who has changed. The world has changed. Uncertainty has Covid restrictions in Israel adjusting daily, sometimes by the minute. This particular week, we are allowed to gather up to 20 people outdoors plus an additional ten indoors. With this allowance, my friend insists I have to be there for her.

One of the best pieces of advice I got early on did not really make sense to me when I first heard it - "If you go to any event, you are better off driving on your own. People will offer to pick you up and drive you, but as hard as it is, drive alone." And I get it now. I don't think one truly understands a situation until one lives it. Now it makes sense, and I am driving alone. I never know when the pain is going to suddenly crawl up, I never know how long I could hold the tears in. When I drove my own car, I was free to leave if it got overwhelming. I was not dependent on someone else's schedule.

I also could not have imagined that just a year after the first wedding I attended, the world would be such a different place.

I arrived at the wedding with a feeling of sadness and detachment. I remembered that Yechiel had stopped attending events, unless his presence was necessary. I realized that he would not be here even if he were alive. Also, all my memories of him are pre-Covid, I cannot even imagine him with a mask on. In some way, that makes it easier. The wedding is surreal; everyone is wearing masks. There is no food or reception, just a small group standing outside waiting for the bride. But it imbues the celebration with a simplicity and humility that I find relatable.

Pre-Covid weddings in Israel had become ridiculously expensive. Often a couple of lesser means would calculate the number of guests and gifts necessary to pay for the wedding. I was shocked the first time I saw a safe at the entrance of the wedding hall, where guests are to 'deposit' their checks for the new couple. At the end of the evening, one would sometimes see newlyweds opening and tallying checks to pay the wedding hall before leaving. So different from the elegant bridal registries I was used to back home.

Now, a small group of twenty people standing outdoors seemed to me, a purer way to a new life as a couple. After the ceremony, there was a simple dinner organized outdoors. The couple had not even planned for music, until someone had the thought of bringing a wireless speaker and connecting it to a phone. Dancing on the small patio next to the table was a beautiful scene.

So simple, so perfect.

The greatest thing in this world is not so much where we stand as in what direction we are moving.

– Johann Wolfgang von Goethe

September 15, 2020

I'm watching the live broadcast as history is being made.

Israel is signing a peace agreement with the UAE and Bahrain, and my heart hurts. *How is Yechiel not here to live this major event*? As I watch, I see many familiar faces who Yechiel socialized with. *He should be sitting there with them.* One of his close friends is interviewed from the White House lawn on Israeli TV. *How is it possible that Yechiel is not there?* This is an incredible day for the world, "A very important day for peace," says the US President. My brain hits a stumbling block. *How is Yechiel not here on this historic day*? It's too surreal. A new era is starting, a day we as Israelis never thought would come. I realize I am crying. *Why am I crying? I should be celebrating.* Yet I am mourning. I am mourning the memories. I am mourning that Yechiel is not here to share in this moment. I am mourning our future that will never be.

Yechiel always signed his messages with *Shalom*, peace. He always prayed for peace. His prayers were answered today, and he is not here to live and see it. Everyone has tears, tears for all our fallen soldiers, tears of emotion for the peace ahead, but I cannot stop my tears for Yechiel. For me. Just ahead of Rosh Hashanah, this is a blessing for the people of Israel. Yechiel would be ecstatic. He would be reciting the prayer, "Blessed are You [...] who has brought us to this season."

Yechiel believed that we have the opportunity to change the world. I think of the words of Psalm 126 carved on Yechiel's grave, "Those who sow in tears will reap with songs of joy." We reap results with our actions. It was one of Yechiel's favorite verses. He got to see results from his actions, and he was always grateful for it. He talked of all the people who became famous after their death and did not live to enjoy the fruit of their actions. He spoke many times of a specific acquaintance who did not live to see the huge following after his death. Yechiel felt he was blessed to see the difference he made in the world, and more than once said, "Ok, I can die now, I did my job." I was horrified to hear him talk like that, but in a way he felt his mission was over. Yechiel sowed in tears and reaped with some joy.

But he missed today. *He should be here today to witness this*. He did not get to live to see the day when his strongest prayer – *Shalom*, peace – was answered.

"We were able to reach this day by not focusing on past conflicts, we need to focus on a vibrant future." Television commentators are still covering this historic event. This is a time to move forward, not to be stuck in past events. This does not mean that we forget our past, but we need to put it aside and look to the possibilities of the future.

Yechiel is not here to enjoy this day, but I must look at the future. There are always those who try to block you, prevent or judge. Yechiel had much opposition in his first years of his work, and this knowledge made the day, and this historic moment, that much harder for me. He should be here to be a part of this. He would have been elated to attend the signing of a peace treaty.

How predictable that even during the signing of this historic agreement, we are being attacked; rockets were launched at Israel at the same time. There are casualties in an outdoor mall in Ashdod. Israeli television is broadcasting both events side by side. Even in celebration, Israel cannot sleep or lower her guard for a moment.

Carve your name on hearts, not tombstones.
A legacy is etched into the minds of others
and the stories they share about you.

– Shannon Alder

I met a friend of Yechiel today. It is heartwarming when people take the time to talk to me about Yechiel. I have not seen him since Yechiel died. I know that he was at the funeral, although I admit I cannot remember seeing him.

He takes the time to tell me about the first time he met Yechiel, when he had just moved to Israel. They had both been invited to speak on a panel about welfare, and he was blown away by this big guy who was like no one else he had ever encountered. He could not figure him out. He was different. Yechiel would actually say about himself. "I don't belong in any box". This was also his answer to any questions on belief or Judaism. Yes, he had *smichah* from Yeshiva University and was officially an orthodox rabbi, but he was his own kind of rabbi. For instance, unlike other orthodox rabbis, Yechiel would shake a woman's hand. For those we were close to, he would hug them goodbye like family.

His friend found that this, somewhat intimidating orthodox rabbi, was actually very accessible and easy to talk to. He told me how surprised he was to find how easily he could discuss difficult issues concerning Israel with Yechiel. Yechiel wanted to help; he often asked mayors and members of the Knesset how he could help, or what the city needed.

Then Yechiel would follow through, and was usually invited everywhere with open arms.

Yechiel was thrilled, except that he was not welcome in the municipality of Jerusalem at the time. Jerusalem was one of the four cities in Israel that had not accepted him, and public opinion did not agree with the work he was doing. They did not believe in building a closer relationship with evangelical Christians, but their views changed after he funded a center to help Jerusalemites during terror attacks. One center led to countless bomb shelters, immigration centers, hospital equipment, programs and supplies for soldiers.

This month we also mark twenty years since the second intifada. Reading the many newspaper articles, watching documentaries of those horrible and terrifying days, I find myself reliving that period when I was a different person. Flashbacks of days when I was so vulnerable and recently divorced. Days when I could barely function, but those seem easier now in retrospect.

Everything is relative.

For every Israeli citizen, those days felt very much like a war, only it was not called a war. A war inside the cities, it impacted everyone, no one was left unaffected. The terrorism in those days was nerve wracking. Just walking down the street was terrifying, and we stayed home whenever possible. The psychological effect on me was numbing. The trauma of those days still remains, the intensity may have lowered, but it still is on our minds and Israel remains vigilant.

Will the trauma that I am now going through last as long? I am afraid it will never be erased, but it will affect the rest of my life. The way the second intifada affected my life, the days where no place felt safe, sitting in a coffee shop was an exercise in bravery. We all got used to looking all around us for suspicious persons, packages; Israelis never entirely relax. Over 120 suicide bombings left a deep scar, and the trauma took years to overcome. I still have flashbacks, triggered when I see a man wearing a jacket in the summer. A nervousness that, scared like in the past, mightI be hiding explosives. Or passing the intersection of Jaffa road and King George street, a major crossing that is always crowded, reminds me of the Sbarro that once stood

there, and horrific suicide bombing that wounded 150, while killing 15, including 7 children and one pregnant woman.

I was lucky. My family was safe, but my coworker was not as lucky. When her daughter was killed by a bus explosion, she left the country. She couldn't bear to live under the stress and horror of all the bombings. I look back at those days and realize how it shaped me, how much stronger I am today, and how I have the tools today to face hardship. We remember, we can never forget. I am reminded of the Winston Churchill quote, "A nation that forgets its past has no future." I watch the Black Lives Matter protests in the US cities where I have friends and I feel the truth of it.

Yechiel was adamant that "never forget" was not enough. It wasn't enough to memorialize, the community needed to live it, to act, to do. I think of this now and know Yechiel would want me to live, to act, to embody, to do. I will never forget him and I also need a life; I want to remember, but I am not going to be stuck in my grief.

It is my choice.

First there is weeping, for we all must weep for what we have lost. Second comes silence, for in the silence we understand solace, beauty, and comfort from something greater than ourselves. Third comes singing, for in singing we pour out our hearts and regain our voice.

– Judy Collins, *Sweet Judy Blue Eyes: My Life in Music*

One year has gone by since last Rosh Hashanah. Emotions vacillate from feeling stronger one day, to seeing a different kind of wave approaching. Some days, a deep paralyzing sadness takes over, and I do not even turn on my phone. One week before the holiday, I shut down for three days. No phone, I don't want to talk to anybody, I feel empty and lie in bed most of the time. Time out.

Now I am ready to face my second Rosh Hashanah without Yechiel.

For Yechiel, it was a stressful month preparing for his High Holy Days sermons. On the first day of the Jewish month of *Elul*, Yechiel started to panic. He had to prepare four sermons, two for each of the two days of *Rosh Hashanah*, one for the start of *Yom Kippur* in the evening, and one for the *Yom Kippur* day. It was all he spoke about at home. He did not enjoy the preparation or the stress of writing, and somehow, every year he accepted the challenge once again. He forgot how hard it was, how drained he got and how every year it took longer to recover. He was pushing himself to his limit, and it was painful to watch. Yechiel worked intensely throughout the year for the organization that he built, but the preparation of those sermons and being "the rabbi" was his hardest job.

He would stay in his office until late at night and write his sermons. Pages and pages of yellow handwritten pages. He would gather jokes throughout the year for possible use during the services, saving them in yellow folders. So many yellow folders… around the house, stacked on every available surface. Labeled "used jokes," or "sermons," all his papers were organized (not always very neatly), inside those folders. He would send me jokes to check if they were 'synagogue appropriate.' Some were typical rabbi jokes, others were random.

I'm reading through his jokes folder, and the memory of him reading some of them in the synagogue makes me smile, "*I love being Jewish because it's such a logical, rational religion! In the past month I blew a ram's horn, ate a fish head, swung a chicken around my head, dressed in a suit and sneakers, then wore a white robe, prayed and fasted for 25 hours, built and ate in a tent with a bamboo ceiling, sometimes in the rain, spent three consecutive days with my in-laws and three more with my parents, walked around with a palm branch and a citrus fruit, whipped willow branches on the floor, ate roughly eight pounds of meat, used four vacation days without leaving my neighborhood, and spent almost as much time in shul as I did in my office!*"

Hearing a large gregarious man say it with such zest made the community laugh even harder. Because it *does* sound like a joke. And we laugh because it is all true.

He would randomly interrupt the service to tell a short story or a joke, often despite the shocked look of the president of the synagogue: "*I constantly tell my children how important it is to stay in school; and yet, every day, they come home.*"

The sermons took everything out of him, he gave himself entirely to the community. There are some who come to the synagogue only on Rosh Hashanah and Yom Kippur, and Yechiel always felt he had to give them the most meaningful experience he could. He felt he had only one chance, once a year, to connect these people to their Jewish identity and bring them closer. It was for them that he wrote such passionate sermons; it was them he addressed. He was dismayed by the fact that outside the synagogue, nobody saw the rabbinic side of him. He wanted to be seen and known as a Rabbi, remembered for his sermons and his position as rabbi of this community. Usually the rabbi is the leader of a community, but our synagogue in Chicago hired one only for the High Holidays. Yechiel sometimes felt he did not receive the respect he deserved here, yet he took his role very seriously.

Yechiel commented many times that the world knew him only as the "bridge builder between Christians and Jews," but he was a rabbi, and he wanted to be known and remembered for being a rabbi. He shared his sermons with a few family members and friends, but the written word never came close to hearing him live. His delivery of the sermons by far exceeded what he wrote. Those were his best performances, but literally risked his life delivering them.

Spending the holidays in Chicago every year was ultimately a very lonely time. Yes, there was the community, but it never felt truly ours. We missed family; we spent most nights just the two of us. Four Rosh Hashanah meals, two full days. The first time that we spent the holidays in Chicago was in 2004, and we were invited into other homes for all the mandatory meals. Yechiel was wiped out by the end of the day, after the six-hour morning service, three-hour lunch, back to the synagogue again, a couple more hours for dinner before we were able to get home to do it again the next day. After that, Yechiel demurred; he wanted just a light meal for lunch so that he could rest before going back to the synagogue again.

So that is what we did. For the years that followed, the only night we went out was the first, and every year we accepted a standing invitation to the home of dear friends. The following three meals we kept light and at home, just the two of us. Yechiel only thought of getting to bed after an exhausting six-hour morning service.

My first Rosh Hashanah without Yechiel was devastating as can be expected. Even with tempering medication, I broke down several times during the service. I was with different friends for every meal, mainly to keep my mind distracted and not be alone. I just needed to get through it.

After each meal, I felt "*okay, one down, three more to go; two down, two more to go.*"

On the first night of Rosh Hashanah, a single woman from the synagogue that I barely knew invited me for a meal. She let me know it would be casual; she was just having over a few friends. It felt right; I could not imagine myself at a table surrounded by married couples or close families. It was a relaxed atmosphere, new people, no memories to well up and threaten my sanity.

In contrast, on the eve of the second Rosh Hashanah without Yechiel, Israel began another lockdown due to Covid19. I felt ready. More prepared. But it was more nuanced than that. Everyone else was shut in and spending the holiday alone. I didn't feel much different than everyone else. I was getting used to being alone, I was not longing to be in Chicago. Everything there was closed too. Lakeshore Drive Synagogue was closed too.

With Covid restrictions around the world, I did not feel like I was missing out on anything. Everyone was on their own - families separated, synagogues semi-closed with very few people attending.

For the first time in 21 years, the cantor of Lakeshore Drive synagogue would not be flying in. Instead, he sent an audio file by email that he had recorded for the community. I pressed play on the file without thinking, and the wave hit me. I was immediately transported to the sanctuary that had been our holiday home for 14 years, and into the holiday prayers. I could see the cantor in the middle of the sanctuary, standing high with his white cantor garb and hat, and Yechiel sitting in front of him, facing him from his seat next to the *Aron Kodesh* – the holy ark. Memories of all those years together on the holidays start flashing by as I listen to the cantor's prayers. Yechiel looked so majestic dressed in his white *kittel* (robe) in his seat facing the congregation. The *kittel* that I would wash and iron every year, then neatly pack in his suitcase as we traveled to Chicago.

I thought of his *kittel*, where was it? I had this sudden urgent need to find it. I got up and nearly ran to his closet. It was the first time I really looked through it. *Where is it?* The images were overwhelming and emotional. I could see him so clearly in that white robe. I find it and I hug it tightly. I cannot take my eyes off it; I feel oddly reverent. And lay it on his side of the bed. I can remember the day I bought it. He had one that was already old, stained and yellow looking, so I had gone into Meah Shearim in Jerusalem to buy a new one, together with a white *kippah* for the holiday. I had not washed the *kittel* since he wore it last and it still smells like him. I will not be ironing it this year. With tears in my eyes, I spread it out on his bed and I left it out during the entire holiday.

The cantor's voice continues with the beautiful melodies of the prayers. A thought brings a smile as I listen. This was the only time of year when Yechiel made a colossal effort to be on time for services. He had to be on time, he had an obligation as the rabbi. Except that days/months/years of not being on time had not given him the tools or capacity to be on time. He always miscalculated the hour. As much as he tried, he was always a few minutes late to synagogue. For him though, it was close enough. In every other matter, he knew he was always late. He arrived late to meetings, always keeping people waiting. The only way I could get him to be on time when we went somewhere together was to tell him the wrong time. He would get lost in time, always rushing out of the house at the last minute. He got up early enough, but forgot the time reading newspapers and having coffee. He would give himself enough time to go over his sermon in the morning before he left to the synagogue. I would hear him in the living room reading his sermon out loud, but in the end, he always ended up rushing.

Even though our apartment was just a ten-minute walk to the synagogue, his rush to get there was enough for him to arrive dripping wet in sweat. Normally, when possible, he would carry a washcloth with him and dry himself off. However, Yechiel was so strict on some issues, yet so lenient in others; and he was strict on the prohibition of not carrying anything on *Shabbat*. Which had surprised me when we first met, asking me to check my pockets when we left home, just in case I accidentally forgot a tissue in my pocket. Tissues then became acceptable when he recalled his mother always having one in her sleeve.

Personally, I always liked to be at the synagogue very early. There is a certain peace and quiet early in the morning that I found very spiritual. Women usually arrive later and the seats fill up, creating a different atmosphere. In Jerusalem, the walk to the synagogue on a holiday or Shabbat morning is unique, you can feel the holiness in the air – in Israel, there is a holiday atmosphere. In Israel, it is common to see people dressed up on a Saturday.

It was different in the United States. I felt a little more alien. On the walk to and from the synagogue, we would pass people hanging out in coffee shops, going to the market, and no one was wearing a suit on a Saturday. We were minorities celebrating a holiday, and the rest of the city was not. Yechiel followed his father's example, who on his path to and from the synagogue, would keep his eyes on the ground. A small courtesy just in case a member of the Jewish community was sitting in a coffee shop, or going to a market, they would not be embarrassed to be caught by the rabbi.

I can picture him sitting in his seat facing the entrance to the synagogue. He would watch me walk in and his smile for me would send a thrill through me. The memory stabs at me.

The Lake Shore Drive Synagogue was set up differently than what I was used to in Israel, or even growing up in Barcelona. There is usually a clear separation between men and women as customary in an orthodox synagogue. In this synagogue, only half of the congregants sat separately, the other half had mixed seating during the holidays. The two areas are separated only by a row of low plants, meaning that everyone could see each other. It was very uncomfortable, but as with everything, eventually I learned to live with it. But I never got used to it; it was always a bit uncomfortable. By arriving early, and the synagogue being almost empty, I could get to my seat easily; but if I had to use the bathroom in the middle of the service, and a full synagogue, I would have to walk through an entire row of men, which I dreaded. Sometimes, I would not return to my seat and just sit in the back, to avoid having to go through the men again. The nice part of such an open space was that Yechiel could come over to me and we could always keep an eye on each other, and especially during Yom Kippur, I could check how he was feeling during the fast.

Yechiel gave two Rosh Hashanah sermons every year, and one was always dedicated to Israel. He felt a deep responsibility, as a rabbi delivering a sermon in the US, to help the community feel connected to Israel. He felt most of the members had only a peripheral attachment to our ancestral homeland. But Yechiel felt strongly about a globally connected community of Jews. Those who did not attend synagogue throughout the year would come in for Rosh Hashanah, and he felt it was an opportunity – his duty – to inspire them about

Israel. In some way or another, every year he spoke about what it meant to be Jewish, and our responsibilities as Jews.

His last Rosh Hashanah sermon in 2018 was different – after many years of talking about it and praying over it, he had finally decided that it would be his last and he said goodbye to the congregation. I don't think the community believed him, but he and I knew it was the last. There was still Yom Kippur, but this was a first goodbye. He just could not do it any more. The days following Yom Kippur were exhausting. There was no time to rest, since he wanted to spend Sukkot at home. For that, we had to fly out the next day.

I saw a real difference that year. He was totally wiped out. He decided, he was done. I could not watch him go through that again. He gave himself entirely to the community to the point where he did not have any spiritual or meaningful moments for himself. He saw his role as rabbi to make it the most meaningful and uplifting for the community, and sacrificed his health.

I realized during my 60-day preparation journey that sometimes the most special experiences last only a moment, that we prepare for these special moments sometimes for hours, only to feel it for a split second. Yechiel had one of those moments, only one minute during the entire service where he reached a higher level and a deep spiritual moment. It was the same moment every year, when he extended his hands and emotionally sang the last words.

It was a deeply emotional moment to watch. My seat in the women's section was just two meters from his side and I could see his tears. The warmth that I felt in that moment ran through my body even in the freezing air conditioning. Every year, he took in that moment, he would turn his back to the congregation and face the ark, but from my vantage point, I could see his eyes close. Just a split moment. Then he would turn around, "You may be seated."

There is a sacredness in tears. They are not the mark of weakness, but of power. They speak more eloquently than ten thousand tongues. They are the messengers of overwhelming grief, of deep contrition, and of unspeakable love.

– Washington Irving

Israel's ever changing restrictions due to Covid kept everyone in a state of confusion. Information was unclear and decisions kept changing, trying to keep up with the shifting spread. One day we are allowed to celebrate only with any immediate family living in the house; the next day, suddenly gatherings are allowed for up to ten family members no matter where they live. We are only allowed to walk out of our homes if we stay within a 500-meter radius; in the last possible moment before the holiday, that radius is extended to one kilometer. Synagogues are restricted to twenty people inside, twenty outside – now it changes to only ten. Most people have just decided to stay home and not attend synagogue this year, not wanting to take the chance or put themselves or family at risk. Many synagogues have arranged temporary outdoor prayer areas in parks, in front of buildings or in backyards. Everything feels different, subdued, this year. The usual hustle and bustle of people rushing, crowded stores with festive shoppers, the scramble to get that last minute perfect gift – gone. The atmosphere is heavy; people are struggling. Even the air feels oppressive, never before has Israel had a heat wave that lasted over two weeks.

At 6:30am the next morning, the morning of Rosh Hashanah, I am awakened by beautiful Sephardic melodies right outside my bedroom window. For a moment I thought I was dreaming, I was back to being a young girl in my synagogue in Barcelona. As I pull my head up and look out the window, I see my next-door neighbor has turned their front porch into a makeshift outdoor synagogue. I thought the blue material cover they were putting up that week was just a protection from the sun, and I was relieved that it would only obstruct my view through the confinement period.

Like most of my female friends, I had not planned on attending services this year. Any outing that was not absolutely necessary was pushed off. All face-to-face meetings were canceled, even if it was in a synagogue or a family holiday meal. But this morning, the synagogue came to me… I was delighted! I could not believe how wonderful, how auspicious, how fortunate I felt. I would be able to attend services. Even at that early hour, I jumped out of bed. All I had to do is go out on my front porch and I would have my own private women's section! I quickly got dressed, slipped on a white t-shirt (it is customary to wear white on the holidays, and even if nobody could see me, I instinctively chose white), and rushed down the stairs. As I waited a few precious seconds for a cup of tea to take with me, I quickly looked through our shelves for a High Holiday prayer book. I was not sure we even had one, since we always spent the holiday away. I gasped when I discovered a Rosh Hashanah and Yom Kippur *machzor* (prayer book). I opened the cover to find his handwriting, "*This is the property of Rabbi Yechiel Eckstein.*" The tears came. Happy and sad. He is with me. I clutch the *machzor* to me and step outside.

In the privacy of my patio, I allow myself to become totally absorbed by the melodies coming from my neighbor's house. Those particular tunes and prayers that I had not heard in over 15 years. I am transported to my childhood synagogue in Barcelona, because these tunes feel so distant, but somewhat familiar. I can remember our rabbi in white garb standing on the *bimah* in the center of our synagogue. The same synagogue where I married Eli all those years ago, that cold winter day while the Gulf war was all we could think of. We canceled our honeymoon plans to go back to Israel as soon as it was possible to do so. Eli had nobody to walk him down the aisle. His sisters were not able to travel and attend the wedding. His parents had both passed away many years ago. My mother suggested she be the one to walk him, and he gratefully agreed. I arrived at the synagogue in a separate car with my father. As I entered the synagogue, I must have looked down for a moment, making my veil fall to the front. My mother was not there to fix it, as she was just walking down with Eli. Nobody other than the photographer was there, and I guess she thought it was normal not to see the face of a Jewish bride.

The melodies bring back some odd memories. I made a note to myself to check the basement to see if I could find the video of my wedding to Eli. Would the children want it now that Eli passed away?

I am carried away further into the past. The women's section in my childhood synagogue was upstairs; we would stand and look down on the men. It had been entirely renovated over the years, but for me, the memories of the old wooden benches remain. In my mind's eye, I can still see my father's seat on the right side of the *bimah*, remembering how I used to sit beside him as a little girl, when I was still allowed to sit in the men's section.

My vision blurs. My heart aches. I'm confused. How different that past was than my more recent memories with Yechiel. How different all of it is from today, sitting outside by myself. I opened Yechiel's *Ashkenazi machzor* and remembered that the Sephardic service is completely different. I'm listening to one service, but reading a different one, and everything is getting mixed up in my mind. As I turn the pages looking for some similarities, Yechiel's handwritten notes appear inside the prayer book – red pen notes, "me", "announce: please respond to the cantor", "explain", referring to the places where he, as the rabbi, would speak to the congregation. Tears follow and freely flow down my face. But they are different now too. They are nostalgic and poignant tears, not the desperately painful tears.

I am creating my own new memories.

These awkward and challenging times will be remembered for generations. Where were you during the 2020 pandemic? How was Rosh Hashanah in those days? I can imagine telling my grandchildren some anecdotes one day, still hoping for Jonathan and Amanda to have children already, how stores ran out of eggs and toilet paper, and about the more serious issue of conflict, distrust and financial crisis. My father was reminding me of the Spanish flu in 1918, a global pandemic that lasted two years, ending just a few years before he was born. Over a third of the world's population contracted it, estimates of up to 100 million died, just one short century ago. How quickly we forget. I think of the four waves of the Spanish flu… is this what awaits us?

Meanwhile, I try to take it one day at a time. There is an unsettling amount of uncertainty, not just in my personal journey but in the world today. So I do whatever it takes every day. On the second day of Rosh Hashanah, I decided to stop by my regular local Ashkenazi synagogue. They have also set up camp outside the neighborhood school, allowing 10 people to sit inside the building. Some chairs are set up keeping the recommended two-meter distance. I could have stayed on my front porch just as the previous day, but felt an urge to connect more to Yechiel, with the prayers more familiar for today. The experience was surreal, not so much because of the service itself, which was cut to half the length from the regular 6 hours, on the recommendation of the rabbis; it was the ten-minute walk to the synagogue that took me by surprise. There were outdoor 'synagogues' at every corner. Small gatherings of ten men everywhere, in backyards, on the street, congregating in the park. Just like my neighbor's, everyone else in the neighborhood had prepared in the same way. The walk to my synagogue felt like walking through one big synagogue.

Covid restrictions had actually brought people out and connected others that would usually not go to synagogue. The religious were dressed in holiday outfits, while the non-religious were in regular clothes, but it was like the entire community came outside to share in the prayers. Even with the terrible situation we were in, the death toll growing every day because of the pandemic, there was such beauty in seeing the connection and love between people. Yechiel would have loved to experience this.

Sitting in a synagogue service with such a small number of people on Rosh Hashanah felt surreal as well. Rosh Hashanah and Yom Kippur, this is the only time of year when the synagogue is packed, and it is very difficult to find a free seat (I hear this is akin to finding seats during Christian services for Christmas and Easter). In fact, outside of Israel, you have to reserve and pay for your seat in advance. Our synagogue in Barcelona had engraved plaques on the back of the seats of all the regular members. The beauty of Israel is that nobody is required to show a ticket to enter a synagogue for the High Holy Days. Everyone is welcome – if you can find a seat.

The main aspect and mitzvah of Rosh Hashanah is to blow, or hear, the blowing of the shofar. This year it could only be blown on the second day since the first day was also *Shabbat*, and we are not allowed to blow the shofar on *Shabbat*. People were concerned if they could not attend services, they would not get to fulfill the mitzvah of the holiday. It was crucial to get out on the second day in order to hear the shofar, but some were in isolation and forbidden to even step outside. But what came next made the walk back from the synagogue amazing. Other years, it was common to hear a shofar here and there; but this year, from the moment I left the synagogue and for the rest of the day, I heard the shofar every few minutes. Rabbis, and people who knew how to blow the shofar, were going to every corner of the city, under every building, in every park, blowing it for those who could not get out, covering the city to make sure that everyone got to hear it.

And boy, did we hear it. I had thought to nap after service, but that was impossible. It was a Rosh Hashanah that will forever be etched in my memory.

Without the possibility of resting, I picked up one of the books that Yechiel was reading. This one was on the top shelf where he kept another stack of books. Another small booklet, he had quite a few of these. Most of them are dedicated, like this one, "For Rabbi Yechiel Eckstein – with gratitude, D." The book was *The Wonders of Solitude.* I wonder how and when they met, or if they even knew each other. Many writers sent Yechiel books to read or as a promotion. *Solitude...* how appropriate for this lockdown.

From the first chapter I was absorbed in the journey of discovering solitude, through being inspired by solitude ending with the power of silence, each quote in the book is more powerful than the next. Yechiel kept a bookmark on page 75. *Thank you for always leading me, my love.* He must have been eating while reading this page as it has marks of grease. I would discover such marks everywhere, no matter how many times I asked him to use a napkin when eating. I smile at those greasy marks today. A sign of where he was and what he touched.

"Solitude can become your most meaningful companion and it can assist you in being a more giving person [...]"

I breathed in. I had not realized how much I needed to read this on Rosh Hashanah. Some believe in messages and signs sent by our spouse. Was this a sign? It felt like it: appreciate the solitude. The paragraph continued, "*...rather than regarding your partner's need for time alone as a threat, see it as a time of renewal that you celebrate. Make every effort to help each other have that space. Treat that space as sacred.*" I am blown away. This is exactly how Yechiel and I lived. We respected that time alone, we gave each other the space we needed and never invaded it. This started very early on in our relationship, at the time when we were dating. Yechiel would 'disappear' for weeks at a time when he was out of the country. I never tried calling him and respected his time away. I learned the concept of letting a man 'stay in his cave as long as he needs to' many years ago from "Men are from Mars, Women are from Venus." I have not only adopted it since, but also recommended it to many friends.

In the middle of passages on solitude, the following quote by Emily Dickinson on page 76 strikes me, "*There is a hush in a home on the morning after death, a silence that would be violated by too many words.*" This is the page following the one that Yechiel was reading. Why is a quote on death in the middle of these inspiring and positive messages on the benefits of solitude and the beauty of love?

The book ends with a very meaningful and powerful series of quotes on the power of silence. From back when I can remember, my mother, like so many mothers, would tell me, '*Keep quiet if you don't have anything nice to say.*" I have not been very successful and only recently have I felt like I keep quieter. The quote from Ecclesiastes 3:7 also mentioned in the last chapter, "*...a time to keep silent, and a time to speak.*" Powerful. I have chosen to remain silent in many circumstances, and especially after Yechiel died. There have been many situations where a reply was just not worth it, an explanation was too exhausting. I have felt the power of my silence being much stronger than words. As Elie Wiesel said, "Certain experiences may be transmitted by language, others – more profound – by silence."

Although silence can sometimes be provoking to others, I have found that only in my silence can I be in control of my emotions. In silence and in solitude, I am on my journey towards healing.

I breathe deeply. *Thank you again, my love, for these moments of peace.*

The *Shabbat* between *Rosh Hashanah* and *Yom Kippur* is called *Shabbat Shuva*, which means to return, named after the *Haftarah* that is read from the portion of Hosea 14:2 starting with the words, "Return, O Israel to the Lord your God." Some also call it *Shabbat Teshuva*, the *Shabbat* of repentance, just before *Yom Kippur.*

Every year, Yechiel and I would be in Chicago for this particular *Shabbat*, and Yechiel had to go to the synagogue. "They know I'm here, I have to go." We would walk together *Shabbat* morning; there was no rush to be exactly on time, since he was not 'on duty.' Yechiel never got the feeling that the community really cared if he attended services on *Shabbat Shuva* or not. There was no real job for him on *Shabbat*, they never asked him to lead the services or even come up to the *Torah*. He felt mostly irrelevant on *Shabbat*, so he offered to give a talk after the *Kiddush*, to answer any questions on Israel.

It never really got to that. All it took was one question and Yechiel would go on for an hour, until the time was up. I would try to get his attention, to take more questions as he originally promised, and he would announce it jokingly to everyone, "Oh! My wife is giving me a look! I better take more questions!"

This *Shabbat Shuva*, I again sat on my front porch listening to the outdoor *minyan* in my neighbor's entrance, grateful for a synagogue within easy reach. Easy reach is an understatement, I could hear the prayers whether I liked it or not. The words of this week's *Torah* portion – *Haazinu* (Deuteronomy 32) are more emotional than ever. We are approaching the end of Moses' life. Yechiel referred to this portion many times in his speeches – "Thank you Lord, I am luckier than Moses. Moses only got to *see* the Promised Land, I walked and lived in it."

I had a light meal after the prayer service outside, in the privacy of my deck. I picked up my friend's recently published book about the lessons from hiking the Israel trail, "Angels and Tahina", by Tzippi Moss.

Beautifully written and insightful, I love her strong, relatable quotes. Many of her passages evoke poignant visceral reactions in me. Very appropriate reading for introspection before *Yom Kippur*. I've only reached page 72, when she describes their arrival at the artist village of Ein Hod. My heart skips a beat. And I am overcome with memories of Yechiel.

It was the beginning of the winter, and Yechiel was arriving in Israel for a week. We did not have much time together, so we decided to go up north for *Shabbat* to an isolated place where we could just be alone. We came across a small village where both of us had never been to, and decided it sounded like the perfect romantic place - away from everything. Tzippi describes the village in her book exactly as I remember it, "*a small center, galleries, cafes and restaurants, and striking sculptures of metal and wood adorning the streets and doorways.*"

It feels like only yesterday we were walking those streets with Yechiel admiring all the art. As we returned to our rooms to prepare for *Shabbat*, taking out the prepared food we had bought on the way, connecting the hotplate we brought with us… and as I had my back to him rinsing some dishes in the sink of the small kitchen area, I heard him say, "Would you be willing to marry me?"

I froze. *Willing*? I did not even turn around. Time slowed down.

"I asked if you would be willing to marry me." Yechiel said again.

I turned around, not sure if this was an actual proposal or not. When I turned, I did not see a ring, nor was he down on one knee. I'm confused.

"Are you asking me to marry you?" I asked.

As with everything, Yechiel then asked, "Is that a *yes* or a *no*?"

He took me totally by surprise. I think he even surprised himself. This is not something he had planned. He told me that at that moment, he just knew. It took him two and a half years to decide.

"Yes, *yes*, it's a yes!"

Time sped up again and we both realized it was getting late fast. *Shabbat* was going to begin. I had to light candles. There was no time to call anyone; we did not make any announcements yet. After prayers and Kiddush we finally sat down at the small table in Yechiel's suite of the Ein Hod bed and breakfast we were staying at. Nothing fancy, but very cozy and perfectly quiet and private. We talked for hours about what had just happened. Were we really going to get married? Did we really want a wedding? If so, what kind of wedding? When? Yechiel was leaving the following week, and would not be back in Israel for at least another month. We spoke long into the night, but it was really very simple. We both wanted a small wedding. We both knew we did not want to make a big deal about it, we just wanted to keep it small and simple.

It was one of the happiest days of my life.

And of course, he did not have a ring.

I did not bring it up. I knew his mind was not thinking about an engagement ring right now. In the following weeks when we would announce our engagement, people would ask me about it, so I started wearing a ring that my mother had given me. Unbeknownst to me, she had a pair of diamond earrings that she had made into two engagement rings: one for when I got married, and one for my brother. But Eli proposed with a different ring so she held onto it. She finally saw an opportunity to give me the ring when my daughter was born, and said, "I'm giving this to you but it is for Amanda." So I had a ring I rarely wore when married to Eli, I had put it away and it largely stayed unseen. I instinctively put it on.

Months into our marriage, we were chatting one quiet *Shabbat* over a vodka and the subject came up. I joked, "You never gave me a ring." He teased back, "Well, you already had a ring." I started laughing, "That is not the way you do it, that is *not* how it's done." He was smiling too, "Do you want a ring?" "Well, *yes*, I want a ring!"

And it became one of our many inside jokes that we teased each other with during vodka nights.

We got married a month and a half after announcing our engagement.

Fast-forward many dinners out and vodka nights later, nearly a year had passed since our wedding when Yechiel suggested a dinner out for Hanukkah. The restaurant was packed when we arrived. Dinner was casual, the restaurant staff lit the candles for Hanukkah, and as we ordered dessert, Yechiel got up from his chair, came around the table and got down on one knee. I kept murmuring, "What are you doing, oh my god, what are you doing??" People stared in anticipation as this huge football player of a guy disrupted the restaurant to open a tiny box in front of me. I was mortified, but he kept smiling mischievously. "Will you marry me?" He asked. I was trying to discreetly hide my suddenly very tight, very obvious *wedding* ring. I'm sure my eyes were huge. The ring was stunning. I did not know whether to laugh, kiss him, or crawl under the table. I think I did a modified combo of all three. He jumped up, turned around to the staring crowd and beamed. "*SHE SAID YES*!!"

The place erupted into "*Mazel tovs*," while I was still desperately trying to hide my wedding band while playing along and thanking the crowd of well-wishers. Yechiel is basking in his surprise. I cannot think of that night without laughing. It was quintessentially *Yechiel*.

From that day forward, Yechiel would always joke, telling people it was our honeymoon whenever we traveled. He created celebrations everywhere. Every day was like an anniversary, especially since he did not give any importance to dates like birthdays. Every day felt festive, any reason was good to go out, or to simply enjoy an evening together.

I wore a wide yet simple plain wedding band for ten years. One day, Yechiel created an elaborate story about a friend of his who owned a jewelry business and wanted to see my collection of gold wire crochet jewelry. Yechiel arranged for a meeting. It struck me as odd, but many things he did were odd as well. I did not question him.

I arrived at his fancy office in Tel Aviv's diamond district, walking through security, feeling underdressed and out of the place. After being escorted to the floor, I was greeted by a secretary who welcomed me into a beautiful waiting room, and offered me a beverage. I asked for water and she was back a minute later with an envelope. I was very confused. I could not figure out what was happening. I opened the envelope and inside was a handwritten note from Yechiel:

"Happy Anniversary my love, choose whatever you want."

"Just because someone carries it well doesn't mean it isn't heavy." – Power of Positivity

– Yom Kippur eve, Jerusalem 2020.

I kept myself busy cooking in preparation for the meal before the fast. As the day progresses, my anxiety rises and memories from past holidays with Yechiel in Chicago start to choke me. I try to find comfort telling myself that this year is different for everyone. Everyone had other plans, everyone would be elsewhere. I am not different. But then it strikes me in the gut: *everyone's husband is still alive.*

It is usual during a holiday for the city to quiet down, especially Jerusalem. On Yom Kippur, even the non-religious adhere to the custom of no driving, fasting, and the city becomes silent in a way one never sees in other cities around the world. This year in lockdown, the silence was smothering. I had trouble driving because the streets were closed, police were everywhere, a curfew was in place due to Covid. We are allowed to deliver food to elderly people even during lockdown, so I am able to reach my parents' house and bring them the food I had prepared for them.

Driving back home was challenging with barriers and police at every intersection, closing off neighborhoods because of the combination of a total lockdown and the prohibition of driving on Yom Kippur.

The quiet is deafening.

The daily study for Yom Kippur eve focused on the ability to access the deepest part of our soul. This is only possible if we create the space for it: by lowering the noise in our life, we will be able to hear our inner voice. This is, of course, meant metaphorically... yet this year we receive the gift of silence. As the sun goes down, there is not one car on the street, no sounds, no music.

Just the sound of prayer.

The holiday in Israel feels a long way from any Yom Kippur we spent together. The route home in Chicago took us through busy Michigan Avenue. Walking by crowded bars, filled with young people and blasting music was weird. We did not belong there. I was aware of the awkward looks from people, as Yechiel stood out with his white *kippah*, suit and tie, and... Crocs (we do not wear leather shoes on Yom Kippur).

'Next year in Jerusalem.' He would say each year. He never made it.

In Jerusalem, the closeness of the community, of the holiday, has everyone outdoors. After evening services, it felt like everyone in the city was milling around outside. It brought out children on their bicycles, the only day of the year where they have all the streets to themselves. The streets were crowded with people, no cars, just all of humanity, pulled out from the oppression of lockdown.

My next-door neighbor's front porch is once again a makeshift synagogue; I decided to stay home and follow their Sephardic service. At first, it is comforting to hear tunes, but I find myself longing for the Ashkenazi service that I had grown accustomed to for the past 15 years. The next morning, I went back to my usual community, not knowing if there were any seats.

The setting is surreal. Ten chairs indoors, ten more outdoors on the women's side. Where is the packed synagogue from last year? How we took it for granted. Who could have ever imagined one year ago that we could not attend services in a synagogue?

The prayers hit me in a different way this holiday. The Jewish people have been reciting the same prayers for hundreds of years.

Nowadays, some prayers are often said figuratively or reflexively, since events like plagues and catastrophes are not in our collective memory. This year, when the cantor cries out "Our father, our king, remove the plague from our land!" - It sounds surreal.

It is the same prayer we pronounce every year, but it suddenly takes a different meaning. A new realization that history can repeat itself. We could not have even imagined that we would be living through a pandemic, and yet, here it is.

A plague? In our times? Who would have thought that we would be crying it out this year? "Send healing to all the sick." We all cried out this prayer in a different way. I get goosebumps. We all felt it. The intensity. The truth of our cries. Ten women, ten men, a few more sitting outdoors, everyone dressed in white. It creates an image I will never forget. Every time I close my eyes, though, I see Yechiel in his white robe in front of the overcrowded synagogue in Chicago. Everything has changed. The world has changed.

As I returned home for a break during prayers, the heat was oppressive. Another heat wave in Israel. After 18 hours into the fast and after walking a few steps, I suddenly felt weak. The streets were eerily quiet, the heat keeping everyone indoors. I felt a sudden fear. I was by myself on the street, just a ten-minute walk away, but feeling increasingly weak and dizzy. I could not faint in the middle of the street in that extreme heat. I took a break in the shade, sat down for a few moments and tried to make my way home, slowly. As I reached the house, I was struck by the realization that if anything happened to me, I was alone.

Yechiel was by himself at home on the day he died. I would not take a chance. I took a few sips of water and lied down. The cat looked at me strangely, as I slowly walked up the steps to my bedroom, one step at a time, holding onto the handrail. She stayed near me. How striking that animals can feel when something is wrong. I rested until the end of the day and felt better.

With the sound of the shofar ending the holiday, and the customary exclamation of, "Next year in Jerusalem!" I am left bereft. There was a level of spirituality and sense of unity during Yom Kippur, and suddenly… there was emptiness. On the one hand, after exclaiming the wish for next year in Jerusalem, I am here – our prayers every year for being in Jerusalem, answered. Obviously, this was not the way I had hoped for. I make a cup of coffee to break the fast. In Chicago, Yechiel and I would stop for coffee at the Starbucks near the synagogue. Every year we broke our fast in the same place, no fancy meals, no family or friends – just Starbucks. When we got back to the apartment, Yechiel would finish his cup of coffee with his all-time favorite: a chocolate covered Entenmann's doughnut.

The neighbors are putting up their sukkah, as is the custom to start building it right after the end of the fast. I have mixed feelings. This will be the first year without a sukkah at home. It will stay stored in the basement. I even contemplated giving it away. Pedro loved putting up our sukkah in our Jerusalem home for the past few years. We usually landed back in Israel just a few hours before the start of Sukkot, and he would have it ready for us, beautifully decorated and with the table set.

My first Sukkot in Jerusalem without Yechiel, I planned to have a full house. My dear friend and her family flew in from Spain, and stayed over for the entire week of the holiday. It was the perfect distraction as we shopped, cooked together, laughed and prepared everything like a family. Her husband was even mopping the living room floor, as her children got the bedrooms ready upstairs. It was a wonderful feeling of togetherness for all of us, and I had not realized I missed so

much. I missed Yechiel terribly, it was supposed to be just the two of us. But honestly, again and again he would just eat and sleep when he could, not accepting any invitations, exhausted from the High Holy Days sermons, no longer wanting to go anywhere. It was sometimes painfully lonely, and on my first *Sukkot* alone, I was grateful for having guests.

I will not be building a *Sukkah* this year though. We are still under lockdown. We cannot have guests over. *Zman Simchatenu* – a time of Joy. "You shall rejoice before the Lord your God seven days… You shall rejoice in your festival... You shall have nothing but joy..." This is what the *Torah* tells us about *Sukkot*, joy is the dominant element and focus of *Sukkot*.

All I can picture is Yechiel singing on the balcony while shaking his *lulav* in all directions. Rejoice? How can I possibly rejoice?

More than *Rosh Hashanah*, this past *Shabbat* felt like the New Year. *Shabbat Bereshit*, Genesis, we start over. Back to the beginning, we start to read the *Torah* again from the start. My mind is mixed up, this is hard. We just finished reading the last portion of *Devarim*, Deuteronomy. No time to stop and think, no time to internalize or take a break, we start over right away. The circle is not to be broken. Finish and start immediately. But how can I start over right away? Another cycle starts and all I can hear is the screaming voice inside me, "Wait, *Yechiel is not here*!" Every beginning strengthens the feeling of leaving Yechiel behind. This *Torah* portion of *Bereshit* is even harder to read. "It is not good that man should be alone; I will make him a helpmate opposite him." (Genesis 2:18).

I stumble. Loneliness is not good. God says it himself. A lonely person is not whole, is incomplete. A column in this week's Jerusalem Post links this *parsha* with loneliness. There are also articles and meditations on the quarantine, calls for the community to adopt each other. Having just made it through another holiday season without Yechiel, these words felt deeply personal. Every year, Jews reread the *Torah*, starting from the beginning; a weekly reading that starts again with Genesis and continues through the Torah culminating at year-end, *Simchat Torah*. Every week of every year, we study the same readings to bring deeper understanding of ourselves, our spiritual journey, our community, and our path in the world.

This particular column examined Genesis 2:18. Why was a lonely person incomplete and what is the significance of God's "a helpmate opposite him"? The marriage solution was not to find a like-minded partner, but to find one that made us complete. To bring two people together who were not identical, to find a partner opposite to ourselves. The expectation is to find an opposite to share life with. "A person who is not open to someone else's perspective on life is a lonely person, even if he or she has many friends. A person who is not willing to hear a different opinion loses out on the richness of life, on the tremendous multitudes of thoughts and feelings. Loneliness is hard because people were meant to be open, ready to acknowledge and accept differences. Man was not created for himself, but to look into the eyes of another and be with them, together, in their life."

Yechiel and I were very different. In our vast differences, we completed each other. Reading over this week's *parsha*, I find a new dimension to the pain of losing a spouse. If man and woman were created and became one flesh, it seems to imply that when one is torn away by death, the remaining one is now half again, the flesh having been ripped apart, ripped out.

I sat with this thought for a long time.

There were also comforting memories in the parsha. Yechiel often referenced another verse. "And the man said, "The woman whom You gave [to be] with me she gave me of the tree; so I ate." (Genesis 2:12)

Whenever Yechiel felt he had done something naughty, like eating more pizza than he should have, he would get a mischievous gleam and blame me jokingly, "That woman you gave me, *she* gave it to me."

And once the storm is over you won't remember how you made it through, how you managed to survive. You won't even be sure, in fact, whether the storm is really over. But one thing is certain. When you come out of the storm you won't be the same person who walked in. That's what the storm's all about.

– Haruki Murakami, *Kafka on the Shore*

I am sitting on his recliner.

I used to dislike it intensely, but Yechiel wanted a comfortable chair. We chose a light color recliner in hopes it would not stand out. Our living room is on the small side, and the television was in the living room. We did not have a separate family room, and the recliner had always dominated the living room. It was Yechiel's chair, no one else sat there. During *shiva* everyone sat on it, I wanted to scream. At first, I could not get myself to sit there, until it became the place where I would sit and cry. I began feeling closer to him when I sat there. How could something that was so painful become a source of comfort?

Looking at the black marks from his newspapers that stain the cream colored leather, the cracked leather on the right side where his arm rubbed more often, I cherish this piece of furniture more than anything else in the house. The remote, his remote, rested in its place next to his recliner. For the first year, I would just look at it. I never turned on the television. We only had one in the house, and it 'belonged' to him. He had total control on what we watched and eventually, I gave up entirely on trying to watch anything that might interest me. He had a peculiar way of watching TV, where he did not actually watch anything. He just switched the channel every few minutes, constantly, for the entire time he stared at it. It made it impossible for me to follow any show or even the news.

However, there was one type of show that captivated his attention. Yechiel was amazed by nature. He would watch shows like National Geographic whenever he could, and would spend hours at night absorbed in them. It was incredible just to see him so captivated by the show, underwater explorations, animals giving birth, jungle hierarchies, species discoveries, or life in Antarctica. No matter the nature topic, he was mesmerized. Usually, it was impossible to watch a show but not with these late night nature shows. As for me, I found myself reading or knitting.

Now, more often than not, the recliner continues to be a place of reflection, reading, and journaling.

As an extremely private person, I never thought I would one day publish my thoughts and experience, but surviving these past eighteen months made me realize how little the world knows about treating widows. Well-meaning people are quick to offer unsolicited advice, but most advice is unhelpful and some hurtful. "Do XYZ, you will feel better." Feel better? Again, I am not sick. This is not something you ever "feel better" about. It is also not the same grief one feels when a parent, sibling, or close family member dies - not more painful or less painful, just different. That gutting of a life gone. Being a widow is compounded by not just that indescribable grief, but by also being robbed of your identity. It is not just daily life being turned upside down; it is the future map of your life, projects and dreams together destroyed.

There is a sudden wave of anxiety. I am staring down the barrel of the two year anniversary. We talk about the difficulties of the first year on social media, but the second year sounds much worse. Personally, I think the lockdown helped since I was able to stay home and do nothing. The rest of the world was doing the same, staying at home, joking how the only exercise they got was going from the bedroom to the living room, or how the dog hid because he was used by all family members as the excuse to go outside. There was no pressure to be "over it" and everyone was struggling.

Death is but a change of circumstances, like moving homes. But a wise person sees to it that the new home is better and nicer than the old one.

– The Lubavitcher Rebbe

I was back in the wave, this time smashing me against the rocks. Everywhere I looked at home was a painful reminder of my life with Yechiel. Slowly, the memories gave me some comfort, but I was heartbroken; the pain was so strong that I felt nothing else. Nothing mattered; I started not caring about anything. Again. The cycle was familiar. Nothing else was as painful, I was living through the worst pain ever all over again.

During the first year, I learned to ask for help, and when I wanted to see someone - I called. When the house felt empty I invited people to stay with me. I grew out of the stage of leaving my home for *Shabbat* every Friday, and I combined it with hosting friends. My cooking skills could use an upgrade, but the company was more important than the food. I also made up for the food with a beautifully set table. I put together a basic menu which I repeated often with minor changes. Sharing a meal on *Shabbat* is about the experience and the spiritual side. As long as I had enough food choices, my guests were happy. The secret was having fresh homemade challah at the table, which everyone enjoys. Homemade challah I can do.

I hosted more and more people over time, and groups of tourists asked to join. The house felt alive again, and I could speak about Yechiel to others. I wanted people to feel comfortable talking about him around me. It hurts when friends avoid the subject, so I talk about him and even tell a joke sometimes to make everyone comfortable. I see the look on someone's face when someone comes to my home for the first time and does not know what to say.

Hosting stopped with the outburst of Covid. Everything was changing around me and inside me.

As I walk through the house, I feel different. It starts as a small blossom of acceptance: *maybe I'm ready for a new beginning.* A place of my own.

It is the first day of winter, in that it is the first cold and rainy day this season in Jerusalem. The weather feels foreboding, and I am extremely sad all over again. It is easy to fall back into depression. The house is dark and chilly, and I am sipping hot tea to keep warm. There is a feeling of déjà vu from last year, it is going to be a long winter ahead and I don't know if I have the strength to get through it again. How do I regain my strength? Is this going to be the rest of my life? The days are shorter now, the evenings so much longer. I need a strategy; I need to get organized in a different way. The restrictions for Covid make it harder to socialize; I need to focus on the small things, repeat the mantra of blessings and gratitude.

There are holes in my memory from the first year. I vaguely recall that six months after Yechiel died I received a call asking me to speak to a group of tourists.

"You're sure you want me?"

"You are his wife, correct?"

"Yes."

"So yes, we would like to have you speak to the group about Rabbi Eckstein."

Me? I am not a speaker.

I said yes to almost anything in the early days. A door that opens is an opportunity. I think of Eli who had taught me first to say yes, first to try, to really try, not just once. Once you have tried, you are allowed to decide if you like it and if you want to continue.

I wanted to practice speaking in public and build my confidence. I wanted to feel comfortable speaking in front of people. As much as I hated it, the only way to get over my anxiety was to keep practicing. The Dale Carnegie course I had taken some time back was a helpful and powerful experience, but I still did not feel ready. *Keep trying. Take every opportunity you get.* So I agreed. It was supposed to be very short, "just a few words about your husband."

How could I possibly sum up Yechiel in just a few words?

I arrived that evening at the event in Jerusalem. It was a small group of Christian tourists, together with Jewish friends, celebrating being together in the Holy Land. I met some very interesting people with whom I have stayed in touch, and was glad I went and had the courage. Warm remarks from everyone, encouragement, and prayers of continued strength gave me the confidence I needed. The hardest part was actually returning home alone to an empty house. The only person I really wanted to share the night and my success with was not there to greet me. In fact, he was not there at all. My good mood deflated. I was left bereft and miserable.

I have come a long way since that day. Although it seems impossible to have survived this long, I am stronger now. I have grown, I have done radio interviews, had newspaper articles written on the work of the Eckstein Fund. Having a purpose is helping me heal. This week, I was approached to speak to a group of Jewish women over zoom.

I felt anxious, but if my journey can help and inspire just one person, I feel like I have done my share. I feel a 'calling' to share with other women what I have learned so far and what has helped me heal.

I start with practicing more gratitude. I am grateful for the technology that allows me to be social online. Zoom has been a lifesaver. Scheduling meetings with friends online. I look forward to my Thursday zoom meeting with my friend to cook together in preparation for *Shabbat.* I see her in her kitchen, she sees me in mine, and we laugh and exchange cooking tips. She is a real pro, and laughs at my mistakes in the kitchen. Last week I forgot to let the dough rise a second time, and my challah came out quite dense... She made sure to remind me about patience when baking bread.

The right attitude makes all the difference; some people strongly dislike video calls - but when it is the only option, practice acceptance and gratitude.

Thursday nights are taken care of. How do I fill the rest of the evenings during the week? My daily evening walks that filled my summer evenings are no longer possible. I am feeling the anxiety level rise by the minute. I am exhausted. I crawl back into bed after a day of fog and uncertainty.

November 6, 2020

Could it be that my body knows on a primal level that it is the 6th of the month again? The first week of the month is always the hardest. I know without checking that it is 21 months today. I feel paralyzed with anxiety. I feel the two-year anniversary of Yechiel's death getting closer, and I don't know how to deal with it. I don't know how it is possible. I don't cry as often any more, but today I cannot stop the tears. My sobs are uncontrollable. I have no filter. I am trying to find new ways to cope.

Old habits will bring the same results. Change your habits if you want new results.

Think new. Try new things. I opened new social media pages today. I would like to raise awareness for widows and share my daily thoughts on grief and growth. New challenge. I look forward to the feedback from strangers around the world. On the one hand, it feels quite liberating; in the past I would not share much about myself and rarely posted any photos. I only prepared personal posts for Yechiel's page which he did not know to do by himself.

Journaling helps with getting feelings off my chest, but also feels like a commitment to myself. Writing about gratitude, positivity or growth, is an incentive to keep trying, but also reinforces the feeling of failure when I am sad.

Today is uncontrollable, I am down in the pit again - the wave hit hard.

How do I ask for help without being pitied and seen as a depressed lonely widow? On the other hand, in order to get support when I really need it, I have to let people know what I am feeling. They will eventually get tired of me if I constantly complain. I am not overly depressed, so I limit my "down" posts to when I really need support. Overall, I aim to be positive, show strength and gratitude.

Today I need help. Asking for help is not a weakness.

Memories pop up on social media. Another unexpected trigger that blows me over. Just five years ago, Yechiel and I attended a gala dinner in Los Angeles. Denial. Surreal. Another life. Only five years, a lifetime ago.

I cannot count time in the same way anymore. Yechiel died 21 months ago. Whatever happened before 21 months is in another world. I still cannot connect both worlds. I can barely recognize the "me" that shows up in that memory from five years ago. I have a hard time remembering that night. I cannot remember the person I was. The woman in the photo from the gala dinner was shy and had little self-confidence. Today I am a strong woman that has survived the worst.

I have a message I want to share, I need to help other widows. Still, on days like today, I need help.

I get an overwhelming response to my shared post, an outpouring of love, messages and calls inviting me for dinner, and I gain my strength. Grief is exhausting, I need more sleep than usual. "Be good to yourself, it's ok to rest". In the middle of the day I fall asleep for two hours. Refreshed, I walked over to my friends following their last minute invitation for Friday night *Shabbat* dinner.

It took courage to reach out for help, and I am grateful for friends that responded.

If you get the inside right, the outside will fall into place.

– Eckhart Tolle, *The Power of Now: A Guide to Spiritual Enlightenment*

Choices. Is everything really a choice? Can I decide to make a conscious choice to be happy every morning? To remember to count my blessings and see good?

Life is rarely that simple.

Some days I am not successful, but I keep trying every day over and over. In the first few months after Yechiel passed away, I would answer "I am going to be ok, I know I am going to be ok." It became my silent mantra, a way of self-soothing. I did not know when or how, but I kept repeating to myself, "I am going to be ok."

I am not a psychologist; I am not a coach. I want to understand, to be more aware of what I am going through. Nearing the end of 2020, the news and social media conversations are still filled with articles on the effects of isolation due to the pandemic, and advice on how to avoid loneliness. My journey through grief felt like a boot camp of isolation.

But I have come to the conclusion that it really is up to us to decide what we want our day to look like, how we want to live our lives. I do not have any research to back me, and yet, I firmly believe it can be done. No one will do it for you. Note to self - study positive psychology one day.

Today, everyone understands that life as we knew it, is over. Life for the generations who lived through this pandemic will never return to the normal before. There is a 'new normal' that is not normal – for everyone. My personal "normal" life ended on February 6th, 2019. I had one year to grieve, before the world turned over. To prepare for the pandemic without knowing I was preparing. I call them the days of "raw" grief, when all I did was cry and scream – under the covers, alone, or in the shower. I felt so alone. Nobody understood. Life continued normally for everyone – busy, normal, everyday lives – except mine. I was hurtling through the dark, wounded and trying to find meaning, purpose, and desperately searching for a hold to guide me.

How could I go on living when Yechiel was gone?

Another really rough day.

A couple of weeks ago my son told me about Apple Music. He tried explaining something about a family plan. I had no idea what he was talking about, thanked him and did not give it any more thought. A week later, he asked me if I was using the new music. He insisted that I needed this. He took my phone, showed me where it was and explained that I had "all the music in the world." I could just search for whatever I wanted, and voila. He typed in some of his choices, and the options seemed endless. Yechiel listened mostly to chassidic or classical music, and my mind tucked away Apple Music for later.

Yechiel had been part of a band when he was younger. It was a joy to hear him sing. My son had said "search for any music you can think of", so I searched for *Kol Salonika* - the name of the band. Later on, he joined another band with friends who had just become rabbis - and called themselves *The Rabbis Sing.* They sang at weddings, bar mitzvahs, and were contracted out for other special occasions. They also made a couple of albums.

Yechiel's voice was unique. I could hear it above all other voices in a crowded synagogue where everyone sang, or in a room full of people. I did not expect to see the name of the band come up on Apple Music. Oddly, it was an album I did not recognize, and the first song took my breath away. It was Yechiel. So strong, so young, his voice so alive. Later in the album he sings a solo, a song I had never heard. It was like hearing him sing for the very first time. It is wedding music. So happy and upbeat. I am sobbing before it is over. I push play, on repeat. I cannot stop crying and I cannot stop listening to this music. I kept pushing the repeat button and hearing him all over again. For hours. I wept myself into exhaustion.

I am lost.

It is never too late to be what you might have been.

– George Eliot

After the High Holidays, I had started to drink myself to sleep. I was drinking vodka every night. Hadas was worried. She knew I was not a drinker and was concerned that I might be self-medicating. She worried I might become an alcoholic. She sat me down. "You are not a drinker. It's fine to have a drink here and there, but this… stop it now!". She made an appointment for a psychiatrist.

I needed that wake up call.

I stopped drinking.

Months later I was back to my usual occasional glass of wine.

I became apathetic with the new medication – I did not care about anything. Nothing mattered. Nothing, who cares what I look like or what I wear anyway?. My diet was less than healthy and I lost interest in everything. The house suddenly felt like too much work, it needed too many repairs and excessive maintenance. I no longer cared about it. Part of me gave up, and part of me wanted something new, but first I had to get through the second anniversary. I panicked at the thought. My doctor adjusted my medication, and helped me prepare.

We are changed, not by what we receive, but by what we give.

- Rabbi Jonathan Sacks.

The social media group for widows was a lifeline for me. I read all the posts and comments from thousands of members. I needed a more personal touch, but I could not find a local widows support group and it became a moot point with the Covid closures. I started looking online for a smaller group that might meet virtually; technology made it possible to meet no matter how far away.

Back in August 2020, I came across a podcast with Carolyn Moore, founder of Modern Widows Club. I guess the word widow attracted me to open it at first, and I was curious. In her very inspiring interview, she mentioned a recent trip to Israel that was canceled, and how she is still looking forward to making the trip one day. The old "me" would have just listened to the interview, but something prompted me to write her a note. I was inspired and I wanted to know more. She was very energetic, I felt hopeful just by listening to her. I needed to hear more of her story.

The old "me" would not have dared. The new "me" had nothing to lose.

I was excited when I received a reply to my message. We set a time to talk on Zoom. We live in a time when meeting someone on a video call has become the norm. The entire world is accessible to us without the need to travel. I did not really know what I wanted to talk to her about; I just wanted to hear her story. I thoroughly enjoyed our conversation;

she told me that she started Modern Widows Club in 2011, about why she was compelled to, nearly ten years ago. We spoke about Israel and her longing to come to this country; about

how she almost made it with a group but had to cancel at the last minute.

She shared how her organization had grown over the years and the impact it had on widows in the United States. During our conversation, I suddenly asked her if she was thinking of expanding internationally.

"Yes! We are! We are currently in the process of starting a community in Kenya," she said. Kenya? I thought to myself. I asked how that came about. She told me that the idea actually came from a widow in Kenya. They had met on a trip and stayed in touch, and then one day the widow in Kenya asked if Modern Widows Club would guide her in opening a widows group in her area.

It was not so much a strategic decision, but an initiative of the widow in Kenya. She was thrilled at the idea of having a community in Jerusalem, and she thought it would be a wonderful incentive for her to travel here. There was only one small issue: only those who had been a widow for two years qualified to start a community for the Club, it was their policy. No exceptions, no other requirements. I would have to wait; I had only been a widow for 18 months when I first spoke to her. I think she could hear my passion and determination; she decided that she would discuss with her team, and one of the regional directors would be in touch with me.

I ended the call bemused and yet excited. *What just happened? Did I just say I was starting a widows group?*

I learned more about the organization, I joined their training program and conferences to start helping and empowering other widows.

Listening to Carolyn talk about it being our time to shine, and how to be a light to others, was inspiring. How those of us bringing widows together were becoming superheroes – running in when everyone else is running out. That by caring to be involved in someone else's life, we enter a new stage of our own; this is our natural transition. How we can focus on rebuilding ourselves by connecting, trusting and embracing others. Creating a new identity takes time, but being authentic in our relationships, learning to rebuild our trust in others and looking to understand others, is the right path.

Those words were very powerful, and took me in a new direction. In late November 2020, I attended their training course, and I believe that is what saved me. I realized how much compassion I had for other widows and how much I wanted to help. I contacted some widows in Jerusalem and asked each one of them if they wanted to meet. Between lockdowns, I was able to have them in my home a few times before we were forced to switch to Zoom gatherings. However different we were, wherever we were on our journeys, we instantly bonded. The strength of that bond stemming from the important factor in our new lives: our pain of losing a spouse.

For the first time in my new reality I felt like things were falling into place. In helping other widows and leading this new chapter, I found my purpose.

I was ready to move forward.

It's my life...it's now or never... I ain't gonna live forever. I just want to live while I'm alive...

– Bon Jovi

Journal Entry, March 23, 2021

It's time to move.

I had resisted for two years, waiting to see if the time would ever be right, when suddenly something dropped. I wanted something new. I was ready. I wanted to move. I needed to move. I opened Yechiel's closet, and started taking out stuff I did not like. What difference can it possibly make? He is not going to wear any of it. It was easier to donate the clothes that I did not like as much. It is confusing, so confusing. "These pants made him look heavier, so they can go. This shirt was tight on him and he could not wear it, so it can go too." I cannot understand how two years ago I was hugging his clothes, smelling him on them, crying and falling apart. I have come a long way.

Once I started, cleaning out his closet took a few weeks. Every moment of it was weird, and I talked to myself the whole time, "He's not going to wear this anymore." I still could not give away his best shirts and suits. I could not part with them. Not yet. Maybe not ever.

I found an apartment faster than I expected.

The move took much longer than the movers had estimated. They did not estimate my house well enough; suggesting seven hours, and they finished in ten. When they were halfway through loading the truck,

I looked at them and told them it was not going to fit. The lead mover said, "It will fit."

It did not fit.

They made two trips. At the end of a very long day, the head guy commented, "Wow, you've been so calm all day." I was calm. It was time. And I was ready.

I was only moving five minutes away. I left a few things at the house in case I wanted to sleep there.

I went back to the house to pick up some last things. I arrived at sunrise, picked up the newspaper. The house was empty. I made myself a cup of tea, one last time in the home we had created together. I walked around the quiet rooms, taking in every detail. Looked out every window, listening to the birds outside, and the familiar comforting sounds.

I sat at our kitchen table for the last time. It was poignant, the end of an era.

As I walked out of our house for the last time, I noticed Yechiel's key was still in the door. My heart stops. Of all things. The key in the door is what caused me the most butterfly anxiety, the emotion. Of all things, his key caught me.

Taking his key out of the door nearly undoes me.

My hand shakes as I do. It is the first time his key is out of the door since his death. I hold his keys to my heart for a moment.

Now… now, it was the end.

Epilogue

Pessach, 2021

The whole meaning of Passover has changed for me. I feel a deeper, more spiritual connection to the holiday now. Passovers past had me busy with all outward preparations of the holiday, the food, taking care of *us* on the holiday. Now, alone, I have the time and space to be aware of where I am in life. Passover is the holiday when we celebrate the freedom from Egypt, so that we do not forget, we celebrate how we became free. This concept got me thinking and analyzing my own opening up, my own growth - freedom in a sense. Instead of seeing grief and sadness, I have a freedom of choice; I can choose to see growth and joy. To see the positive and strive for it.

For the first time, I genuinely feel the freedom that we mark on this holiday – I am free to do whatever I want today. Grief is my Egypt. I leave the grief behind, and instead of pain, I chose growth and purpose. The world feels open. The openness of being able to choose whatever I want for my life.

I feel my purpose in life. Connecting to widows, taking on the mantle of establishing a widow's club in Israel, is where I want to be today. We call it *shlichut*. Christians have a word for it: a calling.

This is where I come alive. This is the ultimate freedom, finding my purpose in life. I am finding my purpose at 50-something. Man's search for meaning. This is what makes me. This is my stability. My security. My spirituality. Realization around Passover. Rather than focusing on the food preparation, where I was going to celebrate, or who I was celebrating with, I was focused on *me*. I have newness and openness in my life.

I am staying in Jerusalem for Passover. Alone. I am taking in the wonders of my city. It took two years to reach this point - I feel blessed.

Acknowledgments

I would not be here without Hadas Tsarfati. Thank you for your continued support and encouragement, and for holding me up until I learned to walk by myself. Words cannot express my gratitude.

Special thanks to my children, Jonathan and Amanda, who continue to drop everything to be by my side whenever I need them.

I started journaling without thinking that I would one day publish my writings. I am grateful to Tonya Derrickson, my dear friend and editor, for the support and superb editing of this book.

I wish to thank all the people who came to comfort me, and especially those friends who continue to check on me.

To the Mizmor Le'David community and Chabad of Baka, thank you for your warmth, countless Shabbat invitations and continued support.

I also want to express my gratitude to all the widows who gave me advice and reassured me that I will be ok. You showed me the light and inspired me to pay it forward. I hope this book can help other widows.

All proceeds from the sale of this book will be used to serve widows in Israel.

For more information, please visit www.ecksteinproject.org

Or follow The Rabbi's Widow podcast on apple podcast, spotify...

For Spanish speakers, you can follow our YouTube channel 'Foro de Viudas'.

For information on support groups and activities in Israel, please contact info@k-eckstein.org

Made in United States
Orlando, FL
10 September 2022

22253569R00161